Simon & Schuster's

GUIDE TO
Butterflies & Moths

by
Mauro Daccordi
Paolo Triberti
Adriano Zanetti

A FIRESIDE BOOK
PUBLISHED BY SIMON AND SCHUSTER, INC.
New York London Toronto Sydney Tokyo

Acknowledgment
The Publisher wishes to thank the Natural History Museum, Milan, and the Natural History Museum, Verona, for their gracious assistance.

Simon and Schuster/Fireside Books,
Published by Simon and Schuster, Inc.
Simon and Schuster Building
Rockefeller Center
1230 Avenue of the Americas
New York, New York 10020

Originally published in Italian under the title FARFALLE by Arnoldo Mondadori Editore S.p.A., Milan

Printed and bound in Italy by Arnoldo Mondadori Editore S.p.A., Verona

10   9   8   7   6   5   4   3   2   1
10   9   8   7   6   5   4   3   2   1   Pbk.

Library of Congress Cataloging in Publication Data

Daccordi, Mauro,
   Simon & Schuster's guide to butterflies and moths.

   Translation of: Farfalle.
   Bibliography: p.
   Includes index.
   1. Lepidoptera.   I. Triberti, Paolo.   II. Zanetti,
Adriano.   III. Title.   IV. Title: Simon and Schuster's
guide to butterflies and moths.
QL542.D3313   1988   595.78   87-26440

ISBN 0-671-66065-9
ISBN 0-671-66066-7 (Fireside book: pbk.)

CONTENTS

EXPLANATION OF SYMBOLS

diurnal lepidopteran

nocturnal lepidopteran

microlepidopteran

Habitat

tropical forests

temperate forests,
parks and gardens

mountain regions

bush and scrub;
subdesert zones

swamps and marshes

plains, cultivated land,
built-up areas

Geographical distribution

The square represents the zoogeographical region to which the species belongs, the colored area the part of this region where the butterfly or moth is usually found.

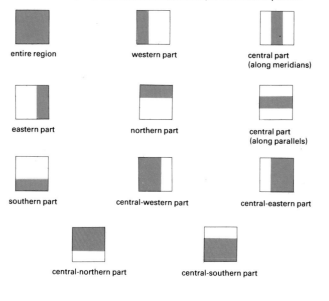

entire region

western part

central part (along meridians)

eastern part

northern part

central part (along parallels)

southern part

central-western part

central-eastern part

central-northern part

central-southern part

NOTE

In the arrangement of the entries the authors have adopted the following procedures:

The species are grouped on the basis of the zoogeographical regions to which they belong, and within these groups they are listed in alphabetical order of scientific names.

The scientific name (genus and species) is given in capital letters, followed by the name of the describer of that species. Where applicable, the common or vernacular name of the species is also given.

When the generic name is simply followed by the abbreviation "sp.", this indicates that the species has not been positively identified.

As regards the accompanying notes to the entries, the following information is given: the family to which the butterfly or moth belongs; geographical distribution; description with wingspan measurements in both inches and millimeters, and a brief comparison with related species; and finally, under "habits," the known facts concerning habitat, diet and period when the adult emerges.

In the section dealing with caterpillars, the references are more generally to the family than to the single species represented.

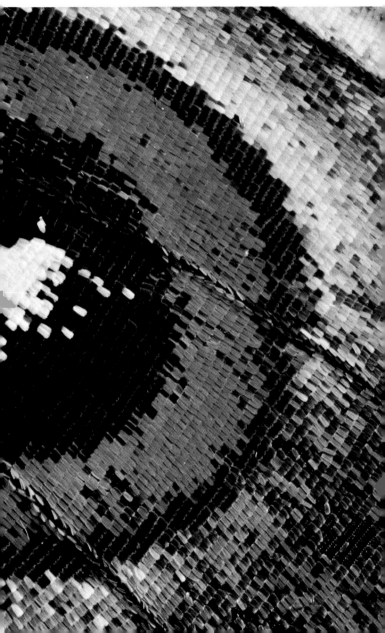

INTRODUCTION

Butterflies and moths are among the best known of all insects, admired even by those who have only the vaguest and most generalized understanding of science. Their splendid colors and graceful flight patterns have always been a source of fascination, although most people know little about their habits. In fact, butterflies and moths play an important role in nature, inextricably linked to the world of plants and thus depending on its changing fortunes. Farming practices, the indiscriminate use of chemical compounds in agriculture, and the draining of swamps are all human activities that have a profound effect on the environment and hence on these insects. Indeed, many species are so intimately linked to particular plants or to groups of plants associated with a particular biotope that they are incapable of responding to deteriorating conditions by dispersing to other areas; the speed and extent of such changes do not enable them to evolve adaptations for survival and therefore they become extinct. In the last few decades a notable decline in the numbers of butterflies and moths has been recorded all over the world, many species becoming rare or vanishing completely. This phenomenon has been verified by individual nations, notably Britain, where documentation on local fauna is continuously updated. This decline, as well as the decline among other groups of animals, is connected with conservation of the environment and thus not easily remedied. Little or nothing, in fact, has been done up to now, the only sign of hope being an increasing awareness of the importance of ecology, which may eventually lead to tangible initiatives.

Despite the threat posed by the advance of "civilization," the order Lepidoptera, to which butterflies and moths belong, is still one of the largest of the class Insecta, with more than 165,000 species identified to date. Their territories range from the equator to the polar regions, checked only by areas of perpetual snow and ice and the searingly hot deserts. Butterflies and moths develop by metamorphosis, a process whereby an organism known as a caterpillar (or larva) emerges from an egg, this creature being completely different from the adult it will become. The differences between the insects in these two growth phases are not restricted to their morphology but also relate to the roles played in their respective functions or ways of life. The larva only exists to feed, accumulating reserves that will enable the adult to concentrate almost exclusively on its function of reproduction. It is also important to remember that the Lepidoptera form part of a group of eight orders (Neuroptera, Mecoptera, Trichoptera, Coleoptera, Hymenoptera, Siphonaptera, and Megaloptera) mainly characterized by the presence of a quiescent phase known as the pupa (chrysalis in moths and butterflies), which marks the transition of larva to adult (holometabolism). The

The Trichoptera (caddis flies) are the closest relatives of the Lepidoptera. There are noteworthy resemblances in the structure of the mouth parts (1) and the positions of the wings at rest (2). The larvae often build a protective case (3) as in some families of Lepidoptera.

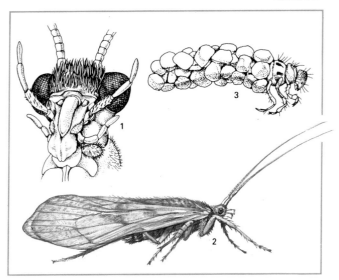

larva, once nutrition and growth stages are complete, becomes immobile and is transformed into a pupa, often spinning a cocoon from which the adult butterfly or moth will subsequently emerge.

Among holometabolic insects, the Lepidoptera are identifiable by certain characteristics, primarily the scales that cover the surface of two pairs of membranous wings. It is the structure of these scales and the pigments they contain that are responsible for the extraordinary colors typical of butterflies and moths. The mouthparts of the adult Lepidoptera almost always exhibit reduction in size of the lower jaw and the transformation of the upper jaw into a sucking apparatus or proboscis, through which the insect sucks flower nectar and other liquids. This proboscis, as well as the powerful chewing equipment of the young larva, are designed for maximum nutritional benefit, mostly from plants.

ORIGIN AND EVOLUTION OF THE LEPIDOPTERA

We have gained little knowledge concerning the evolution of the Lepidoptera. This is hardly surprising if we consider the delicacy and fragility of the body of these insects, the only (and very rare) parts left as recognizable fossil remains. The most rewarding finds have been those that have survived in amber, which is fossil

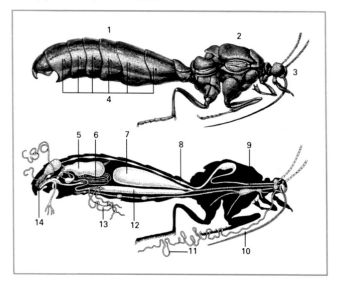

External and internal structure of a lepidopteran. In the top figure the specimen has been drawn without wings, scales and hairs covering the cuticle: 1. abdomen; 2. thorax; 3. head; 4. spiracles; 5. bursa copulatrix; 6. oviduct; 7. stomach; 8. dorsal vessel; 9. esophagus; 10. proboscis; 11. salivary gland; 12. mid intestine; 13. malpighian tubules; 14. hind intestine.

resin. Even the most minute structures have been preserved in this substance, and it has often been possible to interpret the pattern of the wing venation. Recently, amber has furnished the most ancient known finds of Lepidoptera, dating from the Cretaceous (100–130 million years ago). These new discoveries, although they push back in time the hypothetical date when the Lepidoptera first appeared, do not yet make possible a clear reconstruction of their history. This means that scientists can only theorize as to how they evolved, working on the basis of what we know concerning their closest relatives, the Trichoptera (caddis flies). The adults of this group fly at dusk, near fresh water, feeding on various kinds of liquids. The larvae have a varied diet, some living in cocoons of silk and detritus similar to those spun by certain families of the Lepidoptera. Their close relationship is indicated by a number of common features, such as the extreme reduction in size of the lower jaws and the development of the upper jaws, which, in their close relatives Lepidoptera, fuse to form the proboscis, and the similarities of wing venation. The earliest known fossil of the Trichoptera dates from about 250 million years ago (Lower Permian), which is over 100 million years earlier than the first Lepidopteran remains. It seems likely that during this period, Lepidoptera and Trichoptera, deriving from a common ancestor, embarked on separate evolutionary paths. It is interesting to note that the oldest species of angiosperms, the flowering plants upon which butterflies today

A) Head structure of an adult lepidopteran: 1. epipharynx; 2. labrum; 3. clypeus; 4. scape; 5. antenna; 6. labial palpus; 7. compound eye; 8. proboscis. B) Form of the antennae: 9. filiform; 10. clavate; 11. unipectinate; 12. bipectinate. C) Figs. 13–15: forelegs, median legs, hind legs. D) Different types of scales; E) Androconial scales of diverse forms.

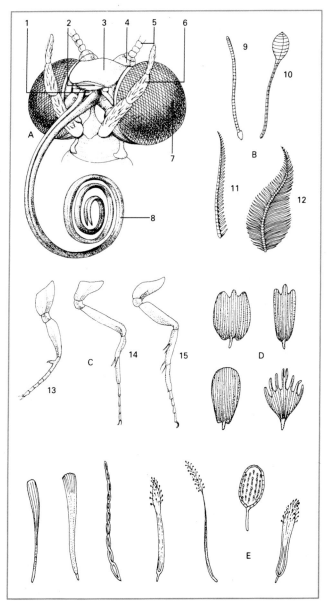

most vitally depend, date back to the Cretaceous. Angiosperms were then already well differentiated, with forms very similar to those of the present day. This suggests that they may have appeared on earth much earlier; some scholars believe that it could have been more than 200 million years ago, in the same period that the Lepidoptera and Trichoptera are thought to have parted company. So it is possible to formulate the hypothesis that butterfly larvae specialized in choosing plant tissues as their source of food, while the adult insects subsequently adapted to a glycyphagous diet based on nectar, the evolution of their mouth-parts taking place parallel to the evolution of angiosperm flowers.

MORPHOLOGY

In everyday speech we refer to butterflies and moths, the former diurnal and the latter mainly nocturnal. In order to identify a species correctly, however, we must verify certain features of morphology and anatomy. In the following pages, therefore, we shall be examining in turn the various stages of development: adult, egg, larva and pupa.

Adult
The body of a lepidopteran, like that of all insects, lacks a true inner skeleton; the supporting function is performed by the outer skeleton or exoskeleton, which envelops the body in a kind of articulated capsule. This covering, the integument, is made up of various layers of which the outermost, the cuticle, gives strength to the entire structure and protects the insect from excessive transpiration or penetration of water, toxic substances, and the like. It is not of uniform thickness but has lines of lesser resistance (sutures), which permit movement and articulation. The body consists of the head, thorax, and abdomen, and is almost completely covered with scales and hairs. The head is rounded, with a pair of large, hemispherically-shaped compound eyes. In some groups there are also two simple eyes (ocelli), the function of which is unclear but certainly relates only approximately to vision. The sense of smell, however, is normally associated with the antennae, situated near the compound eyes (though other body parts are also sensitive to smell). These antennae comprise a variable number of segments and are furnished with numerous muscles, which allow them to move. In the Lepidoptera the length and shape of the antennae are extremely variable, both between different families and between male and female of the same species. They may be threadlike, terminating in a club (clavate), shaped like a comb on one side (pectinate) or on two sides (bipectinate), or very long, as in the case of the Adelidae in which they measure five times the length of the wings. The

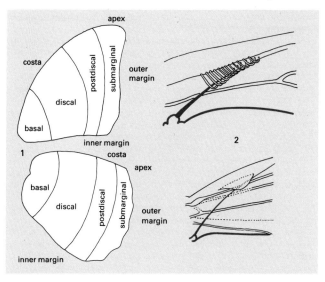

Fig 1. shows the areas into which a lepidopteran's wing is usually divided. Although they are theoretical, the majority of wing patterns conform to these subdivisions. Fig. 2 shows the underside of the wings, in which it is possible to see two types of wing attachment.

females often possess simpler antannae than the males, whose antennae serve principally to find a partner for mating.

The antennae of butterflies and moths bear receptors (sensilla), which enable the males to identify females at a distance of more than 6 miles (10 km), as in the case of *Actias selene*. The mouthparts are usually of the sucking type, derived from a chewing mechanism found in certain fossil families and in the primitive family Micropterigidae. In spite of these evolutionary modifications, it is still possible to distinguish the parts that constitute the primitive mouth arrangement: upper lip, a pair of lower jaws, and a pair of upper jaws equipped with appendages (labial palpi). The lower jaws, however, are atrophied and functionless whereas the outer lobes of the upper jaws (galeae) are extraordinarily long, hollow inside, and perfectly fitted together. This tube is a genuine proboscis through which nutritive liquids are sucked. The organ is composed of numerous strong rings, alternating with bands of membrane as well as many short, oblique muscles; it can fold spirally and when not in use is curled beneath the lower part of the head. The proboscis develops differently in various groups according to their feeding habits: in some Sphingidae it may measure up to 12 in. (30 cm) long, enabling this butterfly to probe into flowers with a very deep corolla that are inaccessible to other butterflies. In *Acherontia atropos* the proboscis is short and thick, used for perforating the operculum of honey cells in hives, while some of the tropical

15

Noctuidae employ it to pierce the skin of fruits. In certain families (Lasiocampidae, Notodontidae, etc.) the proboscis may be completely reduced and the oral aperture closed. These lepidopterans do not feed, but draw the energy they need from reserves accumulated during the larval phase.

The thorax is composed of three segments, the prothorax, mesothorax, and metathorax, each of which has a pair of legs. The prothorax, which bears no wings, is usually small and membranous, often with a pair of dorsal plates (patagia), the color of which sometimes constitutes a characteristic used in classification. The mesothorax is well developed, furnished on the sides with a pair of mobile elements (tegulae), which cover the insertion point of the forewings. The other pair of wings is inserted in the metathorax, smaller and provided with ears or auditory organs (tympana) in some families. As often occurs in flying insects, the legs of many Lepidotera are scarcely suitable for walking, being rather fragile and in certain groups reduced or degenerated. They consist of five different parts: coxa, trochanter, femur, tibia, and tarsus. The front tibia are often furnished with a special platelike appendage, the epiphysis, which serves, as far as we know, to clean the antennae and the proboscis; the middle ones often have a pair of apical spurs while the rear tibia sometimes have one apical and one medial pair. The last segment of the five which normally make up the tarsus terminates in two claws which may be single or bifid.

Butterfly wings are constituted of a double membrane traversed by thick, tubular veins, which stiffen the structure and enable them to resist air pressure during flight. Apart from serving as a framework for the wing scales, the veins also act as ducts for the hemolymph (insect blood), tracheae, and nerves. Although the wing coupling arrangement is quite simple, it offers very important clues to classification. The front and hind wings are interlinked so as to constitute a single surface, but the systems vary a great deal. In many moths, a bristle or bundles of strong bristles (the frenulum), situated on the front edge of the hind wings, engage with or hook or with groups of hooked hairs situated on the hind edge of the forewings. In some more primitive moths, a lobe (jugum) at the base of the forewings overlaps the hind wings. Sometimes there is a combination of both systems, or, as is the case in most butterflies, the edges of the two wings simply overlap. Both wing surfaces, like most of the other parts of the body, are covered with hairs of varying types, and with flattened or platelike hairs called scales. These are inserted in the cuticle on a short stalk and arranged much like roof tiles. The scales have different functions: the androconia are scent scales, which, in the males of some groups, disperse odors secreted by glands, whereas the scales situated along the principal veins, according to some experts, keep the upper edge open and allow atmospheric oxygen to enter the tracheae of the wing.

side views of the female genital apparatus in two different suborders of lepidopteron; above, Monotrysia: 1. rear apophysis; 2. rectum; 3. vagina; 4. front apophysis; 5. bursa copulatrix; 6. ovaries. Below, Ditrysia: 7. anal papillae; 8. rectum; 9. common oviduct; 10. oviduct; 11. ovaries; 12. bursa copulatrix; 13. bulla seminalis; 14. front apophysis; 15. vagina; 16. ductus seminalis; 17. ostium bursae; 18. rear apophysis.

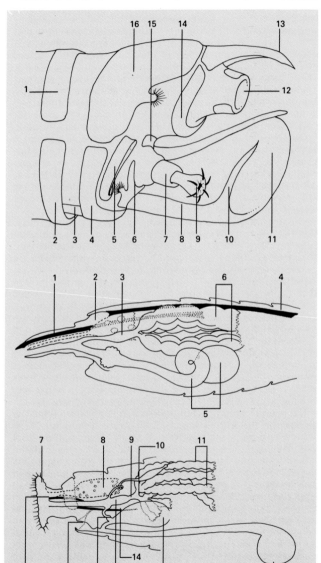

The coloration of the scales, which is responsible for providing the patterns and often glittering hues of the adults, may be due to different types of pigmentation or to the presence of ridges and streaks on the actual surface of the scale. This conformation stimulates the phenomenon of light refraction and other optical effects, whereby the colors change according to the angle of incidence of the light rays. In certain families, such as the Psychidae, the females may be wingless (apterous), while in others, e.g. some species of Geometridae, the wings are short (brachypterous). These phenomena of color are rarely present in both sexes.

The abdomen of adult butterflies and moths lacks legs but it does contain the organs charged with the most important adult function: reproduction. It is made up of ten segments, the last three of which may be strongly modified to constitute the external genital apparatus. The first eight segments are furnished with dorsal and ventral areas that vary in hardness, known respectively as tergum and sternum, connected laterally by a membrane with, as a rule, six or seven pairs of spiracles. These, together with two pairs of spiracles on the thorax, are actually the outer openings of the tracheal system, in other words the lepidoteran's respiratory apparatus. The external sexual organs are extremely variable and complex structures: basically, however, the valves (claspers) of the male, consisting of a sac that is open at the base (and which may assume complicated forms), are found at the tip of the abdomen. The spermatozoa are transferred to the female by means of the penis (aedeagus), which protrudes visibly from the valves. In females of the most primitive groups of Lepidoptera, the Zeugloptera, Dacnonypha, and Monotrysia, there is a single opening, which serves both for laying eggs and for copulation, whereas in the Ditrysia the latter function is performed by the ostium bursae, located lower down and in front of the eighth segment. The genital organs of both males and females are valuable for identifying species and genera.

The internal structure of butterflies and moths does not differ greatly from that of other insects. The nervous system consists of a brain, situated in the head, and of another important cerebral mass known as the suprasophageal ganglion, which controls the mouth apparatus. From it emerges a chain of ganglia that runs the whole length of the insect's abdomen and from which stem lateral nerves that serve the entire body. Some families have an additional characteristic in the form of a pair of hairy papillae, situated on the head near the insertion point of the antennae and provided with nerves connected to the brain; their sensory function is uncertain.

The circulatory system, on the other hand, is quite simple, in so much as it does not connect physiologically with the respiratory system as in vertebrates. There is a dorsal vessel which runs through the abdomen and forms a tubular aorta in the thorax. In the abdomen of some insects this vessel forms tiny chambers in

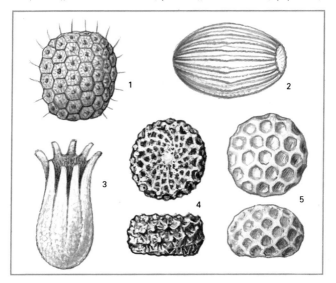

each segment; the structure in its entirety is called the heart. Each chamber communicates with the rest of the body by means of apertures (ostioles), through which flows the hemolymph that circulates in the tissues. The contractions of the muscles in the walls of the heart close the ostioles and at the same time drive the hemolymph toward the aorta, and from here through the terminal aperture back into the body. As mentioned above, the respiratory apparatus consists of a system of tracheae, which communicates with the outside by means of the stigmas. Oxygen is thus transmitted directly to the organs without the need for blood. The digestive system of the Lepidoptera is chiefly characterized by a pharynx provided with powerful muscles, which facilitate the sucking action performed by the proboscis. Leading from the pharynx is the esophagus, which forms a small sac (crop) at the rear acting as a depository for nutritive substances. Sometimes the crop fills with air, and in this condition functions as an aerostatic organ or may be used during the emergence of the adult from the cocoon. Finally, there is the true digestive tube, which has its outlet through the anus.

The reproductive system is fairly simple in the males, but complex and variable in the females. Males have two testes linked by canals to the ejaculatory duct, which has its outlet in the aedeagus. Females have two ovaries (in which the eggs develop), linked by lateral oviducts to a large common oviduct. This may terminate in the anal duct or lead separately to the outside. Other

The outward appearance of butterfly and moth larvae is rather variable. Here are the caterpillars of: 1. Arctiidae; 2. Papilionidae (Iphiclides podalirius); 3. Geometridae; 4. Sphingidae.

organs are the spermatheca and the bursa copulatrix, variously connected to the above-mentioned apparatus, which serve to collect the spermatozoa emitted by the male and release them gradually. The eggs are thus fertilized one by one as they are laid.

Egg

The eggs of the Lepidoptera are covered by a strong membrane (chorion) comparable to an eggshell; they are characteristically ridged or pitted, but can sometimes be smooth, according to species. They are generally round, or – as in many groups of butterflies – conical or fusiform, or even flattened, as in some Noctuidae. In a hollow on the surface of the egg is the micropyle, an opening through which the spermatozoa penetrate; these are channeled toward the aperture by a cluster of microscopic scales. Once the eggs are laid, the micropyle allows the embryo to breathe. The newly laid eggs are yellowish-white and soft, but as the chorion solidifies the coloration changes and may become quite vivid, as in the eggs of the Lasiocampidae.

Larva (Caterpillar)

In the life cycle of the Lepidoptera, the larva (caterpillar) represents an early stage of feeding and growth. Little evidence of the adult fragility and elegance is apparent at this stage; the body of the caterpillar is almost always cylindrical, wormlike, sometimes flattened (as in some Lycaenidae) or shaped like a slug, with a head that may be completely hidden by the thorax (as in the Limacodidae). Like the adults, the larvae are subdivided into segments, which on superficial examination look very similar to one another. Apart from the head, the body has thirteen segments, the first three of which form the thorax and the remaining ten the abdomen. The head, generally rounded, is furnished with a pair of small antennae composed of three or four joints, but the large compound eyes of the adult are absent. The larvae, however, often possess several pairs of ocelli, although these are not found in parasitic species which live for the most part in darkness. The mouth is designed for chewing: between the upper and lower lips are two strong, spoon-shaped mandibles or jaws, the inner margins of which usually accommodate numerous teeth. On the lower lip the duct of the silk glands finds its outlet in a papilla (spinneret); this organ, occurring only in the larvae and not the adults, is in fact a spinning tube with which the caterpillar spins silk or, by emitting liquid, sticks itself to pieces of leaf, bark, and other surfaces. The three thoracic segments are recognizable by the presence on each of a pair of articulated legs. In addition to these, caterpillars have a series of appendages for locomotion, known as prolegs, on the abdomen. These are so called because, even though they function as legs, they are not structured as such but are fleshy cylindrical processes, which terminate in a row or rows of curved hooks. The prolegs are usually situated on the

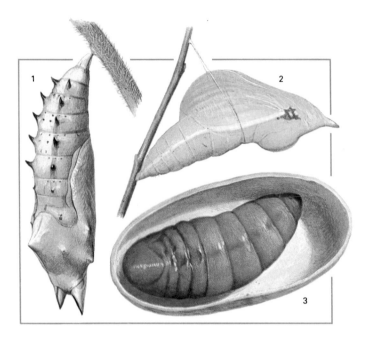

third, fourth, fifth, sixth, and tenth segments. The last pair (anal legs or claspers), in many cases, have been greatly modified so as to become, as in the Notodontidae, whiplike outgrowths, colored at the tip, which have lost their original function and probably serve to confuse predators.

The skin of the caterpillar may be smooth or covered with tubercles, spines, or hairs. The primary hairs may have a sensory function, being stiff and conspicuous in young larvae. Their arrangement, called chaetotaxy, is of great importance in classification. The secondary hairs simply serve as covering and protection.

The internal structure of the caterpillar is similar to that of the adult butterfly or moth, but the glands are more highly developed. In addition to the silk glands, there is in certain groups a jugular gland, situated in the thorax, secreting an acidic liquid, which can sometimes be sprayed for defensive purposes. In the thorax of the Papilionidae there is a Y-shaped appendage (osmeterium), which can be protruded by the caterpillar; linked to this organ is a gland that produces a strong-smelling liquid. The structure is used as a defense against predators but probably also serves for excretion. Other glands produce the hormones that regulate the processes of molting and metamorphosis.

Larvae that lead an aquatic life exhibit some interesting modifications. "Colonization" of this environment is restricted to the larvae of a few species belonging to particular families, including the Pyralididae. This adaptation pertains only to fresh water and is characterized by an initial larval stage in which the insect breathes through the skin or by means of tracheal gills. The gills, although present in other groups of insects, such as the Trichoptera, are simply protrusions of the tracheal tubes, and allow oxygen to be absorbed from the water.

Pupa (Chrysalis)
Caterpillars, once mature, stop feeding and search for a suitable place to transform themselves into pupae. They use silk either to spin various types of cocoons or, if they are butterflies, to make pads or girdles that surround the thorax and provide support in various positions. Having attached itself, the caterpillar remains almost motionless, while inside its cuticle the larval organs are converted into the adult organs.

There are two basic types of Lepidoptera chrysalids. The first has jointed and functional mandibles (jaws), which the chrysalis uses for breaking out of the cocoon (decticous chrysalis), the wings and antennae being free, as are the abdominal segments (exarate chrysalis). This is characteristic of the suborders Zeugloptera and Dacnonypha. The second type of Lepidoptera chrysalid is found in the Monotrysia and Ditrysia. In this type, the mandibles, when present, are unjointed and immobile (adecticous chrysalis), while the various appendages and abdominal segments are, at least to some extent, bound to the body walls (obtect chrysalis). The chrysalis is thus almost totally immobilized, except for movements of the abdomen associated with defense or adjustment. Respiration, as in the caterpillar and the adult butterfly or moth, is effected through the spiracles, while the anal and genital orifices are closed.

DEVELOPMENT

The various transformations that take place in butterflies and moths from egg to adult are collectively known as metamorphosis. Diverse forms of metamorphosis are found in insects, depending on the differences between the juvenile and adult phases. In the case of the Lepidoptera, there is complete metamorphosis – this being typical of the more evolved insects – defined by the four stages of development just described. The differences between the various phases are so great that it is impossible to establish any evident relationship between caterpillar and butterfly or moth unless the entire growth cycle is followed in sequence. This diversity can nevertheless be explained by recognizing the different tasks that each phase must perform. The job of the larva is simply to feed, accumulating reserves for the succeeding phases: this is evident from its mouth parts and its exceptional digestive capacity. On the other

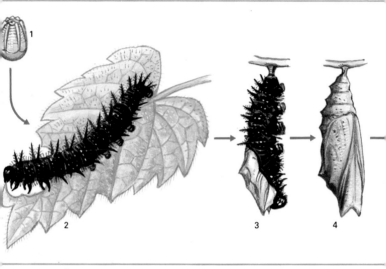

hand, the larva's vision is very poor owing to the absence of compound eyes, walking is extremely slow, and there are no wings. None of this equipment, however, is necessary to the larva because the egg is laid close to or directly upon the food source. By contrast, the adult has to carry out those tasks necessary to perpetuate the species: reproduction and dispersal abroad. A series of adaptations enables the butterfly or moth to perform these functions as efficiently as possible: compound eyes, sophisticated antennae, pheromones to attract the opposite sex, external genital organs for mating, and strong wings, which can carry the insect for hundreds of miles.

The remarkable feeding capacity of the caterpillar results in an increase in weight and body volume. This does not occur in the adult, for the nectar sucked through the proboscis only compensates for the butterfly's or moth's consumption of energy. Larval growth is continuous and might be expected to entail a corresponding increase in the size of the cuticle. But because the latter cannot be extended it is completely and periodically replaced by special phases known as molts (ecdyses). During this process not only are the cuticle of the body and the appendages renewed but tracts of the digestive tube, integumental glands, etc., as well. The shedding of the old cuticle (exuviae) is facilitated by the production of enzymes in the epidermis that digest much of the exuviae, making it softer and more fragile. At this stage, by means of muscular contractions or the accumulation of liquids in

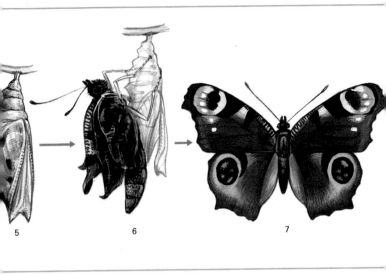

5   6   7

particular spots, pressure is exerted at certain points on the cuticle so that eventually it splits and allows the insect to break free. The molt is controlled by the endocrine system through the production and interaction of two antagonistic hormones: ecdysone, the so-called molting hormone secreted by the prothoracic gland, and the juvenile hormone, produced by glands known as corpora allata, situated behind the brain. In the Lepidoptera there may be from three to five molts, but their number may be influenced both by temperature and food.

During the molting phases, the larva stops feeding and rests for one or two days, a period necessary for the replacement of its cuticle. But there are also other periods in a lepidopteran's life when activity is very slight, metabolism is slowed down, and feeding is curtailed. During these periods the insect lives off its own reserves. Such mechanisms enable the butterfly or moth to survive unfavorable conditions such as sudden drops in temperature, harsh winters, or the rainy season in tropical regions. These resting periods may occur at all stages of development, but assume particular significance in the pre-imaginal stages (those preceding the adult phases). As a rule they may be divided into two types, quiescence and diapause. In the former the state of immobility is an immediate reaction to sudden change in the surroundings, and ends as soon as conditions return to normal. Quiescence commonly occurs among some arctic and mountain species, which live in zones subject to sharp temperature variations even at the height of summer. Diapause, however, is more similar to the winter lethargy experienced by vertebrates: preparations for immobility occur gradually with the commencement of the unfavorable conditions. A variety of factors may bring about this process in the Lepidoptera: length of day, temperature, humidity, shortage of food, etc. Awakening from the period of diapause normally depends upon diverse combinations of the same factors, and if conditions do not improve it will be further delayed until they are suitable. This happened in the case of some Sphingidae and Notodontidae, which, when bred domestically, remained in diapause for years at a time.

VARIABILITY

Examination of any group of living organisms demonstrates that no single individual is exactly identical to another, even though the differentiating characteristics may be quite minute. We only have to look at ourselves. Each of us belongs to the same species of *Homo sapiens*, yet we differ in features such as body build, complexion, eye color, and so forth. The same applies, in a less obvious manner, to other animal groups, and we can verify such variability simply by looking around us. In the case of the Lepidoptera, we need simply to catch a few specimens of the large white butterfly (*Pieris brassicae*) in a field or garden to see how they differ in size, coloration, and wing pattern. This constitutes a good example of variability within a population, the latter defined as a community of individuals living in a particular area and interbreeding with one another. Differences that may occur within a population are essentially of two kinds: genetic, if they are controlled by the particular assortment of genes carried by each individual, or non-genetic, if individual variability is caused by conditions related to the environment.

Genetic variability creates diverse individuals, who differ from one another despite their common, fundamental heredity. This form of variability, known as polymorphism, is due basically to chance variations (mutations) that appear in the genetic makeup of one or more individuals. The variations may, for example, consist of incorrect messages during the duplication of DNA molecules, of which genes are a part. This means that the new individual will be different from the parents in certain characteristics and that this acquired variation will be passed on to the offspring of succeeding generations. The success of the variation will then be established by its interaction with the invironment: polymorphism is almost always regulated by natural selection, which favors one or another variation according to the conditions surrounding the new individual. One of the best-known examples of this process is that of industrial melanism, the subject of a special study in Britain, involving the peppered moth (*Biston*

*These illustrations show the three melanistic forms of the peppered moth (*Biston betularia*); 1. typical; 2. insularis; 3. carbonaria. Note how the typical form camouflages itself against trunks covered with lichen, and carbonaria against trunks blackened by pollution.*

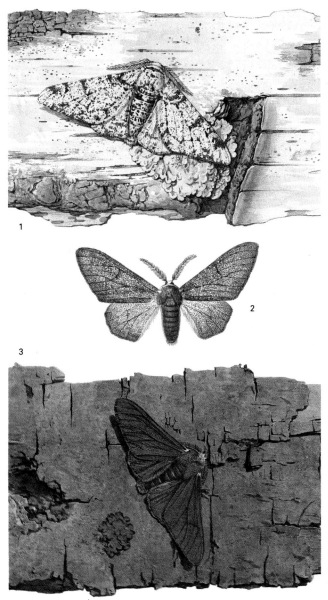

1

2

3

betularia) of the family Geometridae. This species exhibits three main forms: the typical form is white with black speckles, the form *insularis* is gray, and *carbonarius* is completely black. Until the middle of the nineteenth century the two latter forms were rare, and the typical form dominant. In the course of some fifty years, however, the *carbonarius* form became extremely abundant, accounting for around 95% of the population. Tests carried out in other regions of Europe indicated that the melanistic forms were more plentiful in industrialized areas whereas in other zones there remained a high percentage of the typical form. It was eventually discovered that the increased incidence of *carbonarius* and also of *insularis* was associated with the greater protection afforded against predatory birds. Under natural conditions, in fact, the typical form was well camouflaged on tree trunks covered with lichen, while in polluted areas, where trunks were blackened, *carbonarius* was better protected in this respect.

Many of the factors that influence variability in the Lepidoptera are to do with sex. Thus in many species the two sexes are easily identifiable by virtue of differences in wing pattern, coloration and structure of the antennae. This phenomenon is called sexual dimorphism. If, for instance, we examine a male and female large white butterfly (*Pieris brassicae*), we see that the forewings of the male are simply edged with black while those of the female are edged with black but also exhibit tiny round black spots. In some species of Lycaenidae, the upper side of the male's wing is blue, but brown on the female's. Other more spectacular examples are to be found in tropical butterflies, in which the vividly colored males of the large *Ornithoptera* species pursue the drab yellowish-brown females. In many moths, sexual dimorphism is displayed in the form of the antennae or even by the presence or absence of wings. Differences may be so marked that at one time the two sexes were attributed by scientists to different species.

In certain cases, although seldom observed, both male and female characteristics may be found in different parts of the same individual's body. This phenomenon, known as gynandromorphism, may result in the body being split perfectly lengthwise into two halves, one male and the other female. The cause of this aberration would seem to be due to an irregular separation of the sexual chromosomes during the first divisions of the egg cell. This produces two different types of cells in the same individual, one with male, the other with female, chromosomes. In Europe it occurs particularly in *Gonepteryx rhamni*, *Anthocaris cardamines*, and *Argynnis paphia*.

In any given population of Lepidoptera, variability is not always due to genetic factors but may be determined by the environment. Variations of this nature occur, for example, when breeding some species of vanessids, by subjecting the chrysalids to prolonged periods of heat or cold. The small tortoiseshell (*Aglais urticae*), kept for a few days at low temperatures, produces adults very similar to the *polaris* form, which lives in Lapland. The phenomenon is common, too, in different generations of many groups of butterflies. In some Lepidoptera there is only a single generation, the adult taking wing in summer, and in autumn laying the eggs that will become next year's generation. Far more numerous are the species that produce several generations in the course of one year, each in different seasons. One example is the map butterfly (*Araschnia levana*), a nymphalid, whose first generation, hatching in May, is recognizable by its orange wings with blackish markings. The summer generation, on the other hand, has forewings that are almost black, with broad white bands. Should the summer be particularly cool, specimens of the second generation may assume a form somewhere between the two. Examples of this kind are common among tropical species as well, with marked dissimilarities between adults in the dry season (with wings outwardly resembling dry leaves) and those of the rainy season, with wings displaying numerous ocelli and streaks on the reverse side.

Until now we have discussed variability only within a population, underlining the fact that it is impossible to encounter two identical individuals. The same applies to the populations themselves: no two populations, even if contiguous, will be genetically equivalent. To clarify this point, let us discuss the concept of species. A species may be defined as a group of populations that are closely related from a genetic viewpoint, in the sense that they can interbreed and produce fertile offspring. Within a given species, populations vary to a lesser or greater degree, and in this respect the study of geographical variability assumes importance. Such variability may be gradual if the populations are distributed continuously, without physical barriers to subdivide the areas inhabited. In this case genetic exchange is possible among individuals who migrate from one population to another, crossing various but not insurmountable boundaries. Take for instance *Acraea natalica*, whose populations have a continuous distribution in the African continent. If we examine a collection of specimens of this species, we find a continuous variation (cline) of color from northwest to southeast, in which darker forms gradually give way to paler ones.

Geographical variation, however, need not be gradual and is all the more striking where the areas in which the different populations live are geographically isolated from one another. For example, in the cases of groups inhabiting islands or mountain ranges, the various populations may be separated by tracts of sea or deep, inaccessible valleys. It may then happen that single populations take on a genetic and morphological feature that clearly distinguishes one from another. Normally, in such circumstances, these populations will have evolved into distinct subspecies; but it often happens that when geographical isolation is prolonged for a considerable time, the populations

Sexual dimorphism in butterflies and moths is sometimes very striking. Fig. 1 shows the male (above) and female (below) of Plebicula amanda *(Lycaenidae), which differ in wing coloration. Fig. 2 illustrates* Nyssia florentina *(Geometridae); the female (below) is wingless, with filiform antennae, whereas the male (above) is winged, with bipectinate antennae.*

1

2

develop characteristics that result in reproductive isolation and so become distinct species. One such example is provided by the subspecies of *Ornithoptera priamus* in Australia. The area occupied by each subspecies is restricted to groups of islands. The males of the subspecies are characterized by striking variations of wing color: green in *priamus*, blue in *urvillianus*, and gold in *croesus*. From this example it may be deduced that a species can be made up of diverse subspecies or geographical races (polytypical species), each inhabiting part of the entire area of the species.

We have seen how, in the process of forming new species, an extremely important role is played by mechanisms causing genetic isolation. Such mechanisms may be divided into two categories: the first comprises those that prevent copulation, and the second those that reduce the fertility of the resultant hybrids. Mechanisms of the first kind included ecological isolation, whereby individuals occupy different habitats of the same territory (e.g. woodland thickets or clearings, varying altitudes, etc.). Temporal isolation is also significant; this affects populations whose members are displaced during their flight periods so that adults have limited opportunities of encountering one another. The second kind of mechanism involves reproductive isolation (post-copulatory), in which mating sometimes occurs but produces only sterile hybrids. This is the case, for instance, among the Lycaenidae, notably the Adonis blue (*Lysandra bellargus*) and the Chalkhill blue (*L. coridon*); each has a wide distribution in Europe, and hybrids have been found in central Italy and the Pyrenees. The two species, however, as has been verified in the laboratory, differ in their chromosomal structure so that there can be no formation of functional gametes in the hybrids, which are therefore sterile.

HABITS

If we examine the flight of a butterfly or moth and the crawling movements of a caterpillar, we might be tempted to think that most of the activities of these insects are ruled by chance. We should not forget, however, that the Lepidoptera are organisms that interact with other living things, each and every one involved in the struggle for survival and controlled by laws that leave very little to chance. Every action that helps to define the behavior of a butterfly or moth is the result of thousands of years of adaptations, which have been codified in their genetic inheritance. It can be said, therefore, that their life is ruled by instinct. Instinct is not necessarily marked by conventional, unaltering behavior, but tends, in lesser or greater measure (according to the group), to adapt to the needs of unforeseen situations. In this section we shall examine the ways in which butterflies and moths vary in their habits and, in some cases, how they modify them through adaptation.

The complex growth cycle of the Lepidoptera begins with the formation of the embryo at the moment of fertilization; if the eggs are not fertilized, no embryos can develop. Only in exceptional cases, as among certain Psychidae, can unfertilized eggs produce larvae through a process known as parthenogenesis. Inside the egg, the embryo develops in the course of a few days. Having matured, the larva emerges from the egg and from that instant has to fend for itself. In many species it consumes the empty eggshell or chorion, in others it seeks a specific food source. The larvae of virtually all families of Lepidoptera live on plant tissue, while the adults mostly feed on sugary substances. Very few larvae infest lower plants; most of them live on phanerogams (plants that produce seeds), utilizing every part from flowers and fruits to woody stems. In some cases, the larvae of a single species may attack, in the course of successive generations, those parts of the plant that are seasonally available and appetizing. Take, for example, the olive kernel borer (*Prays oleae*), a moth belonging to the family Yponomeutidae. In southern Europe, the larvae, which emerge from eggs laid in the autumn, immediately attack the leaves of the olive, tunneling into them and devouring them from the outside. In early April the chrysalids form on the tree and on the ground. In April–May the first-generation adults appear and the females lay their eggs on the flower buds and on the leaves near the flower heads. The emerging caterpillars penetrate and devour these parts; and in due course the open flowers, too, are attacked. Pupation then occurs in the tangle of dried plant remnants. The adults of the second generation appear in June and lay eggs on the fruits. The larvae burrow their way into the fruit, reaching the seed, and often consume it entirely. When these larvae mature (August–September) they emerge close to the stalk and pupate on the leaves and twigs, or, if the fruit has fallen, here and there on the ground. The third-generation adults take wing from the end of August to mid-October, lay eggs on the leaves and produce hibernating larvae, which begin the cycle over again.

Selective pressure of this kind, together with that of other plant-eating organisms, has induced certain plants, in the course of their evolution, to furnish themselves with special defenses, consisting principally of self-manufactured toxic compounds. Some of these substances are used directly by man to fight insects; an example is pyrethrum, extracted from plants of the genus *Chrysanthemum*. Such defenses have limited the attacks of plant-eating insects but, on the other hand, have caused the latter, too, to develop special adaptations. There may, for instance, be a synthesis of enzymes capable of combating the toxic effects, or the sharpening of the instinct that enables the butterfly or moth to select the host plant. According to this choice, the Lepidoptera larvae may be defined as monophagous when they live off only one plant species, oligophagous when they attack a few different but related species, and polyphagous when they use numerous groups of plant species that belong to different families. An example of how this instinct is actually a choice based on chemical factors is furnished by the Pieridae, which feed on Capparidaceae and Cruciferae. Such plants produce substances that repel many insects but which represent, for these butterflies, a guaranteed signal for recognizing food. The caterpillars, in fact, may be deceived by treating other plant species or even bits of paper with these substances. Such behavior has induced researchers to carry out investigations on the relationships between various plant groups infested by caterpillars with extremely specialized food preferences.

The majority of Lepidoptera larvae feed on the plant tissue, attacking it from the outside; but especially interesting are those species that lead their larval existence inside the tissue. In the case of most miners or borers (species that build tiny tunnels), the eggs are laid inside the leaf tissue. This affords them greater protection and the young larva that emerges need not perforate the plant's strong epidermis. Once hatched, the young larva begins to dig tunnels or mines, without making any holes in either leaf surface. These tunnels take various forms, clearly visible on the leaves, so constituting a helpful taxonomic feature that serves to identify the species. The Nepticulidae (midget

The larvae of butterflies and moths feed on varying substances. The top drawing shows the damage done to an apple by the codlin moth (Cydia polmonella); the lower drawing is of the goat moth (Cossus cossus), whose larvae dig tunnels in the trunks and branches of various trees.

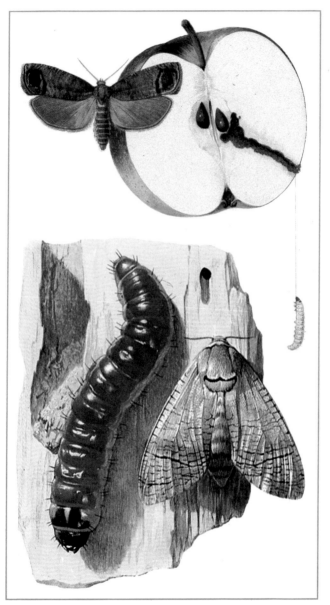

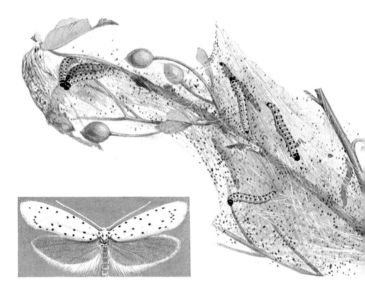

moths) are the best-known group of miners, comprising the tiniest species in the entire order, with a wingspan of 3–4 mm. Far more difficult is the task of the Sesiidae (clear wing moths) and the Cossidae (goat moths) which dig tunnels in trunks and branches, and which live several years before the appearance of the adults (probably due to the low nutritive value of the wood).

Galls can also be used in classifying the Lepidoptera that produce them. These are growths produced by the plant as it reacts to certain stimuli. In the case of many Lepidoptera for example, the simple act of egg-laying triggers the reaction; the larvae that hatch from the eggs develop inside the gall, which is thus used as shelter. The families Tortricidae (leaf roller moths) and Gelechiidae possess the largest number of gall-dwelling species.

A series of complex adaptations has enabled the larvae of certain Lepidoptera (principally Pyralidae) to live underwater. *Nymphula nymphaeata*, which lives on pondweed and water lilies, is one of the best-known examples. The females of this species lay eggs on the underside of these aquatic plants: the emergent larva is, at this stage, a miner living in plant tissues that are almost saturated with water and breathing dissolved oxygen through its cuticle. Following this phase, it builds a case with two leaf segments attached to the leaves of the food plant; in the fall these drop, carrying the larva with them, which then spends the winter completely submerged in water. In the spring, the

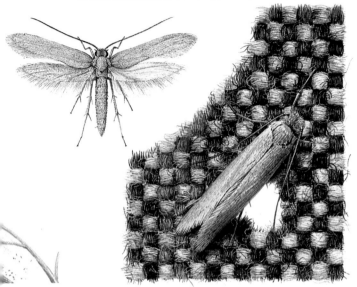

Many species attack plant and animal substances that are man-made. The larva of Tineola bisseliella, *shown here, damages various kinds of material. The group of so-called clothes moths spread rapidly and are found virtually everywhere.*

growing plants bring the lavae back to the surface radically transformed; they shed their aquatic features and assume the capacity to breathe atmospheric oxygen. They construct a new case from the two leaf segments and use it to float on the surface of the water; then, attaching themselves with silk threads to the water plant, they resume feeding. When mature, the lavae build yet another case attached to the stems of the aquatic plants, which are situated under the water's surface. This case is full of air and in it pupation occurs. The construction of protective cases is also found in certain families with terrestrial larvae such as the Psychidae, Coleophoridae, Tineidae, etc. Such a case may be built with a variety of materials, cemented with secretions from the spinneret. The larva lives in the case, carrying it around wherever it goes and enlarging it with new material as it grows. As with mines and galls, such cases are characteristic of individual species, providing useful taxonomic information.

Although most butterflies and moths feed on plants, there are exceptions, which have adapted to truly strange forms of diet. Many Microlepidoptera feed on vegetable substances made by man, such as corks, edible pastes, and flour, paper, and cloth. Substances of animal origin are not immune: they may include wool, fur, feathers, and stuffed animals. Even the excrement of mammals and birds may be used by the developing larvae, especially among the Tineidae. The behavior of one member of the Pyralidae, *Cryptoses choloepi*, is quite astonishing. As an adult it lives exclusively in the fur of the three-toed sloth, an edentate mammal, which feeds on the highest leaves of forests in Central and South America. When the sloth comes down to the ground to defecate, about once a week, the female moths lay their eggs on the fresh dung. The young larvae complete their development in three weeks and are transformed into the adult insect; they then fly up to the forest canopy and begin their quest for sloths. This close link between the adult *Cryptoses* and the sloth is no accident, for it assures the larvae priority in the choice and availability of food as they compete with other dung-eaters on the forest floor.

Some larvae of the Lepidoptera are predatory and carnivorous, as, for example, are certain groups of Asiatic Noctuidae, which attack the eggs and adult Coccidae, of the order Hemiptera. But the most specialized predators are found among the Lycaenidae. *Feniseca tarquinius*, which lives in North America, attacks certain genera of Aphidae. The larvae hide from the ants, which attend the aphids, and launch their attacks when the moment is ripe. Virtually all species that seek out aphids are also myrmecophilous (ie. nest with ants), given that they have to placate the ants before they can get at their prey. The larvae of groups such as the Miletinae and Plebejinae secrete sugary liquids similar to those produced by the aphids. The larvae thus acquires a sort of immunity, and a predator such as *Miletus boisduvalii* is capable of destroying hundreds of aphids at a time. The Palearctic genus *Maculinea* enjoys a mixed diet of plants and flesh. *Maculinea arion* lays its eggs on *Thymus* (thyme), and the larvae start by feeding on the flowers of the plant. After the second molt, they develop myrmecophilous glands and from that moment the ants begin to attend them. After the third molt the larvae are carried by the ants into the ants' nest and immediately begin feeding on the larvae of the host ants, spending the winter actually in their victims' cells. The havoc resumes in the spring and lasts until pupation.

Other carnivores live even more dangerously: the larvae of certain Noctuidae live on the leaves of carnivorous pitcher plants (genus *Nepenthes*). They feed on the plants' victims that have fallen into the leaf hollow of the plant and are being decomposed by the liquid in it. There are also species of Tineidae and Gelechiidae that venture into spiders' webs, consuming the remains of their victims or even their eggs.

Once mature, the caterpillar stops feeding to search for a place in which to transform itself into a chrysalis. This is not necessarily a sheltered spot. Many butterflies, for instance, pupate in the open, attached to any kind of support or propped against the ground inside a few silken threads. In the first case, the caterpillars build a small silken pad, stuck to the selected support, on which they anchor themselves with their prolegs. During the transformation into a chrysalis, these prolegs are replaced by a

variable series of hooks (cremaster), which provides an even stronger attachment to the silk. The suspended chrysalids may adopt two basic positions: either hanging by the cremaster upside-down, or in the opposite position, still attached by the cremaster but provided with extra support by a "safety belt" spun by the caterpillar around its thorax.

Many moths, on the other hand, look for sheltered places such as cracks or holes. Some Noctuidae pupate in the soil, building small cavities often reinforced with silken threads a few inches below the surface. In other cases the caterpillars construct their own cocoon of slender silk thread. The best-known example is that of the mulberry silkworm, *Bombyx mori*, but other groups also use this system, often supplementing the silken threads with hairs or pieces of leaf. The strongest cocoons are those built by certain species of Notodontidae, made from a pasty secretion of the salivary glands stuck to slivers of wood. Having completed the preparations such as these, the caterpillar stops moving and its transformation begins. Inside the cocoon a chemical process, known as histolysis, commences, whereby almost all the caterpillar's tissues dissolve into a formless mass from which, in due course, the adult will emerge from the chrysalis.

Emergence is a rather delicate and painstaking business, in the course of which the insect has to break the cuticle of the chrysalis and, where present, the cocoon as well. Reacting to environmental stimuli such as temperature or humidity, the butterfly's

Courtship phases of the satyrid Hipparchia semele. *In the top figure the male (left) wraps the female's antennae in his forewings, so that they touch his androconial scales. If the female proves receptive, the male makes a semicircle, bringing himself into contact with the tip of his partner's abdomen (lower figure). Copulation then takes place.*

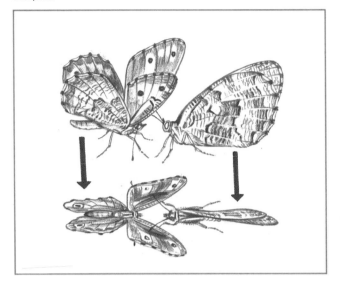

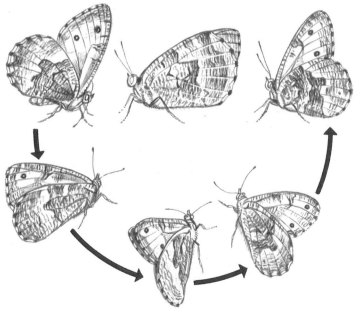

body fluids flow into its head and abdomen, causing the rupture of the cuticle. Pointed processes located on the head and at the base of the wings enable the insect to pierce the cocoon and make its way out. When newly emerged, the butterfly's wings are still soft and barely opened. As the hemolymph is pumped through the veins, the wings gradually spread to their full extent. The veins are then stiffened and the insect is ready to fly. Its principal task is now reproduction.

As already mentioned, butterflies and moths have two sexes. The primary task of the adult male, therefore, is first to find a partner and then to persuade her to couple. For this purpose butterflies have evolved a kind of sexual language based on chemical stimuli, which enable them to overcome difficulties such as distance and visibility, and even the possible reluctance of the partner. In some cases, as with the Rhopalocera (butterflies proper), matters initially proceed quite simply; the male, in fact, seeks out the female visually and will, as has been shown experimentally, follow virtually anything that bears the least resemblance to her. Studies carried out on the satyrine *Hipparchia semele* have established that the males will pursue butterflies belonging to other groups, birds, and objects of various shapes and colors provided the movements are similar to the fluttering flight pattern of their own species. The pursuit of a genuine *H. semele* results in her being brought to ground quite rapidly.

At this point the male commences a dance consisting of movements and wingbeats, culminating in the closure of the forewings over the female's antennae. This is explained by the fact that on the male's forewings there are so-called androconial scales, from which are released sex scents (pheromones), which excite the female. After this operation, the male makes a semicircular movement, bringing the abdomens into contact, so that mating can take place. His first attempt is not always successful: only if the female, slightly raising her wings, exposes her abdomen, can copulation occur. Should this not happen, the male will need to make several attempts to seduce his partner by repeating, sometimes more briefly, the above-mentioned courtship procedure. Females may display various forms of refusal behavior. The female *Pieris brassicae* sometimes allows herself to fall through the leaves, remaining rigid and immobile, wings closed, while at other times she spreads her wings and lifts her abdomen vertically, almost in an attitude of fright. In such a case, the male will hastily retreat. In other groups, like the Danainae, the glands that produce the pheromones are situated in the male's abdomen and the scents are distributed by two tufts of extensible hairs. To excite the female, the male *Danaus gilippus* repeatedly touches her antennae and head with these tufts. Only recently has it been discovered why the tufts are occasionally to be found in a small pouch located in the male's hind wings: evidently such contact is

In some cases close relationships may develop between lepidoptera and plants. For the Liliaceae of the genus Yucca *(1)*, the fairy moth Tegeticula yuccasella *(2)* is the only organism capable of pollinating them. The special mouth parts of the moth *(3)*

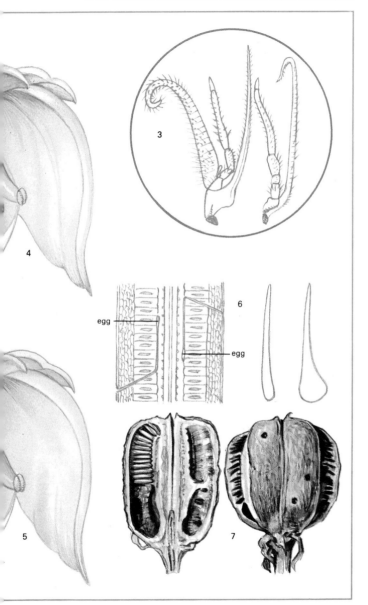

41

During migrations butterflies and moths may travel immense distances. The painted lady (Vanessa cardui), one of the best-known migrants, leaves the shores of Africa in the spring and reaches Iceland and Scandinavia. The species is also known in North America, journeying from Mexico to Canada.

necessary for the synthesis of the pheromone. Among many moths it is the male who always seeks a partner, but sometimes it is the female who attracts the male with her pheromones, even at a distance of some miles. In addition to this attractive capacity, it is worth noting that the high receptivity of the male's antennae may be activated by a single molecule of pheromones. Courtship in these groups is practically nonexistent: mating takes place as soon as the sexes meet.

Other forms of behavior in butterflies and moths increase the likelihood of successful reproduction. They include territoriality, common among many animals. Such behavior implies defense of demarcated territory, occupied by the male of a particular species, against intruders who are generally of the same sex and species. This actually has reproductive significance, since the occupied territory is, as a rule, the best area for the species concerned, both for courtship and for laying eggs. The size of this controlled area may vary a good deal: it can range from 3,000 square feet in the case of the American nymphaline, *Asterocampa leilia*, to just a few square feet for the speckled wood (*Pararge aegeria*), a European satyrine. The male chooses a favorable position, not always high up, from which to launch his attack on an intruder. The peacock (*Inachis io*), for example, takes off from the ground in pursuit of the intruder, while *Charaxes jasius* stations himself, as observed in many instances, at a height of about six feet. *C. jasius* is particularly fierce in the

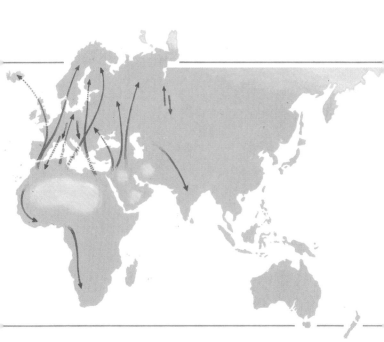

defense of territory: the male has even been observed chasing birds. If the reigning male happens to have strayed some way from his domain, another male is always ready to take his place. In the case of *Pararge aegeria*, territory consists of a few square feet of woodland clearing illuminated by sunlight filtering through the treetops. The new occupant, after a few moments to make sure he is unlikely to be attacked by males who are already there, immediately embarks upon his defense action.

Adult butterflies and moths have no other function apart from mating and dispersal. Even feeding is restricted and usually based on sugary substances. Yet as in the larval stages there are some strange feeding habits. The death's head hawkmoth (*Acherontia atropos*), a member of the Sphingidae, feeds on honey from beehives, while certain Noctuidae perforate the skin of fruit with their proboscis in order to suck the juice. Adaptations for feeding on animal substances are found, not only among the larvae, but also in the adults. Such substances include urine, perspiration, and other secretions. Some tropical Geometridae and Noctuidae attack the eyes of mammals, humans included, inserting their proboscis beneath the eyelashes and feeding on laychrymal fluids. A very famous example is that of the Oriental noctuid, *Calpe eustrigata*, which can pierce the skin of mammals in order to suck their blood.

From the examples given of the habits of butterflies and moths, it is evident that these insects are individualistic; there are no organized communities, as among ants and bees, with appropriate division of labor or care of the young. Yet we do find instances of mass behavior, in which individuals carry out coordinated activities, as in migrations, or, for example, in the single-file expeditions carried out by caterpillars of the pine procession-ary (*Thaumetopoea pityocampa*): some experts describe this phenomenon as gregariousness or the herd instinct. The significance of such mass movements is still unclear. Migratory behavior, for instance, is exhibited almost as soon as the adult takes wing, and would appear to involve a series of preordained stimuli and directives. According to some, it operates in the same manner as in homing pigeons, so that the insects find their direction in flight by using polarized light; however, this is by no means a certainty. As a rule, individuals of migrating species are incapable of completing the entire journey in both directions; one part of the journey is, in fact, made by the next generation. The painted lady (*Vanessa cardui*), for instance, migrates every year, between the spring and the fall, from the shores of North Africa to northern Europe, where it dies with the arrival of winter. Its offspring make the return journey the following spring. This species is also found in North America where it also embarks on mass migrations. An exception to this rule is provided by the Monarch (*Danaus plexippus*). This American danaine is found from northern Canada to Mexico, but in North America it is present only in the summer. In the fall the butterflies form small groups and set off toward the south, increasing their numbers as they go. The journey, as has been verified from marked specimens, is more than 1,500 miles long and the winter quarters are always the same and very circumscribed. Hundreds of thousands of individuals form long garlands on the trees, spending the winter in a state of semi-hibernation and resuming their activity next spring. After pairing, the same adults depart again for the north, repeating their journey of the previous fall in the opposite direction. Soon after their departure or during the journey a new generation appears, and many of the adults travel alongside their offspring.

The migratory phenomenon is most widespread among the Sphingidae, Noctuidae, Danainae, Nymphalinae and Pieridae. It may also be encountered in the larval stages of species that spend their life in colonies, being especially frequent among the Lymantriidae and Lasiocampidae, whereas in other families there are only isolated cases. The caterpillars of the genus *Thaumetopoea*, the processionary moths belonging to the family Lymantriidae, venture out for food in long processions, each individual touching the one in front with its head. These single-file expeditions, as has been experimentally shown, are purely instinctive, with no single individual taking the lead. In fact, if the column is interrupted at any point, the caterpillars immediately

Many diurnal lepidoptera gather in wet places to absorb liquids. The plate overleaf shows some examples of two Neotropical Nymphalidae: In the foreground, left, is Metamorpha epaphus *and, with the two distinctive "figures of eight" on the hind wings,* Diaethria clymena.

follow the individual who happens to be at the front, no matter which direction it takes.

Other types of mass behavior exist, although involving lesser numbers of individuals. Groups of butterflies or moths may often be seen feeding on liquids in wet places or gathering for their nightly rest. Such an assembly appears to constitute a defensive strategy for limiting the harm done in attacks by predators. Predators, in fact, tend to be disorientated by numerous individuals all taking wing together; in the case of unappetizing species, too, defensive odors are certainly stronger in the mass than in isolated individuals. This, however, is merely one of the many defensive adaptations that butterflies and moths can use against predators. Such adaptations are to be found in the larvae as well as in the adults, and for the most part may be defined as passive behavior patterns. Exceptions are very rare: there are some species of Notodontidae whose caterpillars, if disturbed, can spray formic acid for a distance of several inches. But in most instances defense is achieved by means of hairs or irritant spines, by flight, mimicry, warning, coloration, etc. The simplest method is pure concealment: most moths take refuge by day in suitable hiding places. However, predators, particularly bats, also hunt at night. Some moths have evolved very sophisticated mechanisms to cope with this danger; most species of Arctiidae, Noctuidae, and Geometridae have developed, as adults, tympanic organs that pick up the ultrasounds emitted by bats for locating their prey. Reception of such ultrasounds permits the moths to alter flight direction in time to escape attack. Some Arctiidae, on the other hand, respond to the signals of the bats with their own high-frequency sounds, clearly audible to the bats. These may be warning signals, as many members of this family are distasteful to vertebrates.

One of the most common defensive systems used by butterflies and moths is cryptic mimicry or camouflage, which simply entails blending in with the surroundings. The Geometridae are particularly skillful at this; not only do they adopt a cryptic appearance through color but they also eliminate the shadow thrown by their wings by flattening them against the ground, making their body outline less visible. Many species model themselves on various objects, such as green and dry leaves or thorns, for mimetic effect. The larvae of Geometridae can imitate dry twigs to perfection; when at rest, they grip the bark with their anal prolegs, holding the rest of their body stiff and upright, well removed from the supporting surface. Among adults of the tropical genus *Kallima*, which belongs to the Nymphalidae, the upper side of their wings are vividly colored, while the reverse side resembles a dead leaf. The small wing apices, which look like leaf stalks, and the insect's position, complete the similarity so effectively that the butterfly appears to vanish the moment it alights. If disturbed, it opens its wings to display the colored

45

parts: this "flash coloration" startles the predator for an instant, which is usually sufficient time to allow the butterfly to escape. This is a defensive technique also to be found in many Noctuidae, which possess brightly colored hind wings and cryptic toned forewings. When the moth is at rest, the forewings completely conceal the hind ones, which, however, can be suddenly flaunted.

Many Lepidoptera have evolved defense mechanisms involving the production of substances that make them toxic or unappetizing to many predators. The caterpillars of processionary moths have irritating substances on their spines, and many Lymantriidae protect their eggs with irritant hairs. Such substances, whether toxic or repellent, are often part of the actual tissues, which have almost always been absorbed from plant food: a well-known example is the oleander sphinx. The burnet moths of the genus *Zygaena*, however, store hydrocyanic acid in their hemolymph, which is emitted either as a result of an injury or at will from the base of the antennae. These chemical defenses are supplemented by the vivid coloration that characterizes the various species. Unlike the cryptic species, these moths stand out clearly from their surroundings: in fact, the patterns function as warning (aposematic) signals, reminding the predator that the prey is unappetizing. It has been demonstrated that it takes a predator few attempts before learning to recognize such species and to avoid them in future encounters.

46

There is another adaptation, known as phaneric mimicry, in which these protected species are imitated, through similar coloration, by species not provided with defensive chemicals. There are two types of phaneric mimicry, the first of which is called Batesian, named after the scientist Henry Walter Bates who, in 1862, formulated this theory by observation of the insects in the Brazilian forests. He noted in particular that many butterflies and moths looked alike even though they belonged to different families. He was especially struck by certain Pieridae that bore a strong resemblance to Heliconiinae, a numerous group in the South American forests characterized by spectacular colors. Observing the Heliconiinae, he noticed that although the insects were slow-flying and easily identifiable against the forest background, they were never attacked by birds. From this Bates theorized that the Heliconiinae must be distasteful to predators and that the Pieridae, which by the phenomenon of convergent evolution bore similar colors, enjoyed the same advantage. This type of mimicry is most effective when the imitator flies at the same speed and in the same places as its model, and when there are more individuals of the genuine species than of the pretenders. Bates, however, failed to explain why certain species of unappetizing butterflies and moths, systematically unrelated, still resembled each other. It was Fritz Müller, in 1878, who put forward an explanation, defining so-called Müllerian mimicry. He suggested that the more venomous species there were with the

Butterflies and moths often defend themselves in different ways against predators, both at larval and adult stages. Figs 1 and 2 show respectively the caterpillars of Cuculia artemisiae (Noctuidae) and Papilio troilus (Papilionidae). The former imitates the flowers on which it feeds, while the latter takes on the appearance of a snake's head. Similar adaptations are found in adults. Fig. 3 shows the adult of the nymphalid

same warning colors, the more quickly a predator would learn to recognize a particular warning color pattern. Thus there exists, particularly in the tropical regions, a complex chain of mimicry, both Batesian and Müllerian. The groups that exhibit these strategies to the highest degree are the Danainae, Ithomiinae, Heliconiinae, Pieridae and Castniidae. In temperate regions these mimetic systems are less common. In Europe and elsewhere Müllerian mimicry is found not only among Lepidoptera but in insects of other orders mimicking the Lepidoptera. The models are red and black moths of the family Zygaenidae and are imitated by beetles of the genus *Trichodes*, belonging to the Cleridae, and cuckoo spit insects of the genus *Cercopis*.

The behavior of butterflies and moths, like that of other living organisms, is also influenced by the physical conditions of the environment in which they live. Factors such as temperature and humidity can sometimes be more dangerous enemies than predators. We have already seen how these insects have developed mechanisms (quiescence and diapause) that enable them for the most part to overcome such adverse conditions. But there are other adaptations that permit more positive responses. Take, for instance, the activity of flight: its efficiency depends on the ability of the butterfly or moth to heat up its wing muscles to a suitable level, for otherwise it is incapable of flying. The optimal temperature for butterflies is 77°–78°F (25°–26°C). It is clear that if the surrounding temperature rises higher than this, it will cause problems for the insect. But in the contrary case, butterflies and moths have managed to develop "pre-heating" techniques that will enable them to reach, obviously within certain limits, the requisite temperature. The simplest of these systems consists in utilizing radiation from the sun, whereby butterflies warm the surface of their wings and in turn the hemolymph circulating in the tissues. At dawn or on cloudy days, when they cannot resort to solar radiation, they seek shelter and remain there as long as unfavorable conditions last. Crepuscular and nocturnal moths obviously adopt other systems. They regulate their own thoracic temperature by rapidly vibrating or beating their wings against the ground. The necessary temperature for flight, in these groups, varies considerably according to their body dimensions; it may range from 61°–63°F (16°–17°C) in the small Geometridae to 104°F (40°C) and above in the Sphingidae and Saturnidae.

Temperature is the one physical factor that exerts the most influence on the development of lepidopteran eggs and may delay such development from a few days to several weeks. In the case of the silver Y moth (*Autographa gamma*), the eggs develop in three days if exposed to a temperature of 77°F (25°C), in five or six days at 68°F (20°C), and in fifteen days at 59°F (15°C). The minimum and maximum survival thresholds among the Lepidoptera are somewhat variable: in the mountains of northern Europe adults are active at temperatures close to 32°F (0°C), but

Kallima inachus, *which imitates to perfection a dead leaf, while fig. 4 illustrates the* saturniid Automeris io, *with its false eyes.*

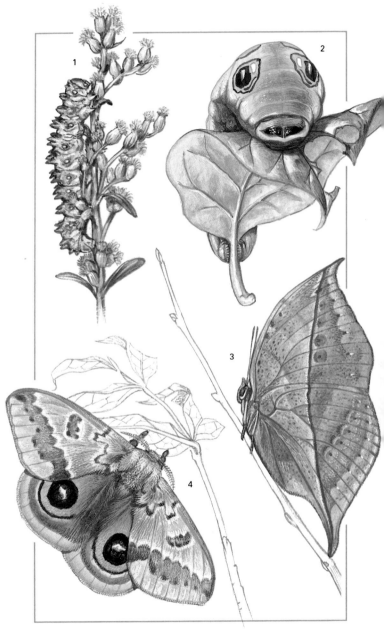

In the Palaearctic region one of the most famous associations of Müllerian mimicry is represented by certain lepidoptera of the genus Zygaena *(1, punctum; 2.* lonicerae; *3.* filipendulae) *and certain beetles and bugs (4.* Trichodes apiarius; *5.* Cercopis sanguinea). *All these species are distasteful, and predators soon learn to avoid those*

obviously such values, especially if prolonged, would prove lethal for species from more temperate climates. Lepidoptera are better able to tolerate downward rather than upward fluctuations in temperature, because of physiological adaptations: temperatures of over 104°F (40°C) are critical for most butterflies and moths whereas the minimum survival threshold for cold-climate species is around −40°F (−40°C). Humidity, too, is another enormously important factor. Some species of Lepidoptera that live in conditions of extreme dryness are furnished with a series of adaptations enabling them to survive, such as larvae covered with dense downy hairs to retain humidity, or a very thick eggshell. By contrast, other groups prefer surroundings with high humidity: for example miner larvae, which live inside the leaves and stems of plants where the humidity is higher than on the outside. Many caterpillars utilize the humidity of the soil, even sheltering there by day when the air is dry.

PREDATORS AND PARASITES

In the life cycle of a butterfly or moth, no stage of development is immune to the attacks of parasites and predators. Among the former, above all, are viruses and bacteria, as yet little known, which are the principal causes of death in caterpillars. Among the latter two orders of insects can be described as the chief parasites of the Lepidoptera: the Diptera and the Hymenoptera.

These parasitic insects do not kill the host individual immediately; instead the female parasite simply deposits her eggs on or inside the host body. The young larvae therefore feed on the caterpillar, which remains alive at least until the parasite is completely developed. It is very common, in the course of breeding butterflies, to see one of these parasitic insects emerge from the chrysalis instead of an adult butterfly. Among the most important families of Hymenoptera to operate in this fashion are the Ichneumonidae, the Chalcidae, and the Braconidae. Particularly active in the last family are the wasps of the genus *Apanteles*, which may parasitize the Zygaenidae, even though, as already mentioned, these moths contain large amounts of hydrocyanic acid used as defense. The wasps are immune to this acid owing to the presence of an enzyme in their tissues, which nullifies its toxic effects.

Among the Diptera are the Tachinidae: the eggs of many of these species of fly are not laid directly on the host but instead, the young larvae attack the caterpillar. Another phenomenon, hyperparasitism, is common, the most specialized of these being the Chalcidae, members of the Hymenoptera. The female chalcid flies lay their eggs in the larvae of other Hymenoptera already in the process of parasitizing caterpillars. Thus a caterpillar may play host to hyperparasites up to four times removed.

51

An example of a discontinuous range is that of Zygaena exulans. *In this instance the discontinuity is caused by the climatic variation that has occurred between the last glaciations and the present day.*

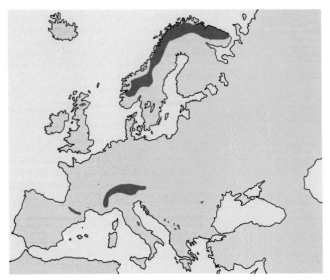

Predators are found among virtually all types of vertebrate; the most important predators of butterflies and moths are reptiles (lizards), bats, and birds. Arthropods such as spiders, mantids, assassin bugs (Reduviidae), tiger beetles (Cicindelidae), and ground beetles (Carabidae) also prey upon lepidopterans.

GEOGRAPHICAL DISTRIBUTION

Butterflies and moths are found on all the continents, and every species occupies its own precise geographical or distribution area. The size of such areas varies enormously; they may cover a few square miles of a mountain region or extend over an entire land mass. In the latter instance the species concerned are described as cosmopolitan; others with a specific range (found nowhere else) are defined as endemic. This diversity depends on various environmental factors: in simple terms, a species is distributed over an area provided it finds no natural barriers (oceans, mountains, etc.) to its dispersal. Geographical or ecological barriers may in fact be found within a distribution area, thus creating discontinuities, characteristic of the majority of Lepidoptera.

A classic example of discontinuous distribution is provided by the European satyrine *Erebia pandrose*. This butterfly is present

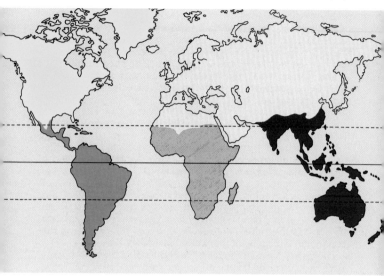

in northern Europe, with an almost continuous distribution from Norway to Finland. But isolated populations are also to be found in central-southern Europe, especially in the Pyrenees, the Alps, and the central Apennines, the Carpathians, the Balkans, and the Altai mountains. The reason for the discontinuity, in this instance, is the variation in climate from the time of the most recent Ice Age to the present day. During the cold periods, those species inhabiting the ice-covered zones were able to expand their range southward along with the spread of the polar icecaps. When in due course temperatures rose and the ice retreated, the relic populations survived only in zones where environmental conditions remained almost unchanged, namely on the summits of the highest mountain ranges.

In addition to environmental and climatic factors, the distribution area of a species depends on its capacity for colonization. Butterflies and moths, being good flyers, are able to disperse far and wide: migratory butterflies and moths, for example, can travel many hundreds of miles. There are exceptions, however, as among the bagworm moths (Psychidae). In this family the females are apterous (wingless) and cannot fly, while the males do not stray far from their places of origin. It is clear that in this case dispersal of the species depends almost wholly on the larvae.

Man sometimes helps to broaden the distribution area by transporting butterflies and moths, either deliberately or unwittingly, from place to place. The common silkworm, for example, is one species distributed deliberately for commercial reasons, whereas the gypsy moth (*Lymantria dispar*), which came originally from Eurasia, was accidentally introduced to the United States in the nineteenth century, and has gone on to become one of the most common insect pests of American forests.

Once the species has overcome obstacles to dispersal, it faces the critical stage of colonization, the outcome of which is almost always unpredictable. The process is affected by many factors, associated either with the species (change of food plant, climatic tolerance, genetic variability, etc.) or with the new surroundings (climate, vegetation, predators, and parasites, etc.). If such factors are positive, they will favor expansion, if not they may lead to a shrinkage in area. A well known example of shrinkage is that of the large copper (*Lycaena dispar*), which inhabits wet zones of the Palaearctic region. In the nineteenth century the eastern part of its distribution area was greatly reduced by climatic changes and the clearance of marshes and swamps by man, thus isolating its populations throughout western Europe. The process is still continuing and some of these populations are now extinct.

Zoologists have subdivided the earth's land areas into large entities known as faunal or zoogeographical regions. These regions (Palaearctic, Nearctic, Afrotropical, Neotropical, Indo-Malayan, and Australian) are mostly bounded by geographical barriers such as oceans, mountain ranges, or deserts, and retain their individual characteristics; but the boundaries between one region and another are not always so clear cut. Thus there are zones where an exchange of fauna is, in varying measure, quite common.

The Palaearctic region comprises Europe, Africa north of the Sahara, and northern Asia, the southern boundary of which is formed by the Himalayas. As might be expected in a territory of such vast size (this region has the biggest land surface), the Palaearctic has a wide variation of environmental conditions, ranging from the scrublands of the Mediterranean to the subtropical forests of Japan and Korea and the arctic tundra of Siberia. In spite of this ecological diversity, there are relatively few species, this being due, as in the Nearctic region, to its climatic vicissitudes. During the Pleistocene, in fact, glaciations that lasted without interruption for about half a million years, and only came to an end some 10,000 years ago, led to extinction or the migration of species. It is not by chance that there are many species adapted to cold conditions to be found not only at extreme latitudes but also scattered among the highest mountain areas of the Palaearctic. As far as is known today, central Asia (that part included in the Palaearctic region), and in particular Tibet, possesses the most species of butterflies (Rhopalocera). This profusion is due principally to the invasion of many characteristic species from the neighboring Indo-Malayan region.

About half the genera of butterflies known to live in Tibet are actually from the latter region. The most important families of Lepidoptera in the Palaearctic, in terms of number of species and diffusion, are the Geometridae (3,000 species) and the Noctuidae (about 2,000 species), together with certain groups of Microlepidoptera such as the Tortricidae, Coleophoridae, Pyralidae, and Nepticulidae. Among the best known and most widely distributed of Rhopalocera are the pierids *Leptidea morsei, Pieris napi, Anthocaris cardamines*, and *Gonepteryx rhamni*; the nymphalines *Argynnis paphia, Apatura ilia, Limenitis camilla, L. populi, Mesoacidalia aglaja*, and *Araschnia levana*; the lycaenids *Lycaena phlaeas* and *Celastrina argiolus*; and the satyrines *Lopinga achine* and *Erebia ligea*.

The Nearctic region comprises North America and part of Mexico north of 20° latitude (Mexico City). Its fauna of butterflies and moths, like the entire animal and plant population, bears a close similarity to that of the Palaearctic. This, among other things, is due to climatic conditions as this region experienced the same Pleistocene glaciations; and here, as well, residual cold-climate populations are to be found in the highest mountain ranges of North America. Many scientists – interpreting the numerous links between the fauna of North America, Europe, and northern Asia as clear signs that animal populations have been exchanged (probably without interruption for thousands of years) – identify a single land mass, known as the Holarctic, comprising all these northern regions. Among the best-known and most widely distributed genera of Holarctic Rhopalocera are *Colias, Erebia, Clossiana, Boloria*, and *Parnassius*. A detailed examination of the North American fauna shows how species from neighboring Eurasia gradually diminish in numbers from north to south. This is due both to climatic factors and to a more intensive faunal exchange with the adjacent Neotropical region. In Florida, for example, about 80% of the species of Rhopalocera belong to Nearctic and Neotropical genera. Among the latter are the pierid *Euremia proterpia*, the papilionid *Papilio aristodemus*, the nymphalines *Danaus plexippus, Dryas iulia, Heliconius erato*, etc. Among the Saturniidae, however, one finds the best-known endemic species of the Nearctic: *Actias luna, Callosamia promethea, Automeris io*, etc. California is also of extreme interest, being one of the zones with the greatest number of endemic species in the entire continent of North America. This may be explained by the presence of formidable barriers (the Rocky Mountains, the deserts of Arizona and New Mexico, and the Gulf of California), which have prevented genetic exchanges with neighboring Lepidoptera populations.

The Afrotropical region comprises the African continent south of the Sahara and the southern part of the Arabian peninsula. Madagascar, with the nearby Comoro, Mascarene, and Seychelles archipelagos, has an exceptionally rich endemic fauna

and is regarded by some experts as a separate region, by others as a subregion. Of some 300 known species of butterflies in Madagascar, about 230 are endemic. Examination of the vegetational types of the whole Afrotropical region indicates that rain forest, savannah, and grassland are most widespread, though in a somewhat discontinuous manner. The tropical rain forest is undoubtedly one of the favored habitants of the Lepidoptera. The forest's fragmentation, due to the alteration in historic times of pluvial and interpluvial periods, has caused the evolution of numerous species, many of them nowadays endemic to the rain forest. The geographical areas richest in Rhopalocera (butterfly) species are Cameroon (1,150), Zaïre (1,000), Ivory Coast (750), and South Africa (200). The Lycaenidae, with some 1,100 species, are the largest represented family, whereas there are comparatively few Satyridae, Riodinidae, and Libytheidae. The closest affinities are with the Indo-Malayan region, especially in terms of the Rhopalocera: examples are the genera *Melanitis, Acraea, Kallima, Charaxes, Neptis*, etc.

The Neotropical region contains a far greater number of species. It consists of Central and South America, the West Indies, and the Galapagos Islands. There is enormous diversity of animal life in this area, by reason of its climatic and topographical complexity. The western boundary, in fact, is the line of the Andes mountain range, with peaks of over 20,000 ft. (6,000 m), while the remaining part is made up of deserts, steppes, high tropical plateaus and extensive rain forests. There are some affinities with the Afrotropical region, particularly evident in the case of the Nymphalidae. According to some experts, this may derive from the fact that until the Cretaceous era South America and Africa were joined, so permitting an exchange of fauna. Among the most characteristically tropical groups are the Morphinae, veritable winged jewels of the rain forest; among the Nymphalinae, the individuals of the genus *Agrias* exhibit an astonishing variety of colors, sufficient to deceive early entomologists, who described numerous species. Recent scholarship has demonstrated that in fact there are only four or five. The Brassolidae include the celebrated genus *Caligo*, very large butterflies with warning signals in the form of owllike eyespots on the reverse side of the hind wings.

The region displaying the most markedly tropical features, however, is the Indo-Malayan, comprising the whole of the Indian subcontinent and Indonesia as far to the southeast as the Sunda Islands. It is densely covered with tropical forest, at one time more extensive than today; only in the western part of the Indian peninsula are there arid zones. The animal population of the Sunda Islands (Sumatra, Java, Borneo, etc.) is particularly fascinating, for here the rise and fall of the sea level over the course of geological eras has led to frequent links and separations of islands. This has encouraged the formation of numerous subspecies, species or groups of species closely related to one another. Examples include the genera *Poritia, Allotinus*, and *Simiskina* among the Lycaenidae, and *Amathusia* and *Tanaecia* among the Nymphalidae.

The Australian region, on the other hand, is partly tropical and partly temperate. It consists of Australia, Tasmania, New Guinea, New Zealand, and minor islands. Of these, Australia and New Guinea have the biggest assortment of Lepidoptera. New Guinea is wholly tropical, as is the northern and northeastern part of Australia, while in the south there are temperate forests. The butterflies and moths of the rain forest are largely Indo-Malayan in origin, but those associated with the eucalyptus and acacia forest areas are much more interesting. There are about 2,500 species of Oecophoridae alone, followed by Tortricidae, Hepialidae, Incurvariidae, Cossidae, Notodontidae, etc.

ASSOCIATIONS WITH MAN

If we were to draw up a list of butterflies and moths, separating the useful species from the harmful ones, we would find the latter to be far more numerous. The essentially vegetable diet of the larvae causes these insects to be both feared and hated by farmers. Nevertheless, it is worth remembering that it is man who has determined that they are either beneficial or harmful according to whether they assist or interfere with his activities; and he alone has usually been responsible, albeit indirectly, for provoking these negative consequences. If we think of any form of natural ecosystem (such as a wood), we see that every organism that inhabits it is actually an integral part of complex food chains in which there is the producer (the plant), transforming inorganic substances into organic substances, the consumer (for example, the caterpillar), which feeds on the producer, and the decomposer (such as bacteria), which demolishes dead organisms. Each of these categories cooperates in maintaining a system of equilibrium within the ecosystem. It is obvious when we look at man's agricultural activities, however, that the same species of Lepidoptera, which in conditions of natural plant growth represented an element of balance, will, when confronted with an overabundance of food as determined by farming practice, increase its numbers beyond all bounds, thus becoming a pest. Hence the evil reputations of the European corn borer (*Ostrinia nubilalis*) and of the codling moth (*Cydia pomonella*), both cosmopolitan. Manufactured goods and foodstuffs also constitute new ecological niches, which have been successfully exploited by many species of Lepidoptera. Particularly well known are the pyralid *Ephestia kuehniella*, which attacks many types of food, and the clothes moth (*Tineola bisseliella*). The list can be extended considerably; recent research has identified

The net for catching butterflies and moths should be easy to fold and assemble. Figs 1–4 show an example. To keep adult specimens in perfect condition and thus obtain the maximum information about their life cycle, it is advisable to raise the caterpillars in special cages, always providing them with fresh food plants (5).

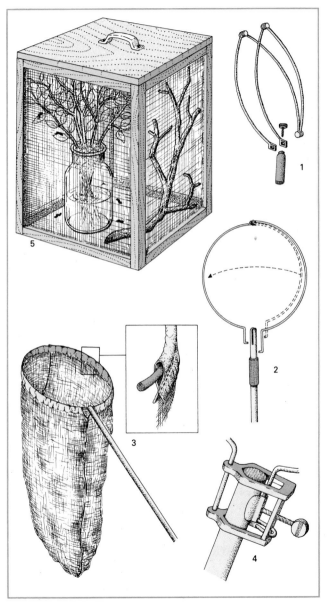

The drawing shows one of the simplest methods of making paper packets for butterflies and moths. Their size will obviously vary according to the dimensions of the insects which are to be caught.

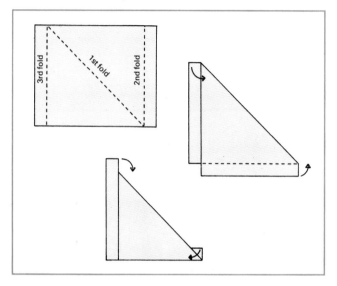

more than 400 species in Europe alone that play an important part in human activities. There are many means of fighting them, ranging from ordinary pesticides to conventional biological methods in which harmful species are controlled by predators or parasites. The two can be combined, as when traps containing pheromones are used for catching the males and a decision made, from the numbers involved, whether or not chemical irradication is necessary.

The list of useful Lepidoptera is much smaller. First place for economic importance is still occupied by the common silkworm (*Bombyx mori*), despite the heavy competition from synthetic textile fibers. Other species are used for biological control, notably the pyralid *Cactoblastis cactorum*. This moth was utilized successfully in Australia and South Africa to check the invasion of the American prickly pear (genus *Opuntia*). Butterflies and moths feature hardly at all in the human diet, except in some parts of the tropics, where people sometimes eat larvae, mainly of species belonging to the families Cossidae, Sphingidae, Satyridae, and Lasiocampidae.

COLLECTION AND CONSERVATION

The method of collecting adult butterflies and moths varies according to their habits of flight, their size, and their structural

Fermented fruit baits are particularly appetizing to diurnal butterflies. Special traps can be used to exploit this attraction; the drawing shows one of the simplest, but collectors can obviously use their experience to modify it.

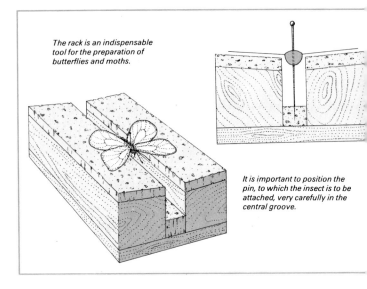

The rack is an indispensable tool for the preparation of butterflies and moths.

It is important to position the pin, to which the insect is to be attached, very carefully in the central groove.

delicacy. Day-flying species, for instance, whether they are Macrolepidoptera or Microlepidoptera, can only be caught with a net. A butterfly net is provided with a handle and consists of a metal ring, about 12–20 in. (30–50 cm) across, which supports a conical net, generally made of nylon, with a minimum depth of 28–32 in. (70–80 cm). A quick rotating movement of the hand folds the net back on itself, preventing the butterfly or moth from escaping. Although somewhat unwieldy, the net can usually be taken apart and folded for carrying, with the handle sectioned or telescoped, and the ring likewise hinged for folding. The handle and the ring can also be conveniently connected by a screw.

Once caught and immobilized in a corner of the net, butterflies should be paralyzed or killed by light pressure of thumb and index finger on the thorax. The specimens can then be transferred into small packets of parchment paper, of varying sizes and shapes, for transport. In the case of the majority of moths, this technique is inadvisable because they are densely covered with delicate hairs and difficult to slip into the packets. Instead, when the insect has been caught in the net, drop the specimen into a wide-necked glass jar, the inner lid of which has been covered in cotton dipped in ether or chloroform. It is also possible to use potassium cyanide but because this can be lethal to humans it is not recommended for use by amateurs. Once the insect is dead, preparations should be made at once for pinning,

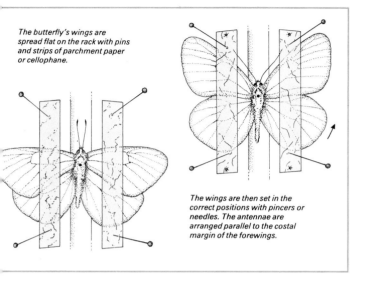

The butterfly's wings are spread flat on the rack with pins and strips of parchment paper or cellophane.

The wings are then set in the correct positions with pincers or needles. The antennae are arranged parallel to the costal margin of the forewings.

keeping the specimen in a suitable box with a soft base. The Microlepidoptera, because they are so difficult to prepare, need to be taken home alive. They should be put into glass tubes directly from the net, and the tubes must immediately be stoppered. Bear in mind that butterflies and moths, once in the net or tube, always try to climb upward to escape.

It is obviously impossible to use a net for catching night-flying moths, so a completely different method is required. This method exploits the fact that very many species are strongly attracted by light. Such behavior has not so far been satisfactorily explained by scientists, but there would seem to be an analogy with the attraction exercised by pheromones. The males appear to be more sensitive to light than the females, and it is noticeable that the approach flight to a light source is conducted in much the same way as when the male is seeking a partner. Far from being haphazard, it follows a steady path in such a manner that the intensity of the reception stimulus is maintained at a high level. The moths can therefore be caught by means of a piece of white cloth attached to suitably fixed stakes. This makeshift screen is then illuminated by a light source consisting of various types of mercury-vapor lamps. Power can be supplied by car batteries or accumulators or even by 200–300 watt generators. It is best to choose warm nights when there is no moon and no wind. The screen should be positioned to make maximum use of the light source, fairly high, perhaps at the edge of a clearing. Any moths that alight on the screen can be collected in jars or tubes, as previously described. Also available, particularly for collecting moths in large numbers and thus to be used with great care, are illuminated traps in which the insects, once close to the light, find their way through an opening and are trapped. Inside, a contraption treated with ether or chloroform kills them immediately. Other traps use bait consisting of fermented substances such as wine, beer, or preserves, erected in places frequented by the butterfly groups to be collected. Two types of traps using pheromones are also very effective. In the first the males are attracted by unfertilized females, kept in small open cages. A single female can sometimes lure several dozen males; this system is particularly successful with the Lasiocampidae, Lymantriidae, and Saturniidae. The second type employs pheromones prepared in the laboratory, used in traps designed for catching species harmful to agriculture.

None of these methods of collection, however, is likely to provide much information about the biology of butterflies and moths. Anyone who wants to carry out such investigations is best advised to collect caterpillars and rear them. This is not difficult, although considerable patience is needed to make minute inspections of leaves, branches, and trunks of trees presumed to accommodate the insects in question. As a rule, faint or prominent traces of damage caused by these species will reveal the presence of caterpillars, though some are hard to catch, living as they do in the soil at the base of the host tree. Collecting them at night with a torch is often effective, for many species are only active in darkness. There are plenty of specialized books to indicate which plants and trees specific caterpillars feed on, how to identify the telltale nibbling signs, and where to look for them. This applies particularly to the Macrolepidoptera since in the case of smaller species, even the identity of the food plant is often unknown.

Having obtained the larvae, the problem now is how to rear them. For young specimens and smaller species, it is best to use glass containers, well cleaned and with the base covered by blotting paper. Check each day that the constituent food plants are not drying out: if so, the dry leaves should be replaced by fresh ones, and at the same time bits and pieces can be removed. It is essential, therefore, to have handy a stock of fresh leaves from the food plant. As the specimens grow, they need to be transferred to bigger containers or into cages covered with wire mesh. Make sure, for each species bred, that there is no overcrowding. Temperature, humidity, and lighting must stimulate as closely as possible the normal conditions of the food plant.

Whatever method of collection is used, and for whatever

purpose, the real preparation begins with the adult actually in hand. To do this without damaging the insect, it must be remembered that the joints have to be kept fairly elastic so that the wings, legs, and antennae can be manipulated into the correct positions. Unless the specimens have just been killed and are therefore still soft, they need to be placed in moist receptacles so that some elasticity can be restored. It is important always to pour in a few crystals of phenol to prevent the formation of mold. In the case of bigger specimens, the wing joints can be softened up by injecting ammonia into the insect's thorax or, in more difficult instances, by making an incision in the side of the thorax. The insect can then be pinned, using pins of a size suited to the thorax of the specimen. These can be bought in various dimensions, starting with tiny pins measuring not more than 2 mm in diameter. The butterfly should be pierced in the center of the thorax so that the body is at right angles to the pin. Special wooden racks can then be used, these consisting of two parallel laths, variously inclined, which border a central groove in which the body of the specimen is placed. The bottom of the groove is lined with cork or polystyrene, and into this the pin attached to the insect's body is fixed vertically. Pincers or needles mounted on wooden holders are then used to spread the butterfly's wings, which are set flat against the rack and secured with a strip of parchment paper or cellophane. After this preparation, the butterfly is left to dry, remaining on the rack for three to four days or as much as two to three weeks in the case of larger specimens. The preparations for Microlepidoptera are more complicated. As mentioned above, they are brought back alive and prepared within a day of being caught. Groups of three or four specimens are transferred from the tubes used for capture into a broad-necked bottle similar to that used for killing Macrolepidoptera. The insects are left only for a few minutes, time enough for them to lose consciousness. They are then removed from the bottle, pinned, and prepared while still alive, using the same methods already described, though with tinier instruments. Before placing the insect on the rack, it is advisable to blow gently on the specimen's abdomen so as to open the wings. The rack in this case will be smaller, about four inches long, and it is then placed in a bottle containing ether to kill the moth. This system is satisfactory for even smaller specimens (Nepticulidae and Gracillariidae), without risk of damage. When the specimen is dry, it is removed from the rack and labeled. This, too, is an extremely important operation considering that the material collected is only of value if information is provided about the circumstances of its capture. This should include the date when found, the name of the region or district where caught, and any other notes relating to its habitat (mountain, river, etc.). Finally, the collector's name should be given, followed or preceded by the Latin abbreviation "leg." (*legit* collected). In the case of specimens that have been reared,

A typical collector's case. This amateur collector has assembled a few specimens of some of the most important tropical species.

another label should be added giving the name of the host plant, the date when the egg or larva was found in the wild, and the date when the butterfly emerged. The labeled specimens may then be kept in a suitable wooden case (usually measuring about $16 \times 10 \times 2$ in.), with a glass lid for viewing. The bottom of the case should be lined with soft material, usually covered by squared paper, into which the pins can be stuck. As a rule, substances (paradichlorobenzene, lindane, organophosphates) but it must be remembered that they are, in varying measure, also toxic for humans and should therefore be used with care.

CLASSIFICATION

Since the earliest systematic subdivision proposed by Linnaeus in his *Systema Naturae* of 1758, the classification of the order Lepidoptera has undergone many important modifications. To this day there remain innumerable unresolved problems, partly due to the advances in knowledge about the morphology and ecology of these insects, and also to the tendency of modern systematics to propose forms of classification that underline the relationships between the various groups. Even so, the old classifications have persisted and it is worth making a brief reference to them here. One example is the division into Rhopalocera (butterflies), comprising forms with club-shaped antennae, and Heterocera, those with other types of antennae. Although this subdivision is justified in the case of the Rhopalocera, grouping together the so-called diurnal butterflies, the same cannot be said of the Heterocera, which is a purely artificial group. Another kind of subdivision, based on the dimensions of the adult, is that of the Macrolepidoptera and Microlepidoptera. Here, too, despite the obvious practical advantages of such a distinction, the division takes no account of morphology and anatomy, nor of the evolution of the different groups of Lepidoptera. Alongside these classifications, some scientists subsequently proposed alternatives, which in fact paved the way for modern systematic arrangement. Examples are the two suborders Jugatae and Frenatae, established on the basis of different systems of wing connection, and Homoneura and Heteroneura, based on whether the front and hind wings have similar or different veining. More recent classification, however, tends to group the Lepidoptera into four suborders: Zeugloptera, Dacnonypha, Monotrysia, and Ditrysia. About 98% of all described species belong to the Ditrysia, which are distinguished from the Monotrysia by the presence in the female of two genital openings (one of which serves for copulation and the other for egg-laying). The Zeugloptera and Dacnonypha, on the other hand, comprise the more primitive groups, often with an adult mouth mechanism of the chewing type.

In each of the four suborders the butterflies and moths are grouped in categories succeeding one another in descending hierarchic order: superfamilies, families, subfamilies, genera, subgenera, species, and subspecies. Species are identified by two Latin names, written in italics. The first, with an initial capital letter, indicates the genus to which that individual belongs; the second, written in the lower case, is that of the species. The Large Tortoiseshell, for example, is known scientifically as *Nymphalis polychloros*. *Nymphalis* represents the genus, which also contains other species: *Nymphalis antiopa, Nymphalis xanthomelas*, etc. To describe the subspecies, the same system is adopted, except that in this case there are three names (for instance, *Parnassius mnemosyne athene*). The taxonomic features generally used for species relate in the main to genital structure and wing color; the genera also employ wing veining, structure of palpi, etc. A family, however, is a grouping of genera: the aforementioned genus *Nymphalis*, together with *Apatura, Vanessa, Polygonia*, etc., make up the family Nymphalidae. Classification of this category or of those above necessitate the complete analysis of structures such as the head (eyes, antennae, palpi), wings (veining, coupling systems), and so forth. Thus it is clear that the categories above species are not natural, considering that they are established on the basis of almost completely subjective criteria. The classification of species, however, as previously noted, is based on the principle of reproductive isolation and this can be verified by experiment.

There are precise rules for naming new taxa, as laid out in the International Code of Zoological Nomenclature. Each taxon, or category, always has a specimen or included subordinate group for reference (in a species it is usually called a holotype) used by the author to describe it. Reassessment of the type material may later be necessary either to describe related taxa or to resolve problems of nomenclature. In fact, with the appearance of new information or with the discovery of new characteristics (or the reinterpretation of those already known), species considered to be different or belonging to separate genera are often found to be identical or at least more closely related than was originally thought. The whole matter becomes more complicated when consideration is given to taxa described prior to the introduction of the first Code in 1961. In such cases many of the earlier authors' descriptions and practices clash with the norms, creating a great deal of confusion between old and new names at every level. Only by patient revision of the various groups will it be possible to bring order to the classification system.

The table lists the most commonly accepted modern classification of butterflies and moths. The columns represent, from left to right, Suborder, Superfamily and Family.

Suborder	Superfamily	Family
ZEUGLOPTERA	Micropterigoidea	
DACNONYPHA	Eriocranioidea	
MONOTRYSIA	Hepialoidea	
	Nepticuloidea	
	Incurvarioidea	
DITRYSIA	Cossoidea	
	Tortricoidea	
	Tineoidea	
	Yponomeutoidea	
	Gelechioidea	
	Copromorphoidea	
	Castnioidea	
	Zygaenoidea	
	Pyraloidea	
	Pterophoroidea	
	Hesperioidea	
	Papilionoidea	
	Geometroidea	
	Calliduloidea	
	Bombycoidea	
	Sphingoidea	
	Notodontoidea	
	Noctuoidea	

Micropterigidae

Eriocraniidae, Agathiphagidae, Neopseustidae,
Lophocoronidae, Mnesarcheidae

Prototheoridae, Palaeosetidae, Hepialidae

Nepticulidae, Opostegidae

Incurvariidae, Prodoxidae, Heliozelidae, Tischeriidae

Cossidae, Dudgeoneidae, Compsoctenidae, Metarbelidae

Tortricidae, Phaloniidae

Pseudarbelidae, Arrhenophanidae, Psychidae, Tineidae,
Lyonetiidae, Phyllocnistidae, Gracillariidae

Sesiidae, Glyphipterigidae, Douglasiidae, Heliodinidae,
Yponomeutidae, Epermeniidae

Coleophoridae, Agonoxenidae, Elachistidae, Scythridae,
Stathmopodidae, Oecophoridae, Ethmiidae, Timyridae,
Blastobasidae, Xyloryctidae, Stenomidae, Cosmopterigidae,
Gelechiidae, Metachandidae, Anomologidae, Pterolonchidae

Copromorphidae, Alucitidae, Carposinidae

Castniidae

Eterogynidae, Zygaenidae, Chrysopolomidae, Megalopygidae,
Cyclotornidae, Epipyropidae, Limacodidae

Hyblaeidae, Thyrididae, Tineodidae, Oxychirotidae, Pyralidae

Pterophoridae

Hesperiidae, Megathymidae

Papilionidae, Pieridae, Nymphalidae, Libytheidae, Riodinidae,
Lycaenidae

Drepanidae, Thyatiridae, Geometridae, Uraniidae, Epiplemidae,
Axiidae, Sematuridae

Callidulidae, Pterothysanidae

Endromidae, Lasiocampidae, Anthelidae, Eupterotidae,
Mimallonidae, Bombycidae, Lemoniidae, Brahmaeidae,
Carthaeidae, Oxytenidae, Cercophanidae, Saturniidae,
Ratardidae

Sphingidae

Notodontidae, Dioptidae, Thyretidae

Ctenuchidae, Hypsidae, Nolidae, Arctiidae, Lymantriidae,
Noctuidae, Agaristidae

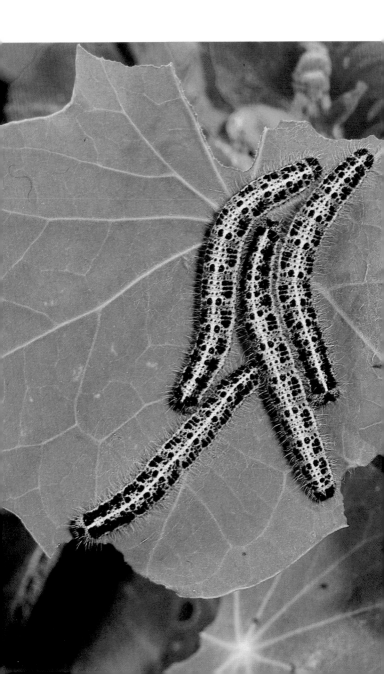

1 ACRAEA SP.

Family Nymphalidae, subfamily Acraeinae.

Geographical distribution Representatives of the subfamily Acraeinae live mainly in Africa, with some 200 species; they are also to be found in the Indo-Malayan region, with only a few species, and in South America, where there are 30 or so species.

Description and related species Caterpillars of the subfamily Acraeinae have feathered elongations on each segment and often live in groups.

Habits The adults of this subfamily produce hydrocyanic acid, which causes them to be poisonous to predators. A poisonous or distasteful insect such as this one evolves bright (warning) coloration so that predators will ignore it and its mimics (Papilionidae, Lycaenidae) after an initial exploratory nibble or peck. Larvae of the Acraeinae feed on various families of plants, members of the genus *Acraea* displaying particular preference for species of the Passifloraceae.

2 ACTIAS ARTHEMIS Brem. & Grey

Family Saturniidae.

Geographical distribution Eastern parts of the Soviet Union, Japan, and Korea.

Description and related species Caterpillars of the family Saturniidae, generally very big, have some striking and bizarre features; sometimes the young larvae are completely different from those in the later stages of development, having a small horn on the eighth abdominal segment as well as other prominent and often branched elongations. These structures, which tend to diminish in later instars (larval stages), are sometimes poisonous. Another characteristic of various saturniid caterpillars is the presence of long hairs. The cocoons protecting the pupae are made of a silk which, although less valuable than that produced by the common silkworm (*Bombyx mori*), is sometimes used for making yarn.

Habits In their larval stage the Saturniidae generally feed on tree foliage. In the case of European species, for example, the caterpillars of the giant peacock moth (*Saturnia pyri*) often feed on fruit-bearing Rosaceae such as apple, while those of the emperor moth (*S. pavonia*) prefer to develop on *Prunus spinosa*. Caterpillars of the Tau emperor (*Aglia tau*) are found on broad-leaved forest trees, and those of the Spanish moon moth (*Graëllsia isabellae*) attack pines.

3 AGLAIS URTICAE L.
small tortoiseshell

Family Nymphalidae.

Geographical distribution Much of the Palaearctic region.

Description and related species Full-grown caterpillars of the family Nymphalidae are of medium or large size and generally have spines on body and head. When spines are not present all over the body, there are usually special processes on the head. The caterpillar of *Aglais urticae* is black, minutely speckled with white, and has two indistinct, interrupted yellow bands along either side. Similar to it are the caterpillars of the peacock (*Inachis io*), which is black with reddish prolegs, and the red admiral (*Vanessa atalanta*), which is black with two distinct yellow bands at the sides.

Habits The caterpillars of the Nymphalidae feed on various plants but display certain preferences. In the Palaearctic region, for example, some species are associated with nettles, such as the map butterfly (*Araschnia levana*), *Inachis io*, *Aglais urticae*, and *Vanessa atalanta*; some Argynninae of the genera *Clossiana, Fabriciana, Argynnis*, and *Meso-acidalia* feed on plants of the violet family; and other species, such as those of the genera *Limenitis, Nymphalis*, and *Apatura* attack tree foliage.

4 AMATA PHEGEA L.
nine-spotted

Family Arctiidae, subfamily Ctenuchinae.

Geographical distribution Central and southern Europe, temperate zones of Asia eastward to the Altais.

Description and related species The subfamily Ctenuchinae, also known by the name Syntominae, has a mainly tropical distribution. The caterpillars are short, cylindrical, and furnished with raised areas bearing groups of hairs. The caterpillars of *Amata phegea* are gray, covered with tufts of gray hairs; the head is reddish-brown with a small black pattern, which is not present in the related *A. ragazzii* of southern Europe.

Habits The caterpillars of this family feed principally on herbaceous plants. In the Mediterranean region those of *A. phegea* have been observed feeding mainly on brambles, dead leaves, and mosses, while those of *A. ragazzii*, in the same zones, prefer the bark, shoots, and young leaves of trees.

5 ACRONICTA MEGACEPHALA Den. & Schiff
poplar dagger

Family Noctuidae.

Geographical distribution Much of Europe and Asia.

Description and related species The enormous family Noctuidae (with some 25,000 species worldwide) is characterized by cylindrical and apparently hairless caterpillars (in fact, all caterpillars are minutely hairy). Exceptions are those of the subfamily Acronictinae. In some genera one or two pairs of prolegs are lacking, hence the larvae move in somewhat the same manner as caterpillars of the Geometridae, sometimes even jumping. Caterpillars of the poplar dagger (*Acronicta megacephala*) are whitish with black patterns spotted red and white. Some other members of the genus *Acronicta* are also quite conspicuous, with long hairs and vivid colors.

Habits The vast majority of noctuid caterpillars feed on herbaceous plants, but there are also species that attack the leaves of trees (*A. megacephala* feeds on the leaves of poplars and willows). As a rule they are active at night and stay hidden near or on the ground by day.

---

6 ARCHIPS SP.

Family Tortricidae.

Geographical distribution Palaearctic region, with some 50 species, and Nearctic region, with about 20 species.

Description and related species The mature larvae are about ¾ in. (2 cm) long and have numerous hairy warts on the body; the head, prothorax, and anal segment are often variously colored green, gray, or black.

Habits The female lays hundreds of eggs, resembling a crust. Each egg is lentil-shaped, about 1 mm in diameter. Almost all species build leaf cases of various forms, chewing away inside, and later attack the fruits. Many species are recognized as pests to orchards; they are nearly always polyphagous and include the European *Archips podana* Sc. and the Palaearctic *A. crataegana* Hb., *A. xylosteana* L., and *A. rosana* L. *A. rosana* L. is biologically the best known, having been introduced into the United States.

7 ARCTIA CAJA L.
garden tiger

Family Arctiidae.
Geographical distribution Europe, Asia, North America.
Description and related species Caterpillars of many species belonging to the family Arctiidae are covered with dense, compact hairs; a few are almost hairless. The larva of the garden tiger (*Arctia caja*) is one of the more characteristic, being covered with long, thick hairs, which arise from short protuberances (verrucae). Those on the back, extending to the line of tracheal spiracles, are black, whereas the ventral hairs are reddish-brown.
Habits Caterpillars of this family generally feed on phanerogams (plants that produce seeds), but one subfamily, the Lithosiinae, attacks lichens. The mature larvae can often be observed wandering over the ground in search of a suitable place to pupate, which occurs in a strong cocoon. The garden tiger is a polyphagous species and the larvae attack both shrubs and herbaceous plants.

---

8 ECTROPIS BISTORTATA Goeze

Family Geometridae.
Geographical distribution Throughout Europe and Asia.
Description and related species The caterpillars of the family Geometridae are extremely characteristic. They possess only two pairs of abdominal prolegs, located on the sixth and tenth abdominal segments. This arrangement gives them a very distinctive type of gait. The insect, in fact, advances like a compass, anchoring itself alternately by the forelegs and the prolegs, so that it seems to be measuring the support on which it is walking. Indeed, the name of the family is derived from the Latin for "earth-measurers" and the larvae are variously known as loopers, stick caterpillars or inchworms. The caterpillar of *Ectropis bistortata* is reddish, with a pair of small dorsal tubercles near the tip of the abdomen.
Habits Geometrid caterpillars, though feeding on a variety of plants, show a certain preference for trees. Those of *E. bistortata* are found on birch, bramble, poplar, oak, silver fir, Norway spruce, and on other shrubs and herbaceous plants.

9 BOMBYX MORI L.
common silkworm or Chinese silkworm

Family Bombycidae.
Geographical distribution Originally from China, not found wild in nature.
Description and related species The silkworm, namely the caterpillar of the nocturnal moth *Bombyx mori*, is whitish all over, with a darker head and its spiracles clearly visible on the sides. There is a pointed protuberance near the rear end.
Habits The species feeds almost exclusively on the leaves of mulberry (*Morus*). Raising of the silkworm began in very ancient times, probably over 4,000 years ago. For more than 2,000 years the technique of sericulture was known only in China, although the ancient Greeks and Romans knew of its existence and prized the silk that arrived in modest quantities from the Orient. The silkworm reached the West in the sixth century A.D., thanks to eggs of the insect that had been hidden by two Nestorian monks within bamboo canes. The raising of silkworms was soon practiced throughout the Mediterranean region and, in the seventeenth century, spread to the United States. From the early part of the present century, however, silk production has once again been confined almost exclusively to the Far East.

10 CARCHARODUS ALCEAE
mallow skipper

Family Hesperiidae.
Geographical distribution North Africa, central and southern Europe eastward to central Asia.
Description and related species The caterpillars of the family Hesperiidae, small in size, are easily distinguished by their large heads and slightly constricted necks. Their bodies are sparsely covered with hairs. *Carcharodus alceae* is stocky, constricted at the tip, a grayish-green to blue. The head is black with a black and yellow collar.
Habits Hesperiid caterpillars construct shelters with leaves and silk, and spin a cocoon of silken threads and pieces of leaf; some species cover themselves with organic detritus. The food plants are varied: representatives of the subfamilies Trapezitinae (Australia) and Hesperiinae (cosmopolitan) feed on monocotyledons; those of other subfamilies chiefly feed on dicotyldons. The caterpillar of *Carcharodus alceae* attacks plants of the genera *Malva, Althaea,* and *Hibiscus*.

11 COSSUS COSSUS L.
goat moth

Family Cossidae.

Geographical distribution Temperate regions of Europe, Asia, and North Africa.

Description and related species Caterpillars of the family Cossidae have plates on the back of the thorax, which relate to the living habits of the insect. Those of *Cossus cossus*, which are more than 2½ in. (6 cm) long, are yellowish-white, tinged with pink, with a broad wine-red band along the back; the first segment of the thorax displays a black pattern. The larvae emit a disagreeable odor.

Habits The Cossidae are generally associated with wood, where the caterpillar may live several years, by reason of the low nutritional value of this type of food. The goat moth is harmful to various trees, as are other members of the family. The wood leopard (*Zeuzera pyrina*), for example, originally from Europe and introduced accidentally to North America, attacks more than 100 different plant species. The red branch borer (*Zeuzera coffeae*) infests coffee and cacao plants; the reed leopard (*Phragmataecia castaneae*), in the larval stage, feeds on reeds in marshes.

12 DANAUS CHRYSIPPUS L.
African monarch

Family Nymphalidae, subfamily Danainae.

Geographical distribution Africa south of the Atlas Mountains, Arabia, and tropical regions from Asia to Australia and Fiji.

Description and related species The caterpillars of the subfamily Danainae usually feed on plants rich in poisonous alkaloids and are themselves poisonous. These substances pass from the larva to the adult, which is therefore avoided by predators. For this reason many adult danaines set the model for chains of mimicry. The color-pattern of *Danaus chrysippus*, in particular, is imitated by various species, such as the females of certain forms of the mocker swallowtail (*Papilio dardanus*), belonging to the family Papilionidae, and of the diadem butterfly (*Hypolymnas misippus*), of the subfamily Nymphalinae. The bright coloration of the caterpillar serves likewise as a warning to predators.

Habits The caterpillars of the migratory North American monarch (*Danaus plexippus*) feed mostly on *Asclepias curassavica*; but occasionally also feed on *Gossypium arboreum* and *Euphorbia mauretanica*; those of *Danaus chrysippus* eat plants of the genus *Asceplias* and other genera of the family Aclepiadaceae.

13 DREPANA FALCATARIA L.
pebble hooktip

Family Drepanidae.
Geographical distribution Central and northern Europe.
Description and related species Caterpillars of the family Drepanidae, whose bodies taper to a point, are notable for the absence of the last pair of abdominal prolegs, so that there are four instead of the usual five pairs. The larvae of the pebble hooktip (*Drepana falcataria*) are brown and greenish in color.
Habits The caterpillars of Drepanidae feed on the foliage of trees and shrubs; those of *D. falcataria* attack birch and alder, as the insects' shape and coloration give them the appearance of little curled leaves of those trees. The chrysalids of the Drepanidae are small and often covered with a bluish waxy bloom.

---

14 GONEPTERYX RHAMNI L.
brimstone

Family Pieridae.
Geographical distribution Much of the Palaearctic region, from Europe to Japan.
Description and related species The caterpillars of the family Pieridae are covered with dense, short hairs. The predominant color is green, often with yellow stripes along the back and sides. The coloration tends to conceal the insect against its background, particularly among solitary species; in gregarious species the colors are brighter.
Habits Pierid caterpillars feed on a variety of plants. The Leguminosae, for instance, are often attacked by representatives of the genera *Dismorphia, Leptidea, Colias*, and others. *Anthocaris, Pieris* and species of other genera, however, prefer Cruciferae; and in tropical regions many species feed on the Capparidaceae. These last two plant families produce bitter tasting substances (thioglucosides), which are stored by the larvae. The caterpillars of *Gonepteryx rhamni* feed on shrubs such as *Rhamnus catharticus* and *Frangula alnus*.

15 HAMEARIS LUCINA L.
Duke of Burgundy fritillary

Family Riodinidae.

Geographical distribution Much of Europe, except for the far north and more southerly regions.

Description and related species The Riodinidae are a family of butterflies living mainly in warm climates and especially in South America. They are for the most part rare and little known, as are their caterpillars, which are often rather hairy, with varied colors ranging from red to green. *Hamearis lucina* is the only European species of the group; its caterpillar, stocky and hairy, is pale brown with a darker spotted band down the middle of the back, flanked by other spotted bands on either side.

Habits There is little information about the food plants of the caterpillars of this family; some species feed on Myrsinaceae and Primulaceae, families that as a rule are little exploited by butterflies. Those of *Hamearis lucina*, in particular, feed on *Primula veris* and *P. vulgaris*, living among the dead leaves at the base of the plant when not active.

---

16 HELICONIUS MELPOMENE L.
postman

Family Nymphalidae, subfamily Heliconiinae.

Geographical distribution From Central America to southern Brazil, Colombia, and Bolivia. Also occurs in the southern United States.

Description and related species The Heliconiinae are a small family of vividly colored mostly Neotropical butterflies. These colors warn possible predators of the presence in the insect's hemolymph of poisonous hydrocyanic acid. Though the caterpillars often blend with their surroundings and possess long spines, they can be brightly colored. Those of *Heliconius melpomene* are white with black spots and branched spines; the head is yellow.

Habits Heliconiinae caterpillars feed on various species of the genus *Passiflora*; cannibalism is also found among the larvae of this family. The caterpillars of *Heliconius melpomene* can be reared in captivity and have been the object of numerous genetic studies.

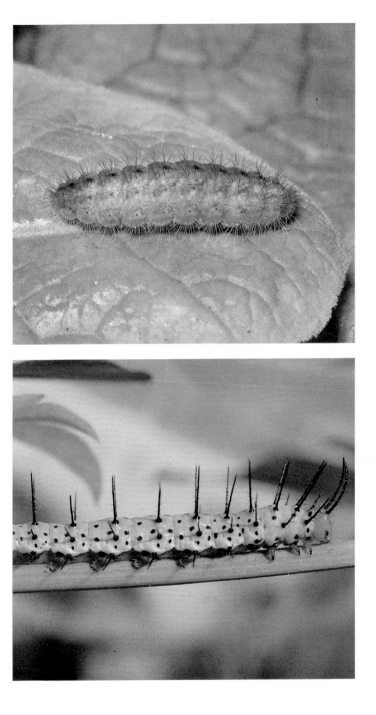

17 HEPIALUS SP.

Family Hepialidae.

Geographical distribution This family contains some 300 species distributed all over the world.

Description and related species Caterpillars of the Hepialidae, long and cylindrical, possess tubercles and a few bristles. Those of the ghost swift (*Hepialus humuli*), the best-known European member of the family, are about 4½ in. (4 cm) in length and have a shiny white or sometimes grayish body with distinct grayish-brown marks.

Habits The Hepialidae are primitive types of moth with greatly varying habits. The caterpillars of some species, such as the orange swift (*H. sylvina*) and the gold swift (*H. hecta*), both European, feed on ferns; others – the vast majority – attack wood and bark, exhibiting very long periods of growth, possibly up to five years. The subterranean caterpillars of the Australian *Oncopera fasciulata* are serious pests on grazing land.

---

18 HYLES EUPHORBIAE L.
spurge hawkmoth

Family Sphingidae.

Geographical distribution Central and southern Europe, and from western Asia to the northern regions of India.

Description and related species The large caterpillars of the family Sphingidae are as a rule very characteristic. On the back of the eleventh body segment there is a long, pointed horn. The name Sphingidae refers to the fact that in some species the caterpillars assume the attitude of the ancient sphinxes of Egypt, with head and thorax raised. They are variously and typically colored. In *Hyles euphorbiae*, for example, the body is black, thinly speckled with yellow, a red line runs along its back and there are yellow or red lines on either flank; the sides also carry white, red, or yellow markings.

Habits The Sphingidae have a varied diet and attack many herbaceous plants and trees. Some show a preference for the families Euphorbiaceae, Solanaceae, and Apocynaceae. The spurge hawkmoth, as its name suggests, feeds on various species of spurge (*Euphorbia ciparissias, E. paralis,* and *E. peplus*), but also on *Mercuriaris annua*.

19   LAELIA COENOSA Hüb.
reed tussock

Family   Lymantriidae.
Geographical distribution   Central Europe.
Description and related species   Caterpillars of the Lymantriidae are generally covered with long hairs, which often form large tufts along the back. Sometimes the hairs have a stinging, irritant effect. The chrysalids are often hairy and protect themselves by fixing their cocoons in the ground or in bark crevices. The caterpillars of the reed tussock (*Laelia coenosa*) are ocherous-brown, with tufts of hair emerging from small protuberances. The first to fourth abdominal segments bear brushlike tufts of hair in the center; additional hair tufts are found on the first thoracic segment and on the eighth abdominal segment.
Habits   The caterpillars of this family feed as a rule on the leaves of shrubs and trees; often they live gregariously in nests. Some species cause serious damage both to forest species and to fruit trees. *L. coenosa* is an exception among the Lymantriidae in that it prefers to feed on reeds and sedges (*Phragmites australis, Sparganium erectum,* and *Cladium mariscus*).

20   MACROTHYLACIA RUBI L.
fox moth

Family   Lasiocampidae.
Geographical distribution   Much of Europe, except for the coldest and hottest regions.
Description and related species   Caterpillars of the family Lasiocampidae are for the most part densely hairy, and often these hairs are irritant. The caterpillar of *Macrothylacia rubi*, which measures over 2½ in. (6 cm) long when mature, has a dark, velvety black body, covered with tufts of reddish-brown hairs on the back and grayish hairs on the flanks. These hairs may cause irritation to human skin.
Habits   In the larval stage the Lasiocampidae live among trees, shrubs, and herbaceous plants. They are generally active by day and are easily identifiable on the upper sides of leaves. Sometimes they are gregarious, living in nests in the early stages of growth. Their chrysalids are found either on the food plants or on the ground, in cocoons that may look like eggs. Fox moth caterpillars attack various plants such as heather and brambles.

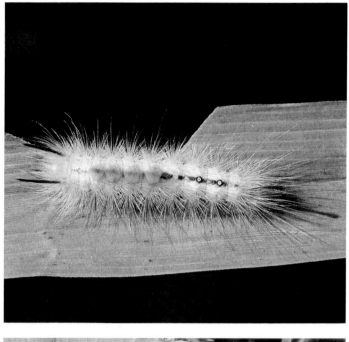

21 OECOPHORIDAE SP.

Family Oecophoridae.

Geographical distribution This family is found all over the world, with more than 300 genera and some 3,000 species known to date; most live in tropical areas and in Australia.

Habits The biology of this family is extremely varied: some larvae live in leaves that have been rolled or stitched together, others live in decaying wood or in bark. Some species are miners: caterpillars of the genus *Depressaria* only exhibit this activity in their final phase and pupate in the mine itself. Those of some groups are saprophagous, feeding on decaying matter; the larvae of *Neossiosynoeca scatophaga*, for example, live in the nests of parrots, feeding on their excrement. The European species are generally recognized harmful to food stocks (Oecophorinae) and to numerous species of Compositae and Umbelliferae, including crop plants.

22 PACHYTELIA VILLOSELLA Ochs.
black muslin sweep

Family Psychidae.

Geographical distribution Europe and Asia Minor, as far as Armenia and Turkestan.

Description and related species The larvae of this family build a complex, robust case. In *Pachytella villosella* it is a silken tube 1¼ in. (3–3½ cm) in diameter, covered with bits of leaves and twigs. The dusky sweep (*P. opacella*) builds a similar case, but much smaller, 3¼ in. long and ¼ in. across (2 cm long and 5–6 mm across). Metamorphosis always occurs within the case and it is interesting to note that the female of this species, which is wingless, remains there during her adult phase.

Habits The species likes warm, dry places and mostly frequents uncultivated land, woodland clearings, etc. During their feeding period, the larvae are found attached to grasses or other plants such as *Calluna* or *Erica*, on which the species feeds; it is active from July of one year to May of the second or third year. For metamorphosis the cases are affixed to stakes, trunks, walls, curbs, etc.

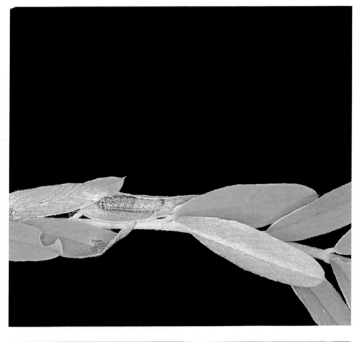

23 PAPILIO MACHAON L.
swallowtail

Family Papilionidae.

Geographical distribution Much of the Palaearctic region.

Description and related species Caterpillars of the family Papilionidae are characterized by the presence of the osmeterium, a forked glandular process protruding from the neck area that produces butyric acid to deter attacks by predators. In other respects caterpillars of this family vary considerably; some are smooth and multicolored, as in the case of *Papilio machaon*, which is mainly green with transverse black bands and red spots. The larva of the scarce swallowtail (*Iphiclides podalirius*) is also green, but it is stocky and fat. The caterpillar of *Parnassius*, however, is hairy, often with red streaks. Some tropical species are known to assume strange and complex shapes and coloration.

Habits Papilionid caterpillars have a variable diet. The Papilioninae (the subfamily to which the swallowtail belongs) feed, for example, on a variety of plants (Rutaceae, Lauraceae, Umbelliferae, Labiatae, and Magnoliaceae); the exotic Troidinae feed on Aristolochiaceae; the Parnassiinae and Zerinthiinae feed on Saxifragaceae, Crassulaceae, Papaveraceae, and Aristolochiaceae.

24 PARARGE AEGERIA L.
speckled wood

Family Nymphalidae, subfamily Satyrinae.

Geographical distribution Europe (except for the far north), North Africa, and central-western regions of Asia.

Description and related species The caterpillars of the subfamily Satyrinae for the most part look alike: the tip of the abdomen is extended into two short protuberances, and green and brown coloration is dominant. The caterpillar of *Pararge aegeria* is yellowish-green with a white-edged dark green stripe down the middle of the back, and alternating light and dark stripes along the sides; there are also two whitish dots near the tip of the abdomen.

Habits Satyrine caterpillars generally feed on grasses (Gramineae). Sometimes they are also to be found on Cyperaceae. They are often polyphagous, attacking many different plant species. The food plants of *P. aegeria* are *Dactylis glomerata, Agropyron repens, Poa annua*, and others.

25 PHALERA BUCEPHALA L.
buff-tip

Family Notodontidae.
Geographical distribution From Europe to the Far East.
Description and related species Caterpillars of the family Notodontidae come in a wide variety of forms. Some are very like those of the Noctuidae, the body having no special modifications; some have one or two humps on the back; and others have the last pair of prolegs modified into a kind of forked tail. The caterpillars of the buff-tip (*Phalera bucephala*) are among the few to possess a noticeably hairy body. Another of their characteristics is the coloration: yellow with blacks bands, the head and abdomen being pure black.
Habits Caterpillars of this species are gregarious for almost their entire growth period. They feed on the leaves of various trees such as limes, oaks, willows, and many others. The larvae of the other Notodontidae likewise live among trees.

26 PYRAUSTA RURALIS Sc.

Family Pyralidae.
Geographical distribution Throughout central-northern Europe and Asia Minor.
Description and related species Caterpillars of *Pyrausta ruralis* are 1¼ in. (3 cm) long. Although the adults look very like those of the related *P. nubilalis*, the larvae are distinctly different. Those of the former species are completely green, whereas those of the latter are a grayish-brown.
Habits The females lay their eggs on the leaves of various plants, especially nettles. The larvae are very agile, rolling the leaves into the shape of a cigar and stitching them together with silken threads. The caterpillars then live inside this leafy roll, gnawing the soft tissue (parenchyma). The caterpillars of species attacking other plants (hemp, hops, hazel, alder, etc.) behave in the same manner. The damage they do is usually slight.

27 SESIA APIFORMIS Cl.
hornet clearwing

Family Sesiidae.

Geographical distribution Temperate regions of Eurasia and North America.

Description and related species Caterpillars of the family Sesiidae are as a rule whitish, apart from the head and the thoracic and anal plates; the body is normally swollen behind the head. They are practically hairless, with a smooth skin. By and large they look quite different from other larvae of the Lepidoptera, more resembling those of other wood-feeding insects, such as the beetles of the family Cerambicidae.

Habits The caterpillars of this family are xylophagous, feeding on wood, except for certain species that infest the roots of Leguminosae and Euphorbiaceae. They attack both healthy and dead wood, digging long tunnels in which they develop slowly, their growth process generally lasting a couple of years. This, again, is because of the low food value of wood. The larvae of *Sesia apiformis* usually live in the trunk and bark of willows and poplars, and, more rarely, other deciduous trees.

28 STIGMELLA AURELLA F.

Family Nepticulidae.

Geographical distribution The British Isles, France, Mediterranean countries, southeastern Europe, and North Africa.

Description and related species The larvae of all members of this family are miners of leaves; the courses of these mines are characteristic for each individual species. As a rule they do little noticeable damage to the vegetation. The species shown here is part of a group (*Stigmella nitens* F., *S. gei* Wo., *S. fragariella* Heyd., *S. dulcella* Hein.), the classification of which still remains to be clarified.

Habits The larva attacks the leaves of various species of *Rubus*, showing preference for the evergreens (*R. fruticosus*). One generation is always active in the winter, feeding when conditions are fairly mild. Its scarcity or absence in regions with harsh winters is due to this absence of a winter diapause or resting phase. It completes its development in March or April. The adults produce a second generation in the summer.

29 THAUMETOPOEA PITYOCAMPA
Denis & Schiff.
pine processionary

Family Thaumetopoeidae.
Geographical distribution Western parts of the Mediterranean region and central Europe.
Description and related species Caterpillars of the Thaumetopoeidae (a group sometimes regarded as a subfamily of the Notodontidae) are known as processionary moths, a name derived from their habit of traveling one behind the other in long lines. Their body is warty and covered with dense down consisting of various types of hairs; some of these, tawny in color, have a strong irritant effect. Related to the pine processionary (*Thaumetopoea pityocampa*) is the oak processionary (*T. processionea*), whose caterpillars are brightly marked.
Habits Pine processionary caterpillars spin silken threads to build their nests, which may be up to 12–14 in. (30–35 cm) long and 8 in. (20 cm) across. As a rule they attack pines, more rarely cedars. The larvae leave the nest to seek food in single files that often comprise hundreds of individuals. When fully developed, they abandon the nest and pupate in underground cocoons. The oak processionary caterpillars attack oak trees, or, more rarely, walnut trees.

30 THECLA BETULAE L.
brown hairstreak

Family Lycaenidae.
Geographical distribution Temperate regions of Europe and Asia.
Description and related species The caterpillars of the Lycaenidae are small and covered with fine, short hairs. They look somewhat like slugs, short, stocky, and often swollen in the center. They sometimes have a dorsal gland on the seventh segment, or extensible organs on the eighth. The caterpillar of *Thecla betulae* – broad, swollen, and flattened at the tip – is green with paler markings.
Habits Information about the food habits of this enormous family is still incomplete; in this respect, the group is extremely varied. It includes species that feed on lichen (the African Lipteninae), others that are predators of ant larvae, such as the Liphyrinae of Africa and tropical Asia, and the Palaearctic *Maculinea* (which in its first stage of growth feeds on plants). Others are even more predatory, like the North American harvester (*Feniseca tarquinius*) whose larvae consume aphids. The remainder are associated with a large number of shrubs and trees. *T. betulae* normally attacks *Prunus spinosa*, but also beech and birch trees.

31 THYATIRA BATIS L.
peach blossom

Family Thyatiridae.

Geographical distribution Throughout the Palaearctic region.

Description and related species The family Thyatiridae comprises some 150 species distributed over Eurasia, North America and southern Africa. The caterpillars, similar to those of the Noctuidae, are almost hairless, cylindrical and pointed at the tip, and sometimes humped. This is the case with the larva of the peach blossom (*Thyatira batis*), which is brownish, with lighter triangular patterns on its back. The body is ridged, and seen from the side it appears indented.

Habits The caterpillars of this family are for the most part nocturnal, living by day in shelters made of the leaves, stitched together, of their food plant. They generally feed on the leaves of shrubs and trees; caterpillars of the peach blossom infest blackberry bushes (*Rubus fruticosus*). Pupation takes place on the plants, on the ground among dead leaves or plant detritus, or in the soil in a pupal cell.

32 TINEA PELLIONELLA Z.
case-bearing clothes moth

Family Tineidae.

Geographical distribution Palaearctic and Nearctic regions, Australia and New Zealand.

Description and related species Whitish body, about ⅓ in. (6–8 mm) long in the final stage. The head is dark brown and there are brownish thoracic plates.

Habits This species often infests human habitation; the females, in fact, lay their eggs on fur, wool, and other materials. The larvae then cut off the hairs at the base and make cases out of them. They stay hidden in these cases, dragging them about when they feed and retiring into them when danger threatens. Pupation occurs within the case, which is thus never abandoned by the larva from the moment it is built. Occasionally the species is found in birds' nests and on a wide variety of stored vegetable products. As a rule there is only one generation, the adult being active from June to October, but in heated places there may be two generations a year.

33 YPONOMEUTA SP.

Family Yponomeutidae.

Geographical distribution A cosmopolitan genus belonging to the subfamily Yponomeutinae.

Description and related species Females of this genus lay eggs individually or in groups, cemented beneath a silky layer, which constitutes a kind of protective shield. The mature larvae are generally about ¾ in. (1½–2 cm) long, their color varying from white to yellow to greenish; the head, legs, and pronotum may be of different colors.

Habits The larvae are usually gregarious by instinct and often form large silky nets, which may envelop a whole plant. This instinct is triggered by a pheromone, which acts as a trail, and is probably emitted by the jugular glands. The larvae remain gregarious up to the final phase. Plants attacked consist mainly of Rosaceae (*Prunus, Crataegus,* and *Malus*), Celastraceae (*Euonymus*), and Salicaceae (*Salix*).

---

34 ZYGAENA SP.

Family Zygaenidae.

Geographical distribution This family contains about 800 species, mainly found in the Old World and especially tropical Asia. The genus *Zygaena* inhabits almost the whole Palaearctic region.

Description and related species Caterpillars of the Zygaenidae are stocky and roughly cylindrical; the head is small and the body is covered in fine down with groups of bristles borne on tubercles. The pupae are fairly characteristic in that they are protected in a cocoon made of a parchmentlike substance, which adheres firmly to the stalks of food plants.

Habits Several species of Zygaenidae are associated in their larval stage with plants of the family Leguminosae. A particularly interesting feature of the caterpillars' development is the winter molt. The moths, in fact, spend the winter in the larval phase, and at the end of that season cast off the old skin and change color (from green or yellowish to brown), reducing the size of their head and also altering the structure of their mouth parts.

35 ABRAXAS GROSSULARIATA L.
magpie moth

Family Geometridae.
Geographical distribution Much of the Palaearctic region, from Europe to Japan.
Description and related species Wingspan approximately 1½ in. (35–40 mm). A very characteristic moth, with a yellowish, black-streaked body and white wings with black spots and small yellow patches. The related clouded magpie (*Abraxas sylvata*) is similar, but has less distinct dark spots and some brown patches. Otherwise the magpie moth cannot be mistaken for any other European species.
Habits This is one of the many Lepidoptera that, although formerly common, is nowadays experiencing a reduction in range. It feeds on the leaves of numerous trees and shrubs such as hazel, peach, plum, etc., but especially on blackcurrant and gooseberry, which it seriously damages. There is one generation a year, with adults emerging between June and August.

---

36 ACHERONTIA ATROPOS L.
death's head hawkmoth

Family Sphingidae.
Geographical distribution Mainly tropical, migrating from Asia and Africa to Europe in the late spring.
Description and related species Wingspan 3¼–5 in. (80–120 mm). This moth derives its common name from the skull-like pattern of scales on the back of the thorax. The forewings bear a complicated brown, tawny, and white pattern, while the hind wings are yellow with two transverse brown bands. The abdomen is largely yellow, with brown bands running crosswise and a bluish stripe down the middle. It cannot be confused with any other European hawkmoth.
Habits Like all migratory species, this species is likely to appear almost anywhere. The caterpillars feed on leaves of Solanaceae, such as the potato. The adults bore with their proboscis into the honeycombs inside beehives for honey. The moths reach Europe in the spring and summer, and if conditions prove favorable, will produce a generation that may survive the winter in its pupal phase.

37 ADELA CROESELLA Sc.

Family Incurvariidae.
Geographical distribution Central–southern Europe eastward to Siberia.
Description and related species Wingspan approximately ½ in. (12–14 mm). The antennae of the males are over twice the length of the wings, while those of the females are only slightly longer than the length of the wings. The wings are basically purplish-bronze, with gold scales set between the veins; a large yellow patch, edged with violet, adorns the apical part of the wing; the hind wings are darker purple. Two very similar species are *Adela degeerella* and *A. congruella*; both, however, are distinguished by their different sizes and by a deeper gold coloration along the wing veins.
Habits There is one generation a year. The adults are diurnal by habit, flying in full sunlight, normally in June or July. The larva lives in a case formed of detritus and pieces of leaves, attacking various plants such as *Ligustrum vulgare* and *Hippophae rhamnoides*.

38 AGLAIS URTICAE L.
small tortoiseshell

Family Nymphalidae.
Geographical distribution Much of the Palaearctic region, from Europe to the Far East.
Description and related species Wingspan 1½–2 in. (40–50 mm). The upper side of the wing is red tending to tawny, with black, yellow, and white marks on the hind wing, and a large dark basal section, blackish on the hind wing; close to the margin there is a narrow band of black and blue crescents. The underparts are brown and yellowish, with patterns that camouflage the butterfly when its wings are folded. It is similar to the large tortoiseshell (*Nymphalis polychloros*), but the latter is bigger and the basal part of the hind wings is tawny.
Habits This species lives in fields and on cultivated land from sea level to considerable altitudes, up to 11,500 ft. (3,500 m) in the Alps. The caterpillars feed exclusively on nettles. One or more generations are produced from the late spring onward. The adults often hibernate and begin flying during the first warm days of early spring.

39 AGROTIS YPSILON Hufn.
dark dart

Family Noctuidae.

Geographical distribution A migratory species, found all over the world.

Description and related species Wingspan 1¼–2 in. (35–50 mm). A fairly inconspicuous moth with indistinctly marked brown forewings. There is a prominent black wedge on the rear part of the wing. The hind wings are light brown, darker along the margin. The other representatives of the genus *Agrotis* are equally subdued in color, including the very common heart and dart (*A. exclamationis*), which has a different pattern on the forewings. All the noctuid moths tend to look alike and are difficult to identify.

Habits Like all migratory species, the species is likely to be found almost anywhere, from sea level to mountainous areas. The caterpillars attack many different plants and often do great damage. Adults are to be found from June to September.

---

40 ALUCITA HEXADACTYLA L.
many-plumed moth

Family Alucitidae.

Geographical distribution The members of this family are mainly to be found in the Afrotropical and Indo-Malayan regions, but this species is widely distributed in Europe and Asia Minor.

Description and related species Wingspan approximately ½–¾ in. (13–16 mm). The wing pattern consists of transverse bands and spots on a light brown ground. The species belongs to a small family (about 100 species), the adults of which are notable for having both forewings and hind wings divided into six fringed, plumelike deep lobes, each strengthened by a vein. The Alucitidae have frequently been associated with the Pterophoridae, but it has now been established that their resemblance in wing structure is simply a matter of convergent evolution.

Habits The caterpillar of this species begins its life cycle as a miner of leaves of *Lonicera* species; subsequently it bores into the stamens and styles of flowers, betraying its presence by a small round hole.

41 AMATA PHEGEA L.
nine-spotted

Family Arctiidae, subfamily Ctenuchinae.
Geographical distribution Central–southern Europe and temperate zones of Asia eastward to the Altais.
Description and related species Wingspan approximately 1½ in. (35–40 mm). Easily identifiable by the coloration of the wings, which are bluish-black with white spots, and the abdomen, which is likewise bluish-black with a yellow patch at the base and a yellow segment near the tip. These are warning colors as the moth is poisonous to birds. This livery is imitated by some Zygaenidae (also toxic to birds), and is thus a typical example of a Müllerian mimic. There are other species of the genus *Amata* in southern Europe, virtually indistinguishable externally, but well differentiated in terms of genetics and ecology.
Habits This species lives in shady places, in woods, on bushy slopes, and similar habitats, especially at low altitudes. The caterpillars are polyphagous and feed on the leaves of brambles, dead leaves, and moss. There is one generation a year, with adults emerging from June to September.

42 ANTHOCHARIS CARDAMINES L.
orange tip

Family Pieridae.
Geographical distribution Temperate regions of the Palae-arctic, from Europe to Japan.
Description and related species Wingspan approximately 1½–1¾ in. (35–45 mm). This species shows marked sexual dimorphism. The upper side of the male's forewing is white, and the apex is orange with a small black spot; the females display no orange at all. The underside of the hind wing exhibits complex greenish designs. There are other species of the genus *Anthocharis*, living in warm regions of Europe, North Africa, and Asia Minor, that have yellow rather than white wings.
Habits This species is found in fields and meadows from the lowlands to mid-mountain regions. There is a single annual generation, with adults appearing early, from March onward. The caterpillars live on various plants of the family Cruciferae.

43 APATURA IRIS L.
purple emperor

Family Nymphalidae.

Geographical distribution Europe and Asia eastward to China.

Description and related species Wingspan approximately 2½ in. (55–65 mm). The upper side of the wing is brown or nearly black; there are white dots on the forewings and a transverse white band on the hind wings. The males, when viewed from certain angles, display a very clear violet iridescence over almost the entire wing surface. The underside of the wing has a varied pattern of multicolored stripes and spots. The similar lesser purple emperor (*Apatura ilia*) always has an orange-circled black mark on the upper side of the forewing; and in many individuals the upper parts are largely brownish-yellow.

Habits This species is found in woods, both in lowlands and mountains, often flying high above the vegetation. The caterpillars feed on willow leaves. There is one annual generation, with adults appearing in July–August.

44 APLOCERA PLAGIATA L.
treble-bar

Family Geometridae.

Geographical distribution Throughout the Palaearctic region.

Description and related species Wingspan 1–1½ in. (25–40 mm). An inconspicuous moth, its forewings grayish-brown with some darker transverse bands and the hind wings entirely brown. It is very similar to *Aplocera praeformata*, which has slightly different patterning on the forewings.

Habits This species frequents plains and hills without being particularly specialized. The caterpillars live on *Hypericum*. There are two annual generations, with adults emerging between May and October.

45　APORIA CRATAEGI L.
black-veined white

Family　Pieridae.
Geographical distribution　Much of the Palaearctic region, from Europe to Japan.
Description and related species　Wingspan approximately 1½–1¾ in. (35–45 mm). Easily distinguished from other European species by its white color and black veining. The forewings of the females, in addition, are nearly transparent and largely without scales. It bears a vague resemblance to *Parnassius mnemosyne*, but the latter has some black spots on the wings, while the inner margin of the hind wing is concave rather than convex.
Habits　This species frequents open spaces with shrubs, from the lowlands to mid-mountain zones. The caterpillars, which are gregarious, feed mainly on the leaves of hawthorn but may also attack other trees and shrubs of the family Rosaceae. There is a single annual generation, and adults appear briefly between May and July, depending on the altitude.

46　APORIA HIPPIA Bremer

Family　Pieridae.
Geographical distribution　Amur and Ussuri regions of Mongolia, to north and northwest China, and Japan.
Description and related species　Wingspan approximately 2½–2¾ in. (64–66 mm). The wings are entirely white, with contrasting black veins. In coloration it much resembles the black-veined white (*Aporia crataegi*), but its forewings are more oblong in shape and the underside has a yellowish tinge. Various races are known of this species, one of which, *japonica*, is indigenous to Japan and is brown at the apex and outer margin of the forewing.
Habits　This butterfly flies slowly and elegantly, being found in sunny places full of flowers, such as fields and meadows. Around Vladivostok the larva has been observed on *Berberis sinensis* and *B. amurensis*, but it is liable to infest many other Rubiaceae. The caterpillars are dark gray with a longitudinal black stripe down the back and a reddish-brown lateral band; they are covered with short, intermingled brown and black hairs, and other longer white hairs. They hibernate in a nest made of leaves rolled together and linked by silk threads.

47 ARCTIA CAJA L.
garden tiger

Family Arctiidae.

Geographical distribution Europe, Asia, and North America.

Description and related species Wingspan approximately 1¾–2½ in. (45–60 mm). The coloration is characteristic but highly variable. The forewings are brown with a network of white lines; sometimes these are so extensive as to make the wings appear white with dark spots, sometimes they are reduced to a minimum. The hind wings, too, are variable; they are basically reddish-orange (rarely yellow), with circular bluish spots of varying dimensions. Other Arctiidae possess equally vivid and contrasting colors, designed for warning purposes, due to the presence of substances toxic to predators in the insects' hemolymph.

Habits This species is found both in lowland and mountainous regions, including cultivated land. The polyphagous caterpillars attack various plants. There is one generation a year, with adults emerging from June to August.

---

48 ARCTIA VILLICA L.
cream-spot tiger

Family Arctiidae.

Geographical distribution Temperate and warm regions of Europe; Asia Minor.

Description and related species Wingspan approximately 1¾–2½ in. (45–60 mm). Like many other species of the Arctiidae, this is a rather variable moth. As a rule it has black forewings with large, round white spots, and yellow hind wings with black spots and streaks. The thorax is covered in black hairs with two white spots and the abdomen is reddish. Sometimes the streaks on the wings are joined by lines; in other instances the forewings are almost completely black. It bears a slight resemblance to the scarlet tiger (*Callimorpha dominula*), but the latter has hind wings that are basically red.

Habits This species is found in the most varied habitats, sometimes even in urban areas. It is polyphagous and feeds on different herbaceous plants. There is one generation a year, with adults emerging in May–June.

49   ARGYNNIS PAPHIA L.
silver-washed fritillary

Family Nymphalidae.

Geographical distribution Europe, North Africa, and temperate regions of Asia to Japan.

Description and related species Wingspan approximately 2½ in. (55–65 mm). The upper side of the wing is basically orange in the males, orangish-brown or grayish-green (*valesina* form) in the females; both sexes exhibit black spots and stripes, but the males possess black lines along the veins of the forewings. The underside of the hind wing is greenish with metallic markings. In the related *Pandoriana pandora* the underside of the forewings is partially reddish.

Habits This common species is found in woods, especially in clearings, from sea level to mountainous regions. The caterpillar feeds on the leaves of violets, and more rarely on other herbaceous plants or shrubs. There is only one generation a year, with adults appearing from June to August, depending on the altitude.

50   BISTON BETULARIA L.
peppered moth

Family Geometridae.

Geographical distribution Europe and Asia.

Description and related species Wingspan approximately 1½–2½ in. (35–60 mm). A very famous species because it exhibits the phenomenon of industrial melanism. The peppered moth is encountered in three main forms: the typical one has white wings with black spots, *carbonaria* is entirely blackish, and *insularis* is gray. In England, prior to the Industrial Revolution, the dark forms were extremely rare. As industrialization spread, however, they became increasingly common until they came to represent over 90% of all individuals. The explanation of this phenomenon is associated with the fact that the dark moths are less likely to be attacked by predatory birds when settled on the trunks of trees blackened by industrial fumes. The related oak beauty (*Biston strataria*) is likewise subject to industrial melanism.

Habits The peppered moth frequents broad-leaved woodlands, infesting oak, birch, elm, beech, willow, and other trees. There is one generation a year, with adults appearing from May onward.

51 BOMBYX MORI L.
mulberry silkworm

Family Bombycidae.

Geographical distribution The silkworm originated in China, where it is not now found naturally but is the result of artificial selection. It is thought to have derived from *Bombyx mandarina*, an inhabitant of the Far East and a producer of good quality silk.

Description and related species Wingspan approximately 1½–2 in. (35–50 mm). The adult moth is inconspicuous, completely white, its stocky body covered with dense down. Like all artificially reared species, genetic experiments have been carried out recently with a view to increasing the silk yield.

Habits The life cycle of the silkworm is briefly summed up as follows: the caterpillar hatches from the egg at the end of winter and develops in four stages. The surrounding temperature must be maintained at 71–77°F (22–25°C) and the only acceptable food consists of leaves of the white mulberry (*Morus alba*). Each silkworm, when fully grown, produces a cocoon of silk, variable in color, diameter, and length. At this stage the pupa has to be killed by means of steam or hot air as otherwise the emergence of the moth would damage the cocoons of silk, which are now ready to be reeled.

52 BRAHMAEA WALLICHII
gray

Family Brahmaeidae.

Geographical distribution Northern India, Sikkim, Nepal, China, Taiwan, and Japan.

Description and related species Wingspan 3½–6 in. (90–155 mm). This moth is colored various shades of brown, with black lines forming complicated patterns of curves and squiggles. On the forewings there are numerous wavy black lines, very close to one another, in the basal zone and lower part of the postmedian and submarginal areas. The marginal area is light brown and there is a small black spot on the apex. In the median zone, bounded by a black line, there is a circular patch and a pattern with jagged edges; both enclose rings arranged along the veins. The hind wings are brownish but near the outer margins of the discal zone there are numerous wavy black lines, set close together, which are a continuation of those on the forewings.

Habits This is a mountain forest species. The caterpillars, smooth-skinned and brightly colored, have a pair of spiral, fleshy appendages on the second and third segments of the thorax and three shorter ones on the terminal part. The lengths of these appendages decrease with age.

53 BRINTESIA CIRCE F.
great banded grayling

Family Nymphalidae, subfamily Satyrinae.
Geographical distribution Europe, Asia Minor, Iran, and the Himalayas.
Description and related species Wingspan approximately 2½ in. (55–65 mm). The upper sides of the wings are mainly black with a white band which on the forewings is made up of large interlinked spots. The underparts display complex patterns. It is similar to some species of the genus *Hipparchia*, notably the woodland grayling (*H. fagi*) and the small grayling (*H. alcyone*) but in these species the white band is never as prominent.
Habits This species lives in places where there are trees, from sea level to moderate altitudes. The caterpillars feed on various species of Gramineae. There is a single annual generation, with adults emerging in June–July.

54 CALLOPHRYS RUBI L.
green hairstreak

Family Lycaenidae.
Geographical distribution Much of the Palaearctic region.
Description and related species Wingspan approximately 1 in. (24–28 mm). Very characteristic species by virtue of the uniformly green underside to the wings, with just a few small white spots on the hind wings. The upper side is completely brown. The outer marginal fringe is well-developed. The only other European lycaenid to resemble the green hairstreak is Chapman's green hairstreak (*Callophrys avis*), a close relative from southwestern Europe and North Africa, whose eyes are surrounded by red instead of white.
Habits The species is found virtually anywhere, either in lowlands or mountains, with a preference for open spaces. The caterpillar is polyphagous but is often found on junipers, heather, gorse, and other shrubs. There is one generation a year, with adults appearing as early as March.

55 CATOCALA NUPTA L.
red underwing

Family Noctuidae.

Geographical distribution Temperate regions of Europe and Asia.

Description and related species Wingspan approximately 2½–3 in. (65–75 mm). The owlet moths (Noctuidae) are usually nocturnal species, which as a rule are fairly inconspicuous. In some instances, however, there are bright colors on the hind wings which, when displayed suddenly by the moth, act to confuse likely predators. The species of the genus *Catocala* are among the most typical and best examples of this phenomenon. The forewings, in fact, are streaked with brown so that, when the wings are folded like a roof over the body, they blend perfectly with the tree trunk on which the moth is settled. The hind wings, on the other hand, are vividly colored with red and black bands (in *Catocala nupta*, *C. elocata*, *C. electa*, and *C. promissa*) or blue and black bands (*C. fraxinis*).

Habits This species is found in wet places where there are trees, often close to water, but sometimes in urban areas. The caterpillars feed on leaves of various trees (willow, poplar, plum, etc.) There is a single annual generation, with adults emerging from July to September.

---

56 CHARAXES JASIUS L.
two-tailed pasha

Family Nymphalidae.

Geographical distribution Along Mediterranean coasts and in equatorial Africa.

Description and related species Wingspan 3¼ in. (80 mm). A large, spectacular butterfly with two tails on each hind wing. The upper side of the wing is mainly brown with a light tawny yellow marginal band. The underside is multicolored and densely covered with brown, reddish, white, yellow, and blue markings. No other European species resembles it, but related species are found in tropical regions.

Habits A typical inhabitant of the maquis, a type of vegetation comprising shrubs and small trees, which grows along the Mediterranean shoreline. The caterpillars feed wholly on leaves of the strawberry tree (*Arbutus unedo*). There are two generations a year, with adults appearing in May–June and August– September.

57 CIDARIA FULVATA Forst.
barred yellow

Family Geometridae.
Geographical distribution Widely distributed in Europe and Palaearctic Asia, ranging eastward to the Altai region.
Description and related species Wingspan ¾–1 in. (20–25 mm). A typical representative of the family Geometridae, with yellowish forewings patterned with transverse bands, the most prominent of which is brown with irregular margins. The forewings are whitish, with a rather darker marginal part. Although other geometrids are smaller in color, the barred yellow is easily identifiable.
Habits This moth frequents various habitats, particularly dry zones with shrubs or sparse tree growth. The larvae feed on roses, both wild and cultivated, and for this reason it is often found in gardens. There is a single generation annually, with adults appearing from June to August.

58 COENONYMPHA PAMPHILUS L.
small heath

Family Nymphalidae, subfamily Satyrinae.
Geographical distribution Europe, North Africa, and western regions of temperate Asia.
Description and related species Wingspan approximately 1–1¼ in. (23–33 mm). The upper side of the wing is mostly ochre, with a narrow dark margin and a small eyespot near the apex of the forewings. The underside of the hind wings is grayish or brown with more or less prominent markings. There are numerous Palaearctic species of the genus *Coenonympha*; the one most closely resembling *C. pamphilus* is the large heath (*C. tullia*), which is slightly bigger and lacks a definite dark wing margin.
Habits This species is extremely common in meadows, pastures, and on cultivated land, from low to high altitudes. The caterpillars feed on various species of Gramineae. There is usually more than one generation annually, with adults in evidence from early spring.

59 COLIAS HYALE L.
pale clouded yellow

Family Pieridae.
Geographical distribution Central and eastern Europe.
Description and related species Wingspan approximately
1½–1¾ in. (40–45 mm). The various species of this genus are difficult to identify because they differ only in minor details. The ground color of the upper side of the wing is pale yellow in the males, whitish in the females; in addition, there are black spots and patterns, and a small orange mark on the hind wings. It is very closely related to Berger's clouded yellow (*Colias australis*), which differs in small details of color, wing shape, and patterning.
Habits The pale clouded yellow is a typical example of a species dependent upon particular herbs and forage plants. In the Mediterranean regions its range is largely determined by the presence of certain Leguminosae such as trefoil, lucerne, and alfalfa. Abandonment of these plants as crops has led to the disappearance of the butterfly over vast areas. The caterpillars feed on many wild and cultivated herbaceous Leguminosae. There are two generations a year, the adults appearing in May–June and August–September.

---

60 COSSUS COSSUS L.
goat moth

Family Cossidae.
Geographical distribution Temperate regions of Europe and Asia; North Africa.
Description and related species Wingspan approximately
2½–3¼ in. (65–80 mm). This is an unmistakable moth with a fairly sturdy body and brownish-gray wings with dense markings of a darker tone; this color pattern has a protective purpose, for it resembles tree bark. The goat moth belongs to a family of primitive moths, with larvae that generally consume wood. It cannot be confused with any other European Cossidae, which are much smaller and bear different colors. Its size is similar to that of many species of the family Sphingidae, but the latter have more slender wings.
Habits This moth lives in woods, orchards, and poplar groves. The caterpillars, which are quite big and have an unpleasant smell, grow in the wood of various broad-leaved trees, both wild and cultivated (poplar, willow, apple, pear, etc.). Larval development takes three or four years. The adults appear in June–July.

61 CYDIA POMONELLA L.
apple codlin moth

Family Tortricidae.
Geographical distribution Almost cosmopolitan.
Description and related species Wingspan approximately
¾ in. (18–20 mm). The wings are ash gray with numerous
thin brown lines running across them; there is a large, dark
eyespot on the distal zone, bordered by a copper-colored
band. The hind wings are uniformly grayish-brown with
copper tints.
Habits The moth is rather difficult to spot in the daytime
because the adults remain settled in the foliage or attached to
tree trunks, blending with them in color. They fly in the
evening, in semi-darkness, the females flitting from tree to
tree (apple and pear) to lay eggs. There are two generations,
the first of which attacks the unripe fruit, the second the ripe
fruit. The larva bores a tiny entrance hole, which immediately
forms a scar so as to render it invisible; the holes to be found
in apples and pears are therefore the exit holes of the adult
caterpillars.

62 DEILEPHILA ELPENOR L.
elephant hawkmoth

Family Sphingidae.
Geographical distribution Temperate zones of Palaearctic
region, from Europe to Japan.
Description and related species Wingspan approximately
1¾–2½ in. (45–60 mm). This species is notable for its predominantly pink and green coloration. The forewings are
olive green with a number of transverse pink lines; the hind
wings are pink with a blackish basal part. The body, too, is
covered in green and rosy scales. The small elephant hawkmoth (*Deilephila porcellus*) is similar but smaller, as its name
indicates, with broader areas of pink on the forewings and
some olive green patches on the hind wings. Both species
differ in color pattern from other European Sphingidae.
Habits This moth is found in hills and mountains up to
medium altitudes, wherever its food plants grow. The caterpillars feed on plants of the genus *Hypericum* but sometimes,
too, on other species, including vines. There is one generation a year, with adults appearing from May to July.

63 DREPANA FALCATARIA L.
pebble hooktip

Family Drepanidae.
Geographical distribution Central and northern Europe.
Description and related species Wingspan approximately 1–1½ in. (27–35 mm). The moths of the family Drepanidae are most abundant in Africa and southeast Asia but some characteristic species are found in Europe. The forewings are as a rule hooked at the apex. The pebble hooktip is distinguished by its complex brown and blackish markings on a beige background. The other *Drepana* species from Europe display a more uniform color pattern.
Habits This moth frequents shrubland and woodland but is also likely to be found in urban areas. The caterpillars feed on birch and alder. There are two generations a year, with adults emerging between April and June, and again in July–August.

64 EMATURGA ATOMARIA L.
common heath

Family Geometridae.
Geographical distribution Europe and Asia, except for the southernmost regions.
Description and related species Wingspan approximately ¾–1¼ in. (22–30 mm). A common species, easily identifiable by its wings, yellowish dusted with brown, each of them bearing fairly straight brown bands. The males have bipectinate antennae.
Habits This species is ecologically undemanding, frequenting both moors and cultivated zones, where it feeds on various plants such as heather and artemisia. One generation appears each year: the eggs are laid in June, the caterpillars are active between June and September, pupation occurs in the soil in the autumn, and adults emerge the following May.

65 EREBIA ALBERGANUS de Prun.
almond-eyed ringlet

Family Nymphalidae, subfamily Satyrinae.
Geographical distribution The Alps, Apennines, and mountains of northern Spain and Bulgaria.
Description and related species Wingspan approximately 1½ in. (35–38 mm). The genus *Erebia* is one of the largest and most interesting groups of Palaearctic and Nearctic diurnal butterflies. It comprises numerous species (some 40 in Europe alone), which are uniformly brown and range from alpine and other mountainous regions to subarctic areas; their distribution is often very restricted, and thus they are markedly endemic. Identification of species is difficult and requires specialized study. *Erebia alberganus* is one of the most characteristic of them because of the orange postdiscal marks, which converge in a band and mostly exhibit a black eyespot.
Habits This is a mountain species found in meadows between 3,000 and 6,500 ft. (900 and 2,000 m). The caterpillars of the genus *Erebia* feed on plants of the family Gramineae. Those of the almond-eyed ringlet have been observed on *Poa*, *Festuca*, and other genera of grasses. There is one annual generation, with adults emerging in June–July.

---

66 ERYNNIS TAGES L.
dingy skipper

Family Hesperiidae.
Geographical distribution Most of the temperate regions of the Palaearctic, from Europe to the Far East; not found in North Africa.
Description and related species Wingspan approximately ¾–1 in. (23–26 mm). The upper side of the wing is brown with indistinct streaks; in the related inky skipper (*Erynnis marloyi*), ranging from the Balkans to Iran, the markings are clearer. The underside of the wing is entirely brown, lighter than the upper side, with a group of white dots not far from the margin. Other European species of the family Hesperiidae that somewhat resemble the dingy skipper belong to the genus *Pyrgus*, but these always display extensive white marks.
Habits This species lives from sea level to high altitudes, in open spaces, mostly on calcareous soil. The caterpillars feed on plants of the Leguminosae (*Lotus* and *Coronilla*), but also on others such as those of the thorny genus *Eryngium* (Umbelliferae). One or two generations emerge each year, according to latitude, with adults flying from May onward.

67 EUPLAGIA QUADRIPUNCTARIA Poda
Jersey tiger

Family Arctiidae.
Geographical distribution Temperate and warm regions of Europe.
Description and related species Wingspan approximately 1½–2 in. (42–52 mm). As in many other members of the family Arctiidae, the colors of this species are highly conspicuous and characteristic. The forewings are brown with yellowish-white lines that mostly run transversely; the hind wings are red with a few deep black spots. The body is predominantly yellow with brown lines and dots. The species is similar to the scarlet tiger (*Callimorpha dominula*), which has white spots instead of lines on the forewings.

Habits The species frequents zones with sparse tree growth both in lowlands and hills. Some adult Arctiidae do not feed, since they have no functional mouth parts. The Jersey tiger, however, visits flowers to sip nectar. The caterpillars are polyphagous and feed on various plants. There is one annual generation, with adults appearing from July to September.

68 EUPLOCAMUS ANTHRACINALIS Lat.

Family Tineidae.
Geographical distribution Central-southern Europe, southern Russia to Armenia, Asia Minor.
Description and related species Wingspan 1–1¼ in. (25–30 mm). The color of the forewing ranges from light brown to brownish-black, with prominent white dots, which may turn yellowish in the aberration *monetella*. There is marked sexual dimorphism, the antennae of the males being pectinate (toothed like a comb) and those of the females filiform (threadlike). The most closely related species is *Euplocamus ophisus*, from southern Europe and Asia Minor. It differs from *E. anthracinalis* in that the forewings are brown, streaked in yellow with strong violet tints and golden yellow dots.

Habits The caterpillar lives in fungi that are found on trees such as beech, oak, hornbeam, alder, and hawthorn, and also in rotten wood.

69 EUREMA HECABE L.

Family Pieridae.
Geographical distribution Widely distributed on many continents; known in India, Sri Lanka, eastern Asia, Australia, and much of Africa.
Description and related species Wingspan 1½–1¾ in. (40–45 mm). This species is predominantly yellow except for a very large blackish band with irregular edges covering the apex and the outer lateral margin of the forewings. On the hind wings this dark band is narrower and more regular in outline, present only on the outer margin. The underside of the wing is yellow, with numerous brownish dots of varying shapes and sizes, arranged unevenly and more plentiful on the hind wings. It is an extremely variable species and many races and varieties have been described. There are also seasonal forms. The male copulatory apparatus provides the surest means of distinguishing it from related species. Very similar is *Eurema blanda*, but in the latter species the underside of the wings is almost wholly yellow.
Habits The apparently hairless caterpillar of this species lives on species of the genera *Cassia* and *Acacia*.

---

70 GASTROPACHA QUERCIFOLIA L.
lappet

Family Lasiocampidae.
Geographical distribution Much of the Palaearctic region, from Europe to the Far East.
Description and related species Wingspan 2–3½ in. (50–90 mm). This is a species with rather drab coloration, wholly reddish-brown with scarcely visible black markings. The shape of the wings, however, is very distinctive, for the margins are toothed, so that when at rest the insect looks like a dead leaf. Other European Lasiocampidae generally have a smooth wing margin (except for those of the genus *Epicnaptera*) and dull brown or grayish colors.
Habits The lappet moth is ecologically undemanding, living in dry woodland from sea level to mountainous zones, and also on cultivated land and in urban areas. The caterpillars feed on the foliage of the sloe (*Prunus spinosa*), but also on hawthorns, willows, and apples. There is one generation a year, with adults appearing in July–August.

71 GONEPTERYX RHAMNI L.
brimstone

Family Pieridae.
Geographical distribution Much of the Palaearctic region, from Europe to Japan.
Description and related species Wingspan 2–2¼ in. (50–55 mm). The characteristic shape of the wing gives this butterfly, when at rest, the appearance of a leaf. The male is lemon yellow, the female greenish-white; and all four wings have a single small orange spot. It is similar to the smaller brimstone (*Gonepteryx cleopatra*), typical of the Mediterranean region, the males of which have a broad orange area on the forewings.
Habits This butterfly is found in open countryside from sea level to mid-mountain zones. The caterpillars feed on shrubs of the genus *Rhamnus*. There is only one annual generation, with adults emerging from June onward; these may survive the winter and reappear in the spring or even on warm winter days.

72 GRAELLSIA ISABELLAE Graëlls
Spanish moon moth

Family Saturniidae.
Geographical distribution A rare and localized species, only found in some regions of central Spain, the Pyrenees, and southern parts of the French Alps.
Description and related species Wingspan 3½ in. (90 mm). One of the rarest and most beautiful of European moths. Its discovery by the Spanish physician Graëlls came as such a surprise that at first it was suspected of being a fake. The moth is yellowish-green with beige and black markings, particularly along the veins. It has typical saturniid eyespots on each wing. It is of special scientific interest as it is regarded as a relic of the tertiary era, since its closest relatives are found in the Himalayas.
Habits This moth lives in established pine forests, the food plants of the caterpillars being *Pinus laricio* and *P. sylvestris*. There is one generation annually, and adults emerge in March. Because of its rarity, it is a protected species.

73 HAMEARIS LUCINA L.
Duke of Burgundy fritillary

Family Riodinidae.
Geographical distribution Much of Europe, except for the most northerly and southerly regions.
Description and related species Wingspan approximately 1 in. (25–28 mm). The basic color of the upper side of the wing is brown with brick red spots, which are more widespread on the forewings. The underside displays a complex pattern of brown and reddish patches and white spots. It can be mistaken for no other European species and is the sole European representative of a family that comprises many tropical species, particularly in Central and South America.
Habits The species frequents clearings and bushy areas both in hills and mountains. The caterpillars generally feed on the leaves of primroses. In southern Europe there are two annual generations, with adults emerging in May and August; in northern parts of the range there is a single generation, the adults emerging in May–June.

74 HELIOPHOBUS RETICULATUS Goeze
bordered gothic

Family Noctuidae.
Geographical distribution Temperate and warm regions of Europe and Asia, eastward to central Asia.
Description and related species Wingspan approximately 1¼–1½ in. (32–37 mm). This is one of the very many representatives of the Noctuidae, which have a fairly unremarkable appearance. The forewings are dark brown with a network of lighter lines; the hind wings are translucent beige with a darker apex. Although it is not difficult to identify, it could be confused with many species of various genera, such as *Hadena*, *Hada*, and *Discestra*. In general, these medium-sized, brown noctuid moths are not easily distinguished from one another and require study of internal structures for reliable identification.
Habits The species frequents various habitats, with a preference for wasteland in populated areas. The caterpillars feed on plants of the family Caryophyllaceae, particularly of the genera *Saponaria* and *Silene*, concentrating on the unripe seeds but also on the leaves. There is one generation a year, with adults appearing in June–July.

75 HEODES VIRGAUREAE L.
scarce copper

Family Lycaenidae.
Geographical distribution Europe, except for the British Isles and the extreme north of Scandinavia; Asia Minor and central Asia, ranging eastward to Mongolia.
Description and related species Wingspan approximately 1–1¼ in. (27–32 mm). This is a species showing marked sexual dimorphism. The upper side of the males' wing is golden red with a narrow dark margin; in the females the ground color is less brilliant and the entire surface is dotted with black spots. The underparts of both sexes are alike, yellowish with black dots. The males of many other species of Lycaenidae have metallic red upper parts to their wings, in particular the large copper (*Lycaena dispar*), which frequents low-lying marshlands, is bigger, and whose wing undersides are differently colored.
Habits The species is found in open spaces, particularly grasslands, and in the southern regions of its range it frequents only mountains; in the north it roams the lowlands as well. The caterpillars feed on plants of the genus *Rumex*. There is a single annual generation, with adults emerging in July–August.

76 HEPIALUS HUMULI L.
ghost swift

Family Hepialidae.
Geographical distribution Temperate regions of Europe and Asia, eastward to Siberia.
Description and related species Wingspan 1½–2¾ in. (40–70 mm). This species belongs to a group of primitive Lepidoptera; the veins of the forewings are similar to those of the hind wings, and the proboscis is either rudimentary or wholly absent. It is distinguished from other European species of the same family by the entirely white coloration of the males; the females, however, are beige with pink markings. In other European species of Hepialidae, the dominant colors are brown and yellowish-brown. The size of the adult ghost swifts is extremely variable from individual to individual.
Habits The species is found mainly in the lowlands, hills, and mid-mountain zones, in open surroundings. The larvae feed on roots of grasses and many herbaceous plants and shrubs, including hops, and for this reason the species is regarded as a pest. The cycle of growth lasts two years. Adults emerge in June–July.

77 HESPERIA COMMA L.
silver-spotted skipper

Family Hesperiidae.
Geographical distribution The Palaearctic region (Europe, North Africa, and temperate zones of Asia) and western regions of North America.
Description and related species Wingspan 1–1¼ in. (25–30 mm). The basic color of the upper side of the wing is yellowish-brown, with a darker margin; there are also some lighter markings. In males a dark, elongated androconial spot on the forewing is immediately apparent. The dominant color on the underside of the wings is olive green, with silvery-white spots and yellowish-brown areas on the forewings. A very similar species is the large skipper (*Ochlodes venatus*), in which the males likewise possess a long androconial spot; the underside of the wing, however, exhibits light, blurred patches.
Habits It frequents grassy places (meadows, wasteland, embankments, etc.), from sea level to fairly high altitudes. The caterpillars are polyphagous and feed on Gramineae and Leguminosae. There is one annual generation, with adults appearing in July–August.

78 HIPPARCHIA FAGI Scop.
woodland grayling

Family Satyridae.
Geographical distribution Central Europe, Italy, and the Balkans eastward to the Soviet Union; locally present on the Iberian peninsula.
Description and related species Wingspan 2½–2¾ in. (60–70 mm). The upper parts of this butterfly are dark brownish-gray, with a lighter postdiscal band, more clearly defined in the female, on which it is largely white. There is a complicated pattern of streaks on the underside of the hind wings, which enables the butterfly to merge with its surroundings, especially tree trunks. A very similar species is the small grayling (*Hipparchia alcyone*), which is usually a little smaller. Certain other species of the genus *Hipparchia* inhabit southern Europe, often with a very limited geographical range.
Habits This butterfly is found in woods or among trees, from low altitudes up to 3,300 ft. (1,000 m). The caterpillars feed on plants of the Gramineae, particularly of the genus *Holcus*. There is a single annual generation, with adults appearing in July–August.

79 HOFMANNOPHILA PSEUDOSPRETELLA St.
brown house moth

Family Oecophoridae.
Geographical distribution A wide-ranging species, known in Europe eastward across Siberia to the Pacific, and in North America. In tropical regions it is found in India, Sri Lanka, Australia, and New Zealand.
Description and related species Wingspan approximately ¾–1 in. (20–24 mm). The forewings are glossy brown with black dots over the entire surface, particularly around the apical margin. The hind wings are gray; the abdomen is uniformly brown in the males, dark gray with an orange border in the females.
Habits The larvae of this moth are active from June until April of the following year. It infests animal and plant refuse, textiles and skins, dead insects, seeds, and many other perishable materials stored, for example, in warehouses. The adult appears from May to September and is often found in human habitations.

80 HYLES LINEATA F.
striped hawkmoth

Family Sphingidae.
Geographical distribution A tropical and subtropical species, found in warm regions all over the world. Being a powerful migrant, it often makes an appearance in temperate parts of Europe and in North America.
Description and related species Wingspan 2½–3¼ in. (60–80 mm). The white lines that run along the veins of the forewings, with their brown and yellowish markings, make this species easy to identify. The hind wings are yellowish and pink with two black spots at the base and near the margin. Other similar species of this genus are the spurge hawkmoth (*Hyles euphorbiae*) and the bedstraw hawkmoth (*H. galii*), but these species lack the white lines on the forewings.
Habits The adult moths of this species are often attracted in the evening to the flowers of ornamental plants of the genus *Phlox*. The caterpillars feed on plants of the genera *Lythrum* and *Galium*. There are usually two annual generations, with adults appearing in May–June and August–September.

81 INACHIS IO L.
peacock butterfly

Family Nymphalidae.
Geographical distribution Temperate regions of the Palaearctic, from western Europe to Japan.
Description and related species Wingspan 2–2½ in. (50–60 mm). The upper side of the wings of this vanessid is deep brick red with a large eyespot on each wing; the underside, however, is entirely blackish with thin, indistinct markings. When its wings are closed, the butterfly blends perfectly with its surroundings. It cannot be mistaken for any other species.
Habits This butterfly is found from sea level to high altitudes, in every type of habitat where there are nettles; it often frequents urban areas, in parks, gardens, and wasteland. The caterpillars feed mainly on nettles. There is one generation a year, with adults appearing in the summer (June–July); however, they often survive the winter and reappear the following spring.

82 IPHICLIDES PODALIRIUS L.
scarce swallowtail

Family Papilionidae.
Geographical distribution Much of the Palaearctic region, from Europe to China.
Description and related species Wingspan 2–2¾ in. (50–70 mm). This butterfly is notable for its white or yellowish-white wings with oblique black bars; the hind wings are extended into long tails and exhibit a black submarginal band with blue crescents and a tricolored patch. It slightly resembles the common swallowtail (*Papilio machaon*), but the wings are more slender, the tails of the hind wing are longer, and the black pattern is completely different. The various generations display appreciable color differences.
Habits This is a common species, frequenting meadows and fields, from the lowlands to subalpine regions. The caterpillars live on shrubs and trees of the Rosaceae (plum, hawthorn, apple, pear, etc.). There are two generations a year, the first in the spring from March onward, the second in August–September. In more southerly regions there may be three generations.

83 LASIOCAMPA QUERCUS L.
oak eggar

Family Lasiocampidae.
Geographical distribution Much of Europe and Asia.
Description and related species Wingspan 1¾–3 in. (45–75 mm). This species shows marked sexual dimorphism. The males, with pectinate antennae, are brick red with a blurred yellowish band towards the outside of each wing; the females, which are larger, are ocher yellow with a less prominent transverse band. Both sexes have a small but distinct light patch on the forewings. The oak eggar bears a slight resemblance to the grass eggar (*Lasiocampa trifolii*), which is a bit smaller and has uniformly colored hind wings without light bands.
Habits This species lives in the lowlands and mountains but is seldom common. The males are often seen flying by day. The caterpillars are polyphagous and have been observed on various trees and shrubs (oaks, willows, bilberries, and heather). There is a single generation annually, with adults emerging from June to August.

---

84 LASIOMMATA MEGERA L.
wall brown

Family Nymphalidae, subfamily Satyrinae.
Geographical distribution Europe, North Africa, and the Middle East.
Description and related species Wingspan approximately 1½–1¾ in. (35–45 mm). The upper side of the wing is orangish-brown with a pattern of black lines; on the forewings there is a large black, white-pupilled eyespot close to the apex, and on the hind wings a row of eyespots along the outer margin. Males have an androconial spot on the forewings. The females are paler in coloration. The underside of the hind wings is grayish with a complex pattern, and there is a line of black eyespots encircled with brown. It is easily distinguished from the other *Lasiommata* species (*maera*, *petropolitana*) by its overall orange hue.
Habits This species is found chiefly in fields, meadows, and gardens, but sometimes also in open woodland, from low altitudes up to 5,000 ft. (1,500 m). The caterpillars live on Gramineae, particularly the genera *Poa* and *Dactylis*. There are two or three generations a year, according to latitude and altitude, with adults emerging from March onward.

85 LEPTIDEA SINAPIS L.
wood white

Family Pieridae.

Geographical distribution Much of Europe, ranging eastward to the Middle East.

Description and related species Wingspan 1¼–1½ in. (30–40 mm). A delicate butterfly, basically white with a dark apical mark on the forewings more prominent in the males. Some generations may to some extent be speckled with gray. It is fairly similar to two other species of the same genus, *Leptidea duponcheli* and *L. morsei*, which may be distinguished by slight differences in wing shape and size. By and large, the wood white differs obviously from all other European pierids.

Habits The butterfly lives in fields and woodland glades, from sea level to mid-mountain zones. Although the specific name suggests an association with mustard (family Cruciferae), the caterpillars feed on plants of the Leguminosae. There are two or three annual generations, with adults appearing in the spring.

86 LIBYTHEA CELTIS Laich.
nettle tree butterfly

Family Libytheidae.

Geographical distribution Much of the Palaearctic region, from Europe and North Africa to the Far East.

Description and related species Wingspan 1¼–1½ in. (30–40 mm). As in all members of the family Libytheidae, the forewings of this species have a conspicuous bulge on the outer margin and, even more characteristically, very long labial palpi which jut out from between the beaklike antennae. The upper side of the wing is brown with orange markings; a small white spot occurs close to the costa of the forewings. The underside is more subdued in color, grayish on the hind wings. It is a very characteristic species, which cannot be mistaken for any other.

Habits The species is found on plains and in hills, wherever its food plant grows. The caterpillars feed on the nettle tree (*Celtis australis*). There is one generation annually. The eggs are laid in the spring, and the new adults appear in the late summer, spending the winter in a sheltered spot and reappearing the following spring to lay their eggs.

87 LIMENITIS POPULI L.
poplar admiral

Family Nymphalidae.

Geographical distribution Temperate zones of the Palaearctic region, from central Europe to Japan.

Description and related species Wingspan approximately 2¾–3¼ in. (65–80 mm). The upper side of this large butterfly's wing is brown with white spots in the middle and orange and black crescents along the margins. Sometimes the white marks are almost totally absent. The underside is for the most part orange, with white spots and black patterns. Other species of the genus living in Europe (*Limenitis reducta* and *L. camilla*), are immediately distinguishable by their smaller size.

Habits This butterfly lives primarily in woods, especially in clearings. The caterpillars feed on the leaves of poplar, especially aspen. There is one annual generation, with adults appearing in June and July.

---

88 LYCAENA PHLAEAS L.
small copper

Family Lycaenidae.

Geographical distribution A vast range, comprising most of the Palaearctic region, certain parts of tropical Africa, and eastern regions of North America.

Description and related species Wingspan approximately ¾–1¼ in. (22–27 mm). One of the few lycaenids in which individuals of both sexes are much alike. The forewings are golden-red with a narrow brown margin and various black markings; the hind wings, however, are brown, with a red band along the apex, and they are also furnished with two short tails. The undersides are lighter, the forewings orange with black spots, the hind wings brownish. The large copper (*Lycaena dispar*) is similar in appearance but larger and more stocky, and the upper side of the male's wing is completely red.

Habits This species frequents open spaces, even fairly arid zones, often close to urban areas. The caterpillars feed mainly on Polygonaceae of the genera *Rumex* and *Polygonum*. There are two or more annual generations except in the north, with adults appearing from February–March onward.

89 LYMANTRIA MONACHA L.
black arches or nun

Family Lymantriidae.
Geographical distribution Temperate regions of Europe and Asia.
Description and related species Wingspan 1¼–2 in. (30–50 mm). A variable species: as a rule the forewings are whitish with a compact pattern of black crescents that serve a mimetic function. There are, nevertheless, individuals in which the coloration is for the most part darker, the wings being blackish. The males are smaller and more slender than the females and have bipectinate antennae. It differs from the related gypsy moth (*Lymantria dispar*) in pattern, abdominal color, and other features. The other European Lymantriidae are extremely diverse; in some species the females have only stumps of wings, while in others they possess a large tuft of hairs at the tip of the abdomen for covering the eggs.

Habits This moth lives in both broad-leaved and coniferous woods. The caterpillars feed on pine needles, causing considerable damage to them, and on the leaves of other trees. There is a single annual generation, with adults emerging from July to September.

90 LYSANDRA CORIDON Poda.
Chalkhill blue

Family Lycaenidae.
Geographical distribution Europe, except for the Scandinavian peninsula and the hottest parts of the Mediterranean.
Description and related species Wingspan approximately 1¼–1½ in. (30–35 mm). In the males the upper side of the wing is a very bright silvery blue (pure blue forms are found in Spain), with dark margins and black and white fringes. The females are brown above, with reddish crescents along the margin. The underparts are gray and brown, with numerous white-rimmed black spots and orange crescents along the margin. These characteristics differentiate the Chalkhill blue quite clearly from other European species.

Habits This species is found in fairly dry grasslands, in hills, and, above all, in the mountains. The caterpillars live on plants of Leguminosae. There is a single generation annually, with adults appearing from July to September.

91 MACROGLOSSUM STELLATARUM L.
hummingbird hawkmoth

Family Sphingidae.
Geographical distribution The Palaearctic region and North America. The species often migrates to more northerly lands and mountain zones.
Description and related species Wingspan 1½–2 in. (40–50 mm). Although fairly inconspicuous, this is a very characteristic species. The forewings are grayish-brown with darker lines; the hind wings are mostly yellowish. There is a dense covering of black and white scales on the flattened tip of the abdomen. The flight pattern is highly individual: the moth is active during the day and, thanks to its extremely rapid wingbeats, often hovers as if motionless in front of flowers, inserting its proboscis into the corolla in order to feed, ready to fly off at speed if disturbed. Such behavior resembles more that of a wasp or bee than that of a moth.
Habits The adult moths may be found almost anywhere, in fields and gardens, even on flowered terraces and balconies. The caterpillars feed on plants of the genus *Galium* (Rubiaceae). Adults appear from the early summer to the late autumn.

---

92 MAMESTRA BRASSICAE L.
cabbage moth

Family Noctuidae.
Geographical distribution Most of the Palaearctic region and North America.
Description and related species Wingspan approximately 1½–2 in. (37–45 mm). A very common and rather inconspicuous moth. The forewings are brown with a complex pattern of black and white lines and crescents; the hind wings are wholly light brown, slightly darker along the margin. The numerous species of the genus *Mamestra* all display the same type of dark, subdued coloration. Many other noctuid moths look much alike and can only be identified by specialists.
Habits The species is generally found on cultivated land, notably orchards and gardens; it ranges from the lowlands to high altitudes. The caterpillars are polyphagous, feeding on various herbaceous plants and trees, but they show a particular liking for cabbages and other cruciferous crops. There are one or more generations a year, depending on the climate, with adults in evidence between May and October.

93 MANIOLA JURTINA L.
meadow brown

Family Nymphalidae, subfamily Satyrinae.
Geographical distribution Europe eastward to the Urals; the Canary Islands and North Africa.
Description and related species Wingspan approximately 1½–2 in. (40–48 mm). This is a rather inconspicuous butterfly. The upper side of the male's wing is entirely brown, with two white-pupiled eyespots near the apex of the forewing; in the female these eyespots are bigger and there is also a tawny area. Similar to the meadow brown is the Sardinian meadow brown (*Maniola nuragh*), which lives only on the island of Sardinia, and the dusky meadow brown (*Hyponephele lycaon*), in which the forewing eyespot of the male is completely black, whereas the female exhibits two eyespots.

Habits This butterfly is common in meadows and pastures from plains to high mountains. The caterpillars feed on Gramineae, especially of the genus *Poa*. There is one generation a year, with a long period when adults are in evidence, from June to August. The females emerge after the males.

94 MELANARGIA RUSSIAE Esp.
Esper's marbled white

Family Nymphalidae, subfamily Satyrinae.
Geographical distribution Southern Europe, with a discontinuous range, and southern Russia eastward to the western regions of Siberia.
Description and related species Wingspan 1½–2 in. (35–50 mm). The upper sides of the wings display a characteristic and complex alternation of black and white areas; on the underside of the hind wings the black is replaced by gray. The veins are outlined in black and there is a series of eyespots along the margin. In the female the basic color is yellowish. The most closely related of the other six European *Melanargia* species is the marbled white (*M. galathea*), which has a different pattern on the forewings.

Habits This species prefers dry hilly places up to an altitude of about 5,000 ft. (1,500 m). The caterpillars feed on plants of the Gramineae. There is one annual generation, with adults emerging in July.

95 MESOACIDALIA AGLAJA L.
dark green fritillary

Family Nymphalidae.

Geographical distribution Much of the Palaearctic region, from Europe to Japan.

Description and related species Wingspan 2–2¼ in. (50–55 mm). This typical fritillary butterfly is characterized by the tawny color of the upper side of the wing, with black markings. The dark green fritillary is easily identified by the coloration of the undersides, the forewings being light brown streaked with black, and the hind wings largely olive green with a reddish-brown postdiscal band and numerous silvery spots arranged in characteristic fashion. The other European members of this group of fritillaries (*Pandoriana*, *Argynnis*, *Fabriciana*, *Issoria*, *Brentis*, *Boloria*, *Proclossiana*, and *Clossiana*) can be distinguished by differences in the color pattern on the underside of the wing.

Habits This butterfly frequents woodland clearings, from sea level to the upper limit of the tree line. The caterpillars feed almost exclusively on the foliage of violets. There is a single generation, with adults appearing in June–July.

---

96 MICROPTERIX AUSTRALIS
heath

Family Micropterigidae.

Geographical distribution This family, comprising the most primitive of Lepidoptera, is subdivided into eight genera that are found in temperate regions all over the world. In Europe it is represented by a single genus, *Micropterix*.

Description and related species Wingspan approximately ½ in. (10–11 mm). All the species of this family possess fully functional mandibles and similar venation on the forewings and hind wings. The wing pattern and coloration of *Micropterix australis* are typical of many other species: the forewings are glossy purple with prominent golden stripes and spots. The shape and arrangement of these markings assist in identification of these moths.

Habits The moths of this genus feed, frequently in large groups, on the pollen of many herbaceous plants, both trees and shrubs. They are very difficult to see in flight and often the only way to capture them is to cut the flowers on which they settle. The caterpillars feed on plant litter or on the mycelia of various species of fungi.

97 NEOPE GOSCHKEVITSCHII Mén.

Family Nymphalidae, subfamily Satyrinae.
Geographical distribution Japan.
Description and related species Wingspan 2½ in. (60 mm). The upper side of the male's forewing has bright ocher yellow veins and spots. In the female this color is more subdued. Inside almost all of the short yellow bands that adorn the postmedian area is a black spot. The underside of the forewing is pale yellow with black streaking and a gray band along the outer margin. The hind wings are gray, the discal area exhibits a dark band with contrasted borders, and the submarginal zone displays a row of eyespots. This is a sturdy butterfly, resembling *Harima callipteris*, another Japanese satyrine; in the latter the colors of the upper side of the wings are more blurred, while on the underside it lacks the black pattern and gray coloration of *Neope goschkevitschii*.
Habits It is very common from the end of July on tree trunks, walls, and the like. It tends to fly at dusk and when at rest keeps its wings folded over the back so as to blend with the surroundings. In September it is the most common butterfly encountered in the gardens of Tokyo.

---

98 NEPTICULA SP.

Family Nepticulidae.
Geographical distribution The species belonging to this genus are found all over the world, even at altitudes of up to 12,000 ft. (3,500 m).
Description and related species The adults are among the tiniest known Lepidoptera, with a wingspan of only ⅛–⅙ in. (3–4 mm). Their principal feature is the tuft of scales that covers the base of the antennae, forming a kind of hood over the eyes. The forewings are relatively large and pointed but the long terminal scales give them a rounded appearance. The hind wings bear cilia that are up to four times the length of the wings.
Habits These tiny moths are very difficult to capture because of their size, and often the only way to obtain adults is to collect the mines and rear the larvae. There are usually one or two annual generations. Identification of the various species is based exclusively on examination of the genitalia or, since they are leaf miners, on study of the mines they produce.

99 NOCTUA FIMBRIATA L.
broad-bordered yellow underwing

Family Noctuidae.

Geographical distribution Europe, especially southern regions, eastward to the Caucasus.

Description and related species Wingspan 1⅓–2¼ in. (45–55 mm). A particularly conspicuous moth. The female's forewings are beige, those of the male are darker, with indistinct patterns; the hind wings, however, are orange with a black band along the margin. It is similar to the lesser broad-bordered yellow underwing (*Noctua janthina*), which is generally darker in color and a little smaller, and to the large yellow underwing (*N. pronuba*), which has a narrower black band on the hind wings. The function of these vivid colors on the hind wings is to disorient predators.

Habits It lives at low levels and in the hills, without any special preference as to habitat. The caterpillars are polyphagous and feed on both shrubs and trees. They have been observed on primroses, docks, violets, hawthorns, plums, birches, and willows. There is only one generation a year and adults appear between June and September.

100 NYMPHALIS ANTIOPA L.
Camberwell beauty

Family Nymphalidae.

Geographical distribution A very wide range, including North America, Europe, and Palaearctic Asia.

Description and related species Wingspan 2¼–3 in. (55–75 mm). A large butterfly with characteristic coloration, violet brown with a series of blue marks close to the broad yellow margin. In individuals that have hibernated as adults the margin turns white. In terms of color and size, the Camberwell beauty cannot be mistaken for any other Holarctic species.

Habits This butterfly is found in fields, meadows and woodland clearings, from lowlands to high altitudes. The caterpillar lives on various trees (willow, poplar, and birch). There is one generation a year, with adults emerging in June–July and sometimes, after hibernating, they will reappear in the spring. This migrant butterfly, after suffering a decline in recent years, now seems to be on the increase again in some regions.

101　NYSSIA FLORENTINA Stef.

Family　Geometridae.

Geographical distribution　Parts of northern and central Italy.

Description and related species　Wingspan 1¼ in. (30 mm). The female of the genus *Nyssia* constitutes one of the rare example of moths that are almost totally wingless; the wings are, in fact, reduced to a couple of whitish stumps (see photograph). The males, on the other hand, possess functional wings, whitish with barely visible dark lines, and have pectinate antennae. Other species of geometrids whose females are without wings or with much reduced wings include the mottled umber (*Erannis defoliaria*), which does a lot of damage in woodlands, and the winter moth (*Operophtera brumata*), the adults of which appear from the autumn to the early winter.

Habits　This moth is found on cultivated land, and sometimes in urban areas. The caterpillars feed on leguminous plants. Adults appear in the early spring, from February onward.

102　OLETHREUTES ARCUELLA Cl.
arched marble

Family　Tortricidae.

Geographical distribution　Deciduous woods from Europe to Siberia; Korea and Japan.

Description and related species　Wingspan approximately ¾ in. (16–18 mm). This is a splendid and quite unmistakable moth. The forewings are deep orange with metallic blue stripes and streaks running across them; on the discal area there is a circular patch, the top part of which is dark gray, the center ocherous-white, and the lower part black with four dots of the same metallic blue color as the stripes. The hind wings are grayish-black. The caterpillar is dark violet gray with a light brown head.

Habits　This moth is very common in oak woods. There is one generation, with adults that fly from May to July during the afternoons and evenings. The caterpillars are active in the spring and summer, developing on leaves that have fallen to the ground.

103 OXYPTILUS SP.

Family Pterophoridae.

Geographical distribution The species belonging to this genus are found all over the world.

Description and related species The adults, like all members of the families Pterophoridae and Alucitidae, are described as plumed moths because of the strange structure of the wings, each of which is divided into ciliated lobes (in the Pterophoridae there are two lobes on the forewings and three on the hind wings).

Habits The adults, as a rule, are not strong flyers. The attitude of the moth when at rest is curious: The forewings and the hind wings are brought close together and held perpendicular to the body. The hind legs are flattened against the abdomen and the moth thus adopts a characteristic T-shape that is typical of the whole family. The caterpillars are not greatly different from those of the Pyralidae, which often have long hairs. These and other features have caused taxonomists to hypothesize that the two families are related.

104 PAPILIO BIANOR Cramer

Family Papilionidae.

Geographical distribution Widespread both in the eastern regions of the Palaearctic (China and Japan) and the Indo-Malayan area (northeast India, Burma, and Indochina).

Description and related species Wingspan approximately 3½–5¼ in. (85–130 mm). This large oriental swallowtail, quite different from the species inhabiting the western part of the Palaearctic region, is notable for its dark color, the males displaying green and blue reflections. In the females the color of the forewings is olive gray and the hind wings exhibit green rather than blue tints. The species is divided into subspecies: the *dehaani* race is found, for example, in Japan.

Habits This butterfly is usually found at low levels, but in the foothills of the Himalayas it may be seen at up to 6,600 ft. (2,000 m). The caterpillar is predominantly green, with two transverse dark bands. Food plants are of the family Rutaceae.

105 PAPILIO MACHAON L.
common swallowtail

Family Papilionidae.
Geographical distribution Throughout Europe, from the Mediterranean to the subarctic region; North Africa; Asia to the Himalayas, and Japan. Replaced by similar species in North America.

Description and related species Wingspan 2–3 in. (50–75 mm). One of the most spectacular and characteristic of European butterflies. It is identifiable by its yellow ground color with black patterns; on the hind wing the postdiscal band displays stripes of blue and a red and blue spot. The various generations differ slightly in coloration. Two related European species of *Papilio* similar to the common swallowtail are *P. alexanor* (sporadic in southern Europe), with a yellow basal area to the forewings, and *P. hospiton*, from Corsica and Sardinia, strongly resembling *P. machaon*.

Habits This butterfly lives in lowland areas up to high levels, in fields, meadows, and glades. The caterpillars feed on various plants of the family Umbelliferae. In northern Europe there is usually a single generation, in central–southern regions there can be two or three generations a year, with adults appearing in April–May and July–August.

---

106 PARARGE AEGERIA L.
speckled wood

Family Nymphalidae, subfamily Satyrinae.
Geographical distribution Europe, except for the northernmost regions; North Africa and the central–western regions of Asia.

Description and related species Wingspan approximately 1¼–1½ in. (32–42 mm). The upper sides of the forewings are brown and orange in the males or yellowish in the females, with alternating stripes and spots; there is a distinct black eyespot near the apex. The hind wings are largely brown with orange marks and clear eyespots in the postdiscal zone. The underside of the hind wings is completely brown and finely patterned. By and large the species is unmistakable, although it bears some resemblance to the large wall brown (*Lasiommata maera*) and the northern wall brown (*L. petropolitana*), in which the color brown predominates, and to the wall brown (*L. megera*), which is mainly reddish-brown. There are also two very similar species to *Pararge aegeria* on the islands of the Canaries and Madeira.

Habits This species frequents woods and shady places as well as parks and gardens, from sea level to mid-mountain areas. The caterpillars live on various species of Gramineae, particularly *Agropyron*. There are three annual generations, with adults emerging from March to October.

107 PARNASSIUS APOLLO L.
Apollo

Family Papilionidae.
Geographical distribution Northern Europe and high ground in central–southern Europe, eastward to central Asia.
Description and related species Wingspan 2½–3 in. (60–75 mm). This extremely variable species is characterized by its basically white coloration, veiled to a certain extent by gray, and its black and red or yellowish spots. It is very similar to the small Apollo (*Parnassius phoebus*), which frequents higher altitudes and is generally much smaller; the latter's black spot, close to the inner margin, is either smaller or absent altogether. The clouded Apollo (*P. mnemosyne*) is even smaller and has no colored markings whatsoever. Because of the geographical isolation of its various populations, the Apollo has been subdivided into a large number of races.
Habits This butterfly is seen in mountain and subalpine meadows; in northern Europe it is also found at low levels. The caterpillars are associated with the Crassulaceae of the genus *Sedum*. There is a single annual generation, with adults appearing in June–August.

108 PHALERA BUCEPHALA L.
buff-tip

Family Notodontidae.
Geographical distribution From Europe to the Far East.
Description and related species Wingspan approximately 1½–2¼ in. (42–55 mm). This moth, when prepared for display in a collection, looks fairly unremarkable; the forewings are grayish-brown with darker markings and there is a large, roundish off-white area at the apex. The hind wings are whitish and the thorax is covered with long, dense, light-colored scales. When settled on a tree or shrub with wings folded, however, its appearance is exactly like that of a snapped twig, representing one of the most striking examples of cryptic mimicry. The large whitish patches on the forewings distinguish the species clearly from other European Notodontidae.
Habits This moth lives both in broad-leaved woods and in parkland. The caterpillars feed on the leaves of trees such as lime, oak, and willow. There is one generation a year, with adults appearing from May to July.

109 PHRAGMATOBIA FULIGINOSA L.
ruby tiger

Family Arctiidae.

Geographical distribution The entire Palaearctic region, from Europe to Japan, and North America.

Description and related species Wingspan approximately 1¼–1½ in. (30–35 mm). One of the most common European tiger moths and also one of the least showy. The wings are sparsely covered with scales and are somewhat translucent; the forewings are brown with two small black dots, while the hind wings are pink, often with a blackish band along the margin. By and large it is a characteristic species which cannot be mistaken for any other inhabiting the Palaearctic region.

Habits This moth lives from sea level to mid-mountain altitudes and does not show any particular preferences as to habitat. The caterpillars are polyphagous and feed on a variety of plants, having been recorded on *Rumex* (Polygonaceae), *Taraxacum*, *Solidago*, and *Achillea* (Compositae). There are often two generations each year, with adults appearing in April–June and July–September.

110 PHYLLONORYCTER BLANCARDELLA L.
apple-leaf midget

Family Gracillariidae.

Geographical distribution Originally Europe and Asia but for approximately the last forty years also found in the United States.

Description and related species Wingspan approximately ⅓ in. (7–8 mm). The basic coloration is reddish-brown with four costal and three dorsal stripes, all of which are pure white and irregularly rimmed in dark brown; there is a large white basal stripe covering up to one-third of the wing. The species belongs to a group which includes *Phyllonorycter cydoniella*, *P. pomonella*, *P. cerasicolella*, *P. mespilella*, *P. sorbi*, and *P. oxycanthae*, all of which attack various Rosaceae. These species are all much alike and can only be identified individually by examination of the genitalia.

Habits The larva is a miner, living among the leaves of various members of the Pomoideae subfamily of the Rosaceae (apple, pear, sorb, medlar, etc.). The mine, as in the case of the majority of *Phyllonorycter* species, is formed from the silken threads of the caterpillar; its lower surface is wrinkled, the rear part strongly curved, and measures about ¾ in. (15 mm) in length. There are four generations a year, the chrysalis hibernating inside the mine of the fallen leaf.

111 PHYLLONORYCTER MESSANIELLA Z.

Family Gracillariidae.

Geographical distribution Central–southern Europe, including the British Isles. Recently it was accidentally introduced into Australia and New Zealand, where it represents a serious threat to oak trees.

Description and related species Wingspan ⅓–½ in. (8–10 mm). The forewings are ocher yellow with white patches (four costal and four dorsal), each with a jagged dark brown border. There is a thin longitudinal white stripe in the basal area. The related *Phyllonorycter quercifolia* is very similar but has a much longer basal stripe, up to two-thirds the length of the wing.

Habits Eggs are laid on oak trees, both evergreen (*Quercus ilex*) and deciduous; they have also been found on *Carpinus betulus*, *Castanea sativa*, and *Fagus sylvatica*. A mine is formed on the lower surface of the leaf; often two or three mines may be found on the same leaf. There are numerous generations, spaced closely together so that larvae are liable to be active from April until December.

---

112 PIERIS BRASSICAE L.
large white

Family Pieridae.

Geographical distribution Western Europe, including islands of the Mediterranean, North Africa, and Asia east to the Himalayas. It often migrates in large numbers.

Description and related species Wingspan approximately 1½–2¾ in. (40–65 mm). The male large white differs from other European cabbage butterflies (*Pieris napi, P. mannii, P. rapae, P. bryoniae*, etc.) in that it is bigger and has a large black apical area on the forewings. The female has a pair of large black dots on her forewings.

Habits This butterfly is found on cultivated land, where it is sometimes very common, from sea level up to an altitude of about 4,500 ft. (1,300 m). The species can be harmful to crops, the larvae attacking many cultivated Cruciferae (cabbages, turnips, etc.). There are many generations each year, up to a maximum of five, according to surroundings and altitude. The various generations display slight morphological differences.

113 PLODIA INTERPUNCTELLA Hb.
Indian meal moth

Family Pyralidae.

Geographical distribution This species, thought to be of tropical origin, is cosmopolitan and one of the most widely distributed Lepidoptera in the world.

Description and related species Wingspan approximately ¾ in. (15–20 mm). The coloration of this moth is characteristic, the basal portion of the forewings being yellowish-white and the proximal part reddish-brown with two or three darker transverse stripes. It cannot be confused with any other species.

Habits This moth's diet is remarkably varied, consisting almost entirely of preserved animal and vegetable products (seeds, flour, dried fruit, dried meat and fish, dead insects, herbs, confectionery, etc.) As a result it is one of the most harmful of Lepidoptera. The number of generations is extremely variable, depending on climatic conditions: possibly six, seven, or even more. The female lays up to 400 eggs on or around a selected food substance, and incubation lasts from a few days to several weeks. The optimal temperature for larval development is between 68°–86°F (20°–30°C).

---

114 POLYGONIA C-ALBUM L.
comma butterfly

Family Nymphalidae.

Geographical distribution Vast areas of North Africa, Europe, and temperate Asia to China and Japan.

Description and related species Wingspan approximately 1½–2 in. (42–50 mm). A butterfly characterized by the toothed shape of its wing margins. The upper side is orange tending to brown, with darker patterns made up of irregular black dots and, frequently, a more or less straight brown margin. The underside of the wings is very dark, with a fairly complex pattern including a small white mark in the shape of a letter "C" on the hind wings. The two annual generations differ in coloration, the later one usually being darker. The related southern comma (*Polygonia egea*), living in southern Europe, has a small white Y-shaped mark on the underside.

Habits This butterfly lives in open places such as the fringes of woods, fields, and gardens, from sea level to mid-mountain regions. The caterpillars feed on nettles, hops, willows, and other plants. There are two generations each year, with adults emerging in June and from late July–August. Individuals of the second generation hibernate.

115 **POLYOMMATUS ICARUS** Rott.
common blue

Family Lycaenidae.

Geographical distribution Europe, North Africa, and temperate regions of Asia; also the Canary Islands.

Description and related species Wingspan 1–1¼ in. (25–30 mm). One of the many lycaenids in which the upper side of the male's wings are blue while those of the female are almost entirely brown. Here the blue coloration of the males tends toward violet, with a thin black line near the margin, which has white fringes; the females have brown wings, with a few reddish crescents along the margin and, sometimes, a light sprinkling of blue. The underparts, however, are grayish, with orange crescents near the margin and black spots encircled with white over the rest of the surface. The other numerous Lycaenidae with blue males are divided into many genera. They include the species of *Lysandra* and *Agrodiaetus*; the silver-studded blue (*Plebejus argus*), a small butterfly with broad black margins to the wings; the Mazarine blue (*Cyaniris semiargus*), dark violet blue; and especially the large butterflies of the genus *Maculinea*, blue with dark spots, whose caterpillars spend part of their life in ants' nests, feeding on ant larvae.

Habits The common blue lives in fields and open grassy areas, even in towns, from sea level to considerable altitudes; in Morocco, for example, it is found at 9,000 ft. (2,700 m). The caterpillars feed on herbaceous plants of the family Leguminosae, for example, *Lotus corniculatus*, *Ononis*, and *Trifolium*. The caterpillar, stocky with pointed ends, can grow up to 5¼ in. (13 cm) in length. It is green and has a dark green stripe with lighter margins in the center of its back; it also has a lighter stripe on each side, just below the tracheal spiracles. It lays its eggs on leaves. Winter is spent in the larval stage and pupation takes place at the base of the food plant. The number of generations varies according to latitude and altitude. In southern Europe there may be three generations, with adults appearing from April onward; in northern Europe there is only one generation a year.

116 PONTIA DAPLIDICE L.
Bath white

Family Pieridae.
Geographical distribution Much of the Palaearctic region.
Description and related species Wingspan approximately 1½–1¾ in. (35–45 mm). The upper side of the wing is white; the apical area of the hind wing is black with white spots and there is a further black mark near the costa. The underside of the wing displays complex greenish patterns. Other species of the genus *Pontia* (*chloridice, callidice*) – much rarer – differ in details of the color pattern. The Bath white is very similar to the female orange tip (*Anthocharis cardamines*), which may be distinguished by the rounded tip of the forewings. Another species resembling *Pontia daplidice* is the dappled white (*Euchloe ausonia*), but the isolated marking on the latter's forewings is more rectangular in shape.
Habits The Bath white is found in fields, even if dry, from low elevations to mid mountains. The species often migrates. The caterpillars feed on various species of the family Cruciferae. There are two or more generations a year, with adults flying from the early spring.

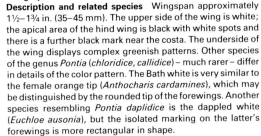

117 PROCRIS STATICES L.
common forester

Family Zygaenidae.
Geographical distribution Throughout Europe, ranging east to the Urals.
Description and related species Wingspan approximately ¾–1¼ in. (22–28 mm). Unlike the representatives of the genus *Zygaena*, which are vividly colored to warn predators of poisonous substances in the blood, the foresters of the genus *Procris* are less showy, with colors that tend to merge with the surrounding vegetation. The forewings are metallic green, the hind wings brown. The various species are much alike and identification is difficult without specialist study.
Habits The common forester is a familiar moth in fields and clearings, especially in damp places, from sea level to the upper limits of the tree line. Its caterpillars feed on plants of the genus *Rumex* (Polygonaceae). There is one generation a year, with adults appearing between May and August, depending on latitude and altitude.

118 PTEROPHORUS PENTADACTYLUS L.
large white plume

Family Pterophoridae.
Geographical distribution Europe, except for the Iberian peninsula.
Description and related species Wingspan approximately ¾ in. (15–16 mm). The pure white color of this moth makes it unmistakable; black scales are rarely found in the median and dorsal areas of the forewings.
Habits The large white plumed moth is fairly common in places with abundant grass and shrubs, in fields, gardens, and uncultivated areas. It flies only at dawn and dusk. The caterpillar lives on *Convolvulus arvensis* and *Calystegia sepium*; it occasionally damages strawberry and soya plants, gnawing the lower surface of the leaves. Infestation is evident from the formation above of brownish patches. Pupation always occurs beneath a leaf. There are two generations a year.

119 PYRAUSTA PURPURALIS L.
common crimson-and-gold

Family Pyralidae.
Geographical distribution From Europe to western Asia.
Description and related species Wingspan approximately ¾ in. (16–18 mm). The color and wing pattern are variable; as a rule the forewings are reddish-brown with numerous yellow spots and the hind wings blackish-brown, with yellow dots and streaks near the base and a pure yellow transverse stripe. Both the forewings and the hind wings bear another thin yellow stripe parallel to the outer margin. A related species, the general purple-and-gold (*Pyrausta aurata*), has only the transverse stripe, without any dots, on the hind wings.
Habits There are two annual generations of this species. The caterpillar lives in a shelter of leaves and silk on *Mentha acquatica*, *M. arvensis*, *Origanum*, *Thymus*, etc. The adult frequents dry, warm, grassy places, close to river banks or in rocky mountain areas.

120 PYRGUS MALVAE L.
grizzled skipper

Family Hesperiidae.

Geographical distribution The Palaearctic region, from Europe to Mongolia; absent in North Africa.

Description and related species Wingspan approximately ¾–1 in. (18–22 mm). The genus *Pyrgus* comprises a dozen or so European species, which are all very similar and can only be identified for certain by examination of the male genitalia. The males possess a groove in the costa of the forewings in which there is a structure that produces sex pheromones. *P. malvae* is one of the most common species of its genus. The upper side of the wings is brownish-black with white markings; the underside of the hind wings is brown, with green or yellowish tints.

Habits This species frequents wet, grassy places, from sea level to high altitudes. The caterpillars are polyphagous, feeding principally on plants of the family Rosaceae (including the genera *Potentilla*, *Fragaria*, and *Agrimonia*) but also on Malvaceae (*Malva*). There may be only a single annual generation in the colder parts of its range, with adults appearing from May; in warmer zones there may be two generations, with adults appearing in April and July.

---

121 QUERCUSIA FUJISANA Matsumura

Family Lycaenidae.

Geographical distribution Japan.

Description and related species Wingspan approximately 1¼–1½ in. (34–36 mm). The male's forewings are entirely greenish; on the outer margins there is a clear black patch, and another one, less distinct, on the hind wings. The costal region of the hind wings is brown. There is a short curved tail close to the lower end of each hind wing. The underside is whitish with a few short, thin dark patches in the median zone. In addition, there is a series of dark dots on the submarginal area and a similarly dark marginal patch. On the hind wings a brown band runs across the discal area; and a yellow patch enclosing two black spots marks the anal zone. The female is dark brown above, while the color pattern of the underparts is similar to that of the male, with alternating light brown and white patches. The species is similar to *Favonius yuasai*, but in the latter the underside of the wings is practically devoid of light brown while the anal zone is orange instead of yellow.

122 SAMIA CYNTHIA Drury
Cynthia silkmoth

Family Saturniidae.

Geographical distribution Originally from the Far East, it was imported to and has become acclimatized in various parts of Europe and North America.

Description and related species Wingspan 5–5¼ in. (120–130 mm). This silkmoth cannot be mistaken for any other European species, its characteristic features being the wavy outer wing margin, the olive brown color of the wings, and the presence on each of a prominent black-rimmed pink band and a large, translucent half-moon. In overall appearance it resembles the huge Atlas moth (*Attacus atlas*), a southeast Asian species with females whose wingspan can reach 12 in. (30 cm).

Habits This silkmoth was introduced to Europe and North America several decades ago for the silk produced by its caterpillar, but the quality of its silk proved much inferior to that of *Bombyx mori* and rearing of the species was soon abandoned. The moth has prospered in certain regions where its food plants, ailanthus and castor oil, grow. Adults emerge in June–July.

---

123 SASAKIA CHARONDA Hewits.

Family Nymphalidae.

Geographical distribution Japan.

Description and related species Wingspan 3¾–5 in. (95–120 mm). On the upper side of the male's wings the basal and discal areas display an extensive blue sheen. From the post-discal zones to the margins, the color varies from pale green to a light greenish-brown. The wing surfaces are sprinkled with white spots of varying size but always smaller toward the margins. There are two marks, almost linked, close to the anal area. The inner marginal area of the hind wings is light brown. The female is brown, without the blue sheen on the wings. Several subspecies have been described by taxonomists.

Habits This species can fly rapidly. The caterpillars feed on plants of the genus *Celtis*. In the more northerly part of its range, as on the island of Hokkaido, adults do not appear until July, but in more temperate zones they are already flying in June. This species – often depicted by artists – is regarded by the Japanese as their national butterfly.

124 SATURNIA PYRI Schiff.
giant peacock moth

Family Saturniidae.

Geographical distribution Central–southern Europe, North Africa, and temperate regions of Asia.

Description and related species Wingspan 4–6¼ in. (100–160 mm). This is the largest of all European butterflies or moths, especially in the size of its wings. The coloration is predominantly brown with zigzag patterns; the wing margin is lighter in color and on each wing there is an eyespot in alternating tones of black, cyclamen, and beige. The males are distinguished from the females by their bipectinate antennae. In general appearance it much resembles the emperor moth (*Saturnia pavonia*), but the latter is smaller, with a wingspan of not more than 2½ in. (60 mm), and the hind wings of the males are chestnut orange.

Habits This moth frequents areas with trees and shrubs but is often found, too, in urban areas. The very large caterpillars feed on the leaves of trees, especially fruit trees. There is one generation a year, with adults appearing from April to June.

125 SCOLIOPTERYX LIBATRIX L.
herald

Family Noctuidae.

Geographical distribution Almost the whole Palaearctic region and North America.

Description and related species Wingspan 1½–1¾ in. (40–45 mm). This moth is characterized mainly by the shape of the forewings, which have a jagged outer margin, their outline resembling that of certain vanessid butterflies. The color of the forewings is hazel with lighter transverse lines and orange patches; the hind wings are uniformly brown with a slightly darker transverse stripe. The species is thus clearly distinguishable from other noctuids.

Habits This moth frequents moist ground, especially areas close to water, where its food plants grow, from sea level to mountain zones up to 3,300 ft. (1,000 m). The caterpillars feed on the leaves of willows and poplars. There are one or two generations annually, with adults flying virtually all year round. The herald often hibernates and it is not uncommon to find groups of individuals in sheltered spots such as cellars and lofts.

126 SESIA APIFORMIS Cl.
hornet clearwing

Family Sesiidae.
Geographical distribution Temperate regions of Europe, Asia, and North America.
Description and related species Wingspan 1¼–1½ in. (30–40 mm). The wasp or clearwing moths of the family Sesiidae have wings that are largely devoid of scales and a brightly colored body. The hornet clearwing represents one of the most typical cases of Batesian mimicry; the shape and color of its wings and legs imitate, in a remarkable manner, those of a wasp, particularly of the hornet (*Vespa crabro*), in order to keep possible predators, especially birds, at bay.
Habits This moth is generally found near water where its food plants grow. The caterpillars feed on the roots of poplars and willows, their period of development lasting two years. The adults appear between May and August.

127 SMERINTHUS OCELLATA L.
eyed hawkmoth

Family Sphingidae.
Geographical distribution Throughout Europe and the western regions of Asia.
Description and related species Wingspan 2¾–3¼ in. (70–80 mm). This is a very characteristic moth, the only European representative of a genus with widespread distribution in temperate regions of the Orient. The pattern of the hind wings, with two black and red eyespots on a pink ground, is extremely conspicuous and probably serves to frighten or at least confuse potential predators. In fact, the moth, having settled, often does not fold the forewings protectively over the body and clearly displays part of the hind wings. It cannot be mistaken for any other European species.
Habits This moth frequents a variety of habitats, from the lowlands to fairly high altitudes. The caterpillars live on the leaves of different trees, particularly willow and poplar. There is one annual generation, with adults emerging from May to July.

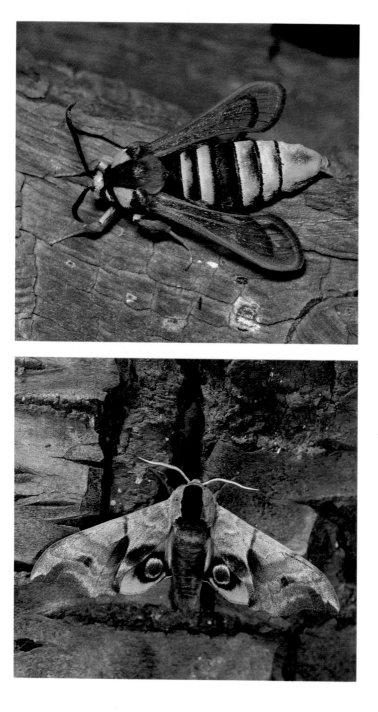

128 SPHINX LIGUSTRI L.
privet hawkmoth

Family Sphingidae.

Geographical distribution Throughout the Palaearctic region, from Europe to Japan.

Description and related species Wingspan 3½–5 in. (90–120 mm). The forewings of this hawkmoth are brownish or whitish with a darker postdiscal area. There are some blackish lines along the veins. The hind wings are pinkish-white with three black transverse bands. The abdomen is covered in pink scales, with black bands running across and a brown line down the middle. Overall it is fairly similar to the convolvulus hawkmoth (*Agrius convolvuli*), a migratory species with denser and more complex patterns on the wings and less distinct bands across the hind wings.

Habits This moth lives in natural shrubland as well as in parks and gardens. The caterpillars are polyphagous and feed on leaves of various shrubs (privet, sorb, lilac, etc.). There is a single annual generation and adults appear in May.

---

129 STRYMONDIA PRUNI L.
black hairstreak

Family Lycaenidae.

Geographical distribution Temperate regions of the Palaearctic, from Europe to Japan.

Description and related species Wingspan approximately 1 in. (25–28 mm). The upper side of the wing is mainly brown, with a blurred yellowish patch on the forewing and a series of orange crescents near the margin of the hind wings. The underside is a lighter brown, with crescents and reddish, black, and white spots along the wing margin, which is edged by a thin, jagged black and white line. This pattern on the underside of the wing distinguishes the black hairstreak from other European species of *Strymondia*, such as *S. spini* and *S. w-album*.

Habits It is found at low altitudes in shrubby areas. The caterpillars feed on shrubs and trees of the genus *Prunus*, especially the sloe or blackthorn (*P. spinosa*). There is one generation a year, with adults appearing from May to July.

130 THECLA BETULAE L.
brown hairstreak

Family Lycaenidae.
Geographical distribution Temperate regions of Europe and Asia.
Description and related species Wingspan approximately 1¼–1½ in. (32–37 mm). The upper side of the wing is dark brown, as are the short tails protruding from the hind wings. The males display an oblique brick red patch on the forewings. The underside is yellowish with transverse brick red bands and thin black and white lines. The larger size and the coloration of the underside of the wings clearly separate the brown hairstreak from other related genera of Lycaenidae (*Strymondia, Callophris*, etc.).
Habits This species is found in open woodland, on hills, and mountains. The caterpillar is polyphagous and lives on trees (Rosaceae, Betulaceae, and others). There is one generation a year, with adults emerging in June–July.

---

131 THYATIRA BATIS L.
peach blossom

Family Thyatiridae.
Geographical distribution Almost the entire Palaearctic region.
Description and related species Wingspan approximately 1¼–1½ in. (32–38 mm). One of the fifteen European species of Thyatiridae, a small family comprising fewer than 150 species on all continents apart from tropical Africa and Australia. The peach blossom is unmistakable because of the coloration of its forewings, which are brown with white-rimmed pink spots; the hind wings are uniformly brown.
Habits It frequents both broad-leaved and coniferous woodlands in hills and mountains. The caterpillars live on blackberry (*Rubus fruticosus*). Depending on the climatic conditions, there may be one or two generations a year, with adults appearing from May to August.

132 TINEA PELLIONELLA Z.
case-bearing clothes moth

Family Tineidae.
Geographical distribution Palaearctic and Nearctic regions, Australia, and New Zealand.
Description and related species Wingspan variable, from 3¼ in. (8–15 mm). The forewings range in color from ocherous gray to grayish-brown, with two darker spots in the median zone and another farther back; particularly notable are the areas covered by transparent scales, both on the upper side and underside of the wing, close to the base, below the costa. The hind wings are a glossy pale gray. This moth belongs to a group comprising many very similar species whose identification is only possible by the study of their genital apparatus. They include *Tinea translucens, T. dubiella, T. lanella, T. flavescentella, T. murariella*, etc. The most closely related species, however, is *T. columbariella*, which lacks the two median spots on the forewings.

133 TORTRIX VIRIDANA L.
green oak tortrix

Family Tortricidae.
Geographical distribution Europe, the Mediterranean shores of North Africa, and Asia Minor.
Description and related species Wingspan ½ in. (10 mm). The adult is unmistakable: entirely brilliant green, apart from the hind wings, which are grayish with yellow hairs. It is common, nevertheless, to come across a variety in which the moth is wholly pale yellow instead of green.
Habits The moth flies both by day and night, particularly in the afternoon. The females lay eggs in the fissures of oak branches; the eggs are covered with detritus and scales stuck together. The young larvae curl up and attack leaves in various ways, gnawing away from the inside. They move from one leaf to another, leaving only the principal veins intact. The species is often responsible for large scale infestations, during which entire oak woodlands are stripped of leaves.

134 TYRIA JACOBAEAE L.
cinnabar moth

Family Arctiidae.

Geographical distribution Western regions of the Palae-arctic, from Europe to central Asia.

Description and related species Wingspan approximately 1¼–1½ in. (32–42 mm). A graceful and elegant tiger moth of characteristic appearance. The forewings are grayish-brown with a deep pink line along the costa and the inner margin, and two round patches of the same color close to the outer margin. The hind wings are uniformly dark pink. The coloration is slightly like that of a burnet moth (Zygaenidae), but the shape of the wings is totally different.

Habits This moth is found in dry meadows and wasteland both at low elevations and in mid-mountain zones. The caterpillars tend to live in groups and attack plants of the family Compositae in particular. There is a single annual generation, with adults appearing from May to July.

135 VANESSA ATALANTA L.
red admiral

Family Nymphalidae.

Geographical distribution An extremely wide distribution including Europe, North Africa, the Canary and Azores Islands, Asia Minor, North America, New Zealand, and Haiti.

Description and related species Wingspan 2–2½ in. (50–60 mm). The name "vanessid" is sometimes applied to a group of Nymphalidae placed in various genera, characterized by the vivid, contrasting colors of their upper parts and their sometimes conspicuously irregular wing margins. Among them the red admiral may be distinguished immediately by its predominantly black coloration with an oblique red band on the forewings and an orangish-red band near the margin of the hind wings; some white spots appear at the apex of the hind wings. The underparts are inconspicuous by comparison, with complex brown patterns that probably have a protective function.

Habits This species frequents fields and meadows but is also found in gardens and parks. The caterpillars usually feed on nettles. There can be two or three annual generations except in the north of its range, with adults appearing throughout the summer and autumn.

136 VANESSA CARDUI L.
painted lady

Family Nymphalidae.

Geographical distribution Found almost all over the world, except South America.

Description and related species Wingspan 1¾–2½ in. (45–60 mm). The upper side of the wing is reddish-orange; on the forewings there are black patterns and a few white marks near the apex, and on the hind wings there is a series of black eyespots in the postdiscal area. The undersides of the hind wings display complex brown markings and a prominent group of colored eyespots. It cannot be confused with any other European species, but it much resembles the American painted lady (*Vanessa virginiensis*), which displays two very big eyespots on the underside of the hind wings, and which is found not only in North America but also in the Canary Islands, on Madeira and occasionally reaches Europe.

Habits This species frequents a variety of habitats but shows a preference for open spaces, from sea level to high altitudes. It is also a typical migratory species. The caterpillars feed on thistles, nettles, and probably other plants as well. The life cycle varies according to latitude and climate; in the Mediterranean region, for example, there are probably three generations a year.

137 YPONOMEUTA EVONYMELLA L.

Family Yponomeutidae.

Geographical distribution Throughout the Palaearctic region.

Description and related species Wingspan approximately ¾ in. (17–20 mm). The forewings of this very characteristic moth are satiny white with lines of black dots; the hind wings are gray. In Europe there are nine known species belonging to this genus, all of them much alike both in morphology and biology. They can be distinguished only by careful examination of structural and biological features at various stages of development, and identification is assisted by knowledge of the food plant concerned. *Yponomeuta evonymella*, however, is distinguishable by the fact that the black dots are smaller, closer together, and arranged in five rows rather than three.

Habits There is only one generation a year, with adults emerging in June–July. The moth's favourite food plants are hawthorn (*Crataegus*) and *Prunus*.

138 ZEUZERA PYRINA L.
leopard moth

Family Cossidae.

Geographical distribution Europe and Asia; in the nineteenth century it was accidentally introduced to North America.

Description and related species Wingspan approximately 1½–2½ in. (35–60 mm). The wings of this striking moth are largely white with numerous black spots; the thorax is covered with woolly white scales, set off by six black marks. The abdomen, too, displays black and white stripes. Individuals are variable in size, depending on the food intake of the larvae. In Europe its shape and coloration cannot be mistaken for that of any other species.

Habits This moth lives in various habitats where trees grow; the caterpillars will attack many different species. Although these are polyphagous, they often bore into the trunk and branches of fruit trees and do considerable damage. The cycle of growth lasts two years and adults appear in June.

---

139 ZYGAENA CARNIOLICA Scop.

Family Zygaenidae.

Geographical distribution Temperate, warm regions of Europe and of western and central Asia.

Description and related species Wingspan approximately 1¼–1½ in. (33–40 mm). The burnet moths of the family Zygaenidae are highly characteristic, with vivid black and red (more rarely black and white) colors. *Zygaena carniolica* is readily distinguished by the white-rimmed red spots on its forewings; often there is a red patch, too, on the abdomen. The hind wings are red with a narrow black margin. The other species of the genus, though fairly alike, always tend to be variable. Sometimes, as a consequence of mimicry, populations of the same species may exhibit completely different forms of coloration.

Habits This moth frequents hills and mountains, usually in open, dry areas of calcareous soil. The caterpillars live on leguminous plants (*Lotus, Onobrychis, Hedysarum,* and *Ononis*). There is one generation a year, with adults emerging from June to August. The bright colors warn predators of repellent toxic substances in the insects' blood.

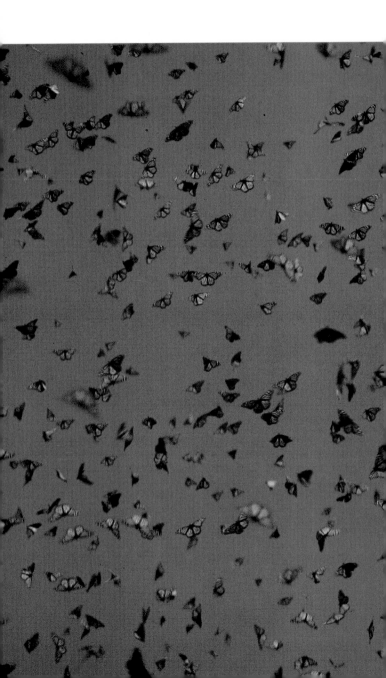

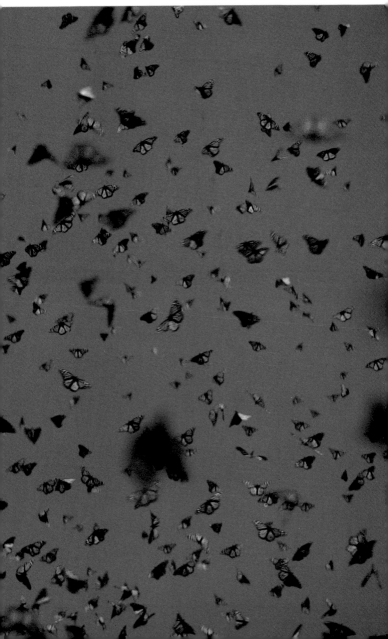

142 ALYPIA OCTOMACULATA F.
eight-spotted forester

Family Noctuidae.
Geographical distribution The United States and south-eastern Canada.
Description and related species Wingspan 1–1¼ in. (26–33 mm). The color of this forester is black except for eight spots (two on each wing). On the forewings the spots are pale yellow; the outermost ones, ellipsoid in shape, are at right angles to the costal vein. Those spots on the hind wings are white, the outermost ones, in the median area, being smaller than the inner ones, which are located in the basal zone. The sides of the thorax, at the attachment of the wings, are enveloped in yellow down; the front and middle legs are covered with orange scales. It is very similar to *Alypia wittfeldii*, but in *A. wittfeldii* the terminal part of the abdomen is speckled with yellow and the yellow spots on the forewings are all elongated crosswise. Some specimens of *A. octomaculata* from Canada lack the white basal spot on the hind wings.
Habits This species flies during the day. The caterpillar does considerable damage to its food plants *Vitis, Lonicera* and *Parthenocissus*. In the north there is only one generation, from April to June; in southern states there is a second generation in August.

143 ANTHERAEA POLYPHEMUS Cramer
polyphemus moth

Family Saturniidae.
Geographical distribution Southern Canada and the United States.
Description and related species Wingspan 4–6 in. (100–150 mm). The color of the upper side of the forewing ranges from brownish-yellow to cinnamon to reddish-brown with the submedian areas edged in pink or white. There are two elongated black marks on the apical area and a wide dark gray band along the submarginal zone of the hind wings. In addition, there are four transparent ovoid spots (one on each wing), situated in the discal area. Those on the hind wings are surrounded by an area of black, which extends to the outer margin of the basal area.
Habits This is the most common of the saturniid species. The caterpillar lives on over fifty species of trees and shrubs. It is green with red tubercules, much like that of *Actias luna*. There is one generation from May to June in northern regions, two from April to September in southern regions. The cocoons of some Oriental species of this genus are used in the silk industry.

144 GRAMMIA VIRGO L.
virgin tiger moth
(formerly APANTESIS VIRGO L.)

Family Arctiidae.

Geographical distribution Eastern Canada and parts of the United States.

Description and related species Wingspan approximately 1¾–2½ in. (45–60 mm). The wings are black with numerous narrow cream-colored bands which vary in length according to the veins, originating at the base, getting thinner, and intersecting one another in the postmedian and marginal areas. The hind wings are cinnamon red with large black spots, irregularly bordered, stemming from the discal area. The abdomen is reddish with a black stripe on the back. Because of its size and color pattern it cannot be confused with any other species of the genus *Grammia*.

Habits This is a species distasteful to and avoided by birds. The adults are able to emit repugnant secretions from their thoracic glands. The very hairy caterpillars feed on various plants, especially *Asclepias*, from which they derive the toxic substances transmitted via the pupae to the adults. They are thus protected from predators, warning them of this toxicity by the particularly vivid coloration on their wings and body.

---

145 APPIAS DRUSILLA Cramer
pure white

Family Pieridae.

Geographical distribution Widespread in the Neotropical region; in the United States found only in south Texas and Florida, rarely migrating north to Nebraska and New York state.

Description and related species Wingspan 1½–2½ in. (40–60 mm). The male of this species is one of the few examples of a butterfly with wings entirely white on both sides, except for the dark costal margin of the forewings. The females, however, are variable; they may either be whitish or display a dark band along the outer margin of the forewings, with pale orange hind wings. Another characteristic of the pure white is that the outer margin of the forewings is slightly concave. Because of its peculiar coloration, it cannot be confused with any other species.

Habits This butterfly lives in warm places such as evergreen riverside forests and open flowery areas. The caterpillars feed on various plants including those of the genera *Capparis* and *Drypetes*. In the southern regions of its range it flies all year round.

146 ATLIDES HALESUS Cramer
great blue hairstreak

Family Lycaenidae.

Geographical distribution Much of the United States, especially the south, but also northern regions as far as Oregon and New York.

Description and related species Wingspan approximately 1¼–1½ in. (32–38 mm). The coloration of the upper side of the male's wing is particularly striking: an iridescent metallic blue with a black margin and a small black spot near the costa of the hind wings; in the female the blue coloration is a little more restricted. The hind wings are furnished with two long, thin, curving tails. The underside of the wings is less brilliantly colored, predominantly brown, with some red spots near the base and an area with alternating white patches and black bands close to the tails. The lower part of the abdomen is red. Similar to this species is *Parrhasius m-album*, which is smaller and does not possess red basal spots underneath.

Habits This species is found in open spaces close to trees infested by plant parasites of the genus *Phorandron*. There are two generations a year, with adults emerging from February to October.

---

147 AUTOGRAPHA CALIFORNICA Packard

Family Noctuidae.

Geographical distribution Western United States.

Description and related species Wingspan approximately 1½ in. (35–40 mm). The genus is widely distributed in the Nearctic region. It is a typical noctuid moth with a cryptic coloration; the pattern and color of the forewings perfectly conceal the insect when it is resting on tree bark. The coloration varies from gray to brown with a silvery pattern of streaking and veining.

Habits The caterpillars feed on cabbages and other low-growing plants. The absence of front prolegs gives them a characteristic looping gait, which resembles that of most Geometridae. The adults, whose flight is rapid, are nocturnal by habit and are attracted to lights. The larvae, too, remain hidden by day, feeding exclusively at night. Like other members of the huge Noctuidae family, they do considerable damage to crops.

148 AUTOMERIS IO F.
bull's eye moth

Family Saturniidae.

Geographical distribution Canada, the United States, and Mexico.

Description and related species Wingspan 2–3¼ in. (50–80 mm). This species is easily recognizable by the two large eyespots, black and dark blue with white centers, on the hind wings. In typical specimens the color of the male's forewing is yellow with small irregular brownish spots; in the female the spots are reddish-brown and there are thin yellowish halfmoons characteristically arranged along the postmedian area. The eyespots are bounded on the outside by a thin black line on the submarginal area. The margins are varying shades of brown.

Habits The bull's eye moth belongs to a vast genus of which more than 100 species have been described, most of them found in tropical parts of Central and South America. The greenish caterpillars possess many irritant spines. Among the many plants attacked are birch, maple, oak, and willow, but also trefoil and cereals. There is one generation in the north, with adults appearing from May to September; two or three generations emerge each year in the south.

---

149 BASILARCHIA ARCHIPPUS Cramer

Family Nymphalidae.

Geographical distribution North America south of Hudson Bay, from the Great Basin westward to the eastern part of the Pacific coast states.

Description and related species Wingspan approximately 3–3½ in. (75–85 mm). The basic color of the upper side of the wing is reddish-brown with black lines that follow the wing veining; the outer margin of all four wings is also black, with small white dots on the apical area of the forewings. The underside, except for slight differences in color, is similar to the upper side. In coloration and size it resembles the monarch (*Danaus plexippus*), but differs from it in having a black submarginal line on the hind wings. This is a classic example of Batesian mimicry, because predators find the monarch (danaine) distasteful and consequently leave it alone – they are duped by *Basilarchia archippus*'s color pattern and ignore it too, regardless of the fact that they have rejected an edible mimic.

Habits The butterfly almost always lives close to swamps, lakes, canals, and rivers. The larvae prefer to feed on willow leaves but will also attack poplars, apples, and plums. There are two or three generations a year, with adults appearing from April to September, and even later in southern regions.

150 BASILARCHIA ASTYANAX F.

Family Nymphalidae.
Geographical distribution From North and South Dakota and Colorado eastward to New England; southward to central Florida; and westward to Arizona and Mexico.
Description and related species Wingspan approximately 3–3½ in. (75–85 mm). The upper side of the wing is largely varying shades of black; the submarginal area, especially of the hind wings, is iridescent blue or green, giving way to a black band bordered by alternating iridescent blue and black marginal crescents. On the underside, which is brownish, there is a series of orange crescents on the submarginal area and other irregular orange spots towards the base. It resembles the female of *Speyeria diana*, which has more rounded wings and lacks the orange markings.
Habits This species lives in open woodland, on the fringes of forests and often close to rivers and streams. In southwestern parts of its range it may also be found in canyons. Known food plants of the species include trees or shrubs such as willow, poplar, apple, hornbeam, and hawthorn.

151 BATTUS PHILENOR L.
pipe vine swallowtail

Family Papilionidae.
Geographical distribution Southern Mexico northward to California, Colorado, and northwestern regions of Canada.
Description and related species Wingspan approximately 2¾–3½ in. (70–86 mm). The upper side of this splendid butterfly is largely blackish or dark gray with strong metallic blue reflections. The underside is also mainly black or bluish with many conspicuous colored markings; on the forewings a series of submarginal yellowish dots appear, and on the hind wings a spectacular group of orange spots encircled in black and streaked with white. The species, unpalatable to predators, is imitated by the females of various members of the genus *Papilio* (*P. polyxenes, P. glaucus,* and *P. troilus*).
Habits This species was probably well distributed before the Europeans colonized America, and it is likely to be found wherever Aristolochiaceae – the food plants of the caterpillars – are grown. Very probably there are two generations a year in the northern part of its range, three in the south.

152 CALEPHELIS VIRGINIENSIS Guér. Mén.
little metalmark

Family Riodinidae.

Geographical distribution Southeastern lowlands of the United States from the Gulf of Mexico to Texas.

Description and related species Wingspan approximately ¾ in. (16–19 mm). A small butterfly which is brick red or orange above, with a continuous silvery submarginal line and numerous other broken lines, more or less silvery, over the remaining wing surface. The northern metalmark (*Calephelis borealis*), a related species not easily distinguished from *C. virginiensis*, is bigger and slightly different in color. Other North American representatives of the genus are likewise not easily distinguished from *C. virginiensis*.

Habits This butterfly is found in open grasslands and also around brackish water. The caterpillars have been observed on *Cirsium horridulum*. There may be three generations a year, with adults emerging in May, July, and September; in the south it can be present throughout the year.

---

153 CATOCALA SP.

Family Noctuidae.

Geographical distribution Most species inhabit the temperate region of the northern hemisphere, but some may be found in Central America, India, Taiwan, and southeast Asia. The majority of species (more than 100) live in North America.

Description and related species Wingspan approximately 1½–3 in. (35–75 mm). The forewings are cryptic both in color and pattern. Normally they are folded so as to cover the abdomen and the hind wings. The hind wings, however, are usually brightly colored with conspicuous black stripes or spots on a ground of orange, yellow, scarlet, red, blue, or possibly completely black.

Habits Potential enemies are surprised and confused, even if only temporarily, by the dazzling effect of the brilliant hind wing color. The mechanism is just as effective in the reverse situation where the attacker, attracted by the moth's vivid colors, is thrown off balance when the colorful hind wings are suddenly concealed by the closing of the forewings. The adults are strong flyers. The caterpillars are squat, cylindrical, and minutely hairy, normally with five pairs of prolegs. They feed on the leaves of various trees and shrubs.

154 CELASTRINA LADON Cramer

Family Lycaenidae.

Geographical distribution Much of North America, from Alaska to Panama. It is a counterpart of the related European holly blue (*Celastrina argiolus*).

Description and related species Wingspan approximately ¾–1¼ in. (20–32 mm). There are slight seasonal variations. The males, however, are varying shades of blue above; the females have a large black outer margin running along the costa and dark spots along the margin of the hind wings. Underneath the color is variable, with more or less clear patterns on a gray ground. The apparent variability of the species may be due to confusion about the identity of *C. ladon* – perhaps more than one species is involved.

Habits This species frequents various habitats, from open woodland to roadsides. The caterpillars feed on many plants (*Cornus, Viburnum, Ceanothus, Vaccinium, Cimifuga, Spiraea*). Generations vary in number according to climatic conditions.

---

155 CERCYONIS PEGALA F.

Family Nymphalidae, subfamily Satyrinae.

Geographical distribution Much of North America, from central Canada to California, Texas, and Florida.

Description and related species Wingspan approximately 2–3 in. (52–73 mm). This is an extremely variable species, to which many names have been given. The upper parts range from light to dark brown, generally with two eyespots – sometimes very large with a white or blue pupil – on the forewings; around these there may be a yellow area of varying extent. On the underside of the wings marbling on a brown background camouflages the butterfly when its wings are closed. It resembles *Cercyonis sthenele*, which is, however, smaller.

Habits This species frequents open woods of conifers and broad-leaved trees, and is also seen in grassland and along river banks. The caterpillars feed on various Gramineae. There is a single annual generation, with adults appearing from June to September, depending on the locality.

156 CHLOSYNE HARRISI Scud.

Family Nymphalidae.
Geographical distribution In Canada from Nova Scotia eastward to Manitoba and the state of Wisconsin; southward to northern regions of Illinois, Indiana, Ohio, and the Appalachian mountains, and western parts of Virginia.
Description and related species Wingspan approximately 1½ in. (35 mm). The upper side of the wing is mainly tawny with a black margin. In both pairs of wings there are networks of black lines in the basal zones. In the postbasal area, however, only the veins are outlined in black. On the hind wings there are small black circular patterns close to the margins. The markings of the undersides are more complex; on the hind wings alternating yellowish and orange areas are bounded by lines, which emphasize the veining. White crescents adorn the outer margin. This species closely resembles western North American species of the same group, although the pattern of the underside is different.
Habits There remains much to be discovered about the early stages of development in this species, but it is known that the larvae of the typical form feed on *Aster umbellatus*.

---

157 CITHERONIA REGALIS F.
regal moth

Family Sarturniidae.
Geographical distribution The eastern United States, from Massachusetts and Kansas south to Florida and Texas.
Description and related species Wingspan 4–6 in. (100–150 mm). Forewings are grayish-green with yellow spots variable in form and size, mostly in the postmedian area. The veins are orange and stand out against the background color of the wings. The hind wings are largely orange with yellow streaks on the basal and discal areas and particularly along the costa and inner margin. The body is orangish-brown with yellow rings on the abdomen and yellow lines on the thorax. The regal moth is similar to *Citheronia splendens*, which is more red, has a greater number of yellow spots, and more orange on the hind wings and abdomen.
Habits The caterpillars have long, curving red spines – which are completely harmless – on the thorax. In the late summer they leave the food plants and pupate in the soil. At the beginning of the twentieth century they were considered harmful to cotton, but their principal food plants are walnut, hickory, ash, and sycamore. It is a common species in southern regions, rarer in the north, and the single annual generation is on the wing from June to September.

158 CLOSSIANA SELENE Den. & Schiff.
small pearl-bordered fritillary

Family Nymphalidae.

Geographical distribution A Holarctic species also found in Europe and Asia. In North America it lives from Alaska eastward to Newfoundland and south to Oregon, New Mexico, Illinois, and North Carolina.

Description and related species Wingspan approximately 1½–2 in. (35–50 mm). The upper side of the wing is tawny; black lines and dots form a complex pattern on the basal part, and there is a series of black spots on the submarginal area. The complicated design on the underside of the wings consists of silvery-white spots on a yellow and ocher ground, punctuated with other black marks and dots. It is distinguished from other North American species of *Clossiana* by the presence of silvery spots on the underside of the hind wings.

Habits This butterfly lives in damp meadows, often near woods. One colony found in the Columbia River basin in a humid enclave of the desert may be a relic of past glaciations. In North America known food plants belong to the genus *Viola*; in Europe the caterpillars have also been found on *Fragaria* and *Vaccinium*. There may be one to three generations a year, with adults appearing from May to September.

159 COLIAS PHILODICE Latr.
common sulphur

Family Pieridae.

Geographical distribution Much of North America, although becoming rarer in the south; absent in many parts of Florida.

Description and related species Wingspan approximately 1½–2 in. (35–50 mm). The upper side of the wing is a vivid lemon yellow, with a clear black margin in the males and broken by yellow dots in the females. There is also a small black spot on the forewings and an orange one on the hind wings. The underside of the wing is lighter in color, without the black band, and there are rows of dark spots close to the margins. This characteristic distinguishes this species from its relatives.

Habits This species frequents all types of open spaces but, owing to its feeding habits, it prefers cultivated land. The caterpillars feed exclusively on plants of the family Leguminosae, and probably the increased acreage devoted to such crops has helped to expand the range of the species. There are numerous generations each year, with adults appearing from the beginning of the spring until the winter.

160 COPAEODES MINIMA Edw.

Family Hesperiidae.

Geographical distribution From the southern United States southward to Panama.

Description and related species Wingspan approximately ½–¾ in. (13–19 mm). The smallest North American representative of the Hesperiidae. The upper side of the wing is basically orange, darker along the veins, and the underside is lighter orange. A feature characteristic of the species is the light longitudinal line across the lower surface of the hind wings. This feature distinguishes *Copraeodes minima* from many other similar hesperiids.

Habits This species lives mainly in open fields and on grassy banks. Little is known of its life cycle although the larvae have been recorded on *Cynodon dactylon*. There are several generations a year and where climatic conditions are favorable the adults may fly all year round.

---

161 DANAUS GILIPPUS Cramer
queen

Family Nymphalidae, subfamily Danainae.

Geographical distribution Southern parts of the United States, from California to Texas, Georgia and Florida; then ranges southward to South America.

Description and related species Wingspan approximately 3¼ in. (80–83 mm). The upper side of the wing of this large butterfly is dark reddish-brown, with a narrow black margin, small white dots, and prominent veining. There are also two curved series of white dots across the forewings. It is smaller, with less well-marked veining, than the monarch (*Danaus plexippus*) and lacks the transverse black line that is present on the hind wings of *Basilarchia archippus*.

Habits This butterfly frequents open spaces such as grassland, river banks, and semi-desert areas. The larvae are associated with *Asclepias amplexicaulis* and *Sarcostemma hirtellum*. Unappetizing to birds, the queen is mimicked by certain southern populations of *Basilarchia archippus*, whereas in the north the latter mimics *Danaus plexippus*. There are successive generations, which in Texas may be present all year round.

162 DANAUS PLEXIPPUS L.
monarch

Family Nymphalidae, subfamily Danainae.

Geographical distribution Practically all of North America, with one distinct subspecies in parts of Central America and the northern regions of South America.

Description and related species Wingspan approximately 3½–4 in. (89–102 mm). A large and well known species, notable for the bright tawny color of the upper side of the wings, the black veining, and the black margin with white spots. Underneath, the black lines along the veins are much more prominent and the tawny coloration lighter. The related queen (*Danaus gilippus*) is smaller, with less prominent veins. Its Batesian mimic, *Basilarchia archippus*, has a black line across the hind wings.

Habits This is a classic migratory species. In the fall the butterflies head south, forming swarms that grow ever bigger until they comprise several thousands of individuals. There are two principal migration routes, one of them from the northwest region of North America southward to the mountain zones along the coast of California between San Francisco and Los Angeles. The conditions of their traditional winter habitat are very circumscribed: the butterflies form dense masses on eucalyptus and pine trees and spend the winter in a state of semi-hibernation. In the spring they mate and then set out on the return flight northward. Eggs are laid on any *Asclepias* or, more rarely, *Apocynum* plants that are encountered on the journey. It is the adults that result from these spring broods that resume the northward flight. Other generations may follow and these subsequently reach the most northerly limits of the species' range. The populations from the eastern parts of the United States that follow the second principal migration route have a similar cycle, but until quite recently nothing was known about their winter resting place. Marking procedures were adopted with a view to determining the specific routes and speed of flight. It was established that the butterflies headed for Mexico, and in 1976 the place where they spent the winter was discovered. This was a valley, at an altitude of about 10,000 ft. (3000 m), in the state of Michoacán, where some 14 billion individuals were found on the trunks and branches of trees, over an area of only about 4 acres (1.5 hectares)!

163 DRYAS JULIA F.

Family Nymphalidae, subfamily Heliconiinae.

Geographical distribution Southern parts of the United States (Texas and Florida); across the tropical zones of Central and South America.

Description and related species Wingspan 3¼–3½ in. (80–90 mm). A large, characteristic species. The upper side of the wing is orange, brighter in the males; often there is a thin black margin almost entirely surrounding the wings and a black spot near the costa of the forewings. The underside is light brown with indistinct markings. It vaguely resembles the Gulf fritillary (*Agraulis vanillae*), which also inhabits the southern United States but is blacker on the upper side of the wings along the veins, and spots that have a white pupil occur near the costa of the forewings.

Habits This species is found in various habitats, including gardens. The caterpillars live on passion flower foliage. There are two generations a year, but adults may be encountered all year round where the climate is favorable.

---

164 EACLES IMPERIALIS Drury

Family Saturniidae.

Geographical distribution Southern Quebec in Canada, east of the Great Plains in the United States, and Mexico.

Description and related species Wingspan approximately 3¼–7 in. (80–175 mm). The wings of this large species are yellow, variously spotted and striped in orange, brown, and pink. Even in forms with uniform coloring of the forewings there are always two dark spots, one in front of the other on the median area near the costa, and one more toward the discal area of the hind wings. The males, especially those from southern regions, are more extensively marked with brown than the females. The related *Eacles oslari* is densely covered with brown markings, including two bands, one from the apex of the forewing to the inner margin, the other extending from the costa to the inner margin. Various subspecies of *E. imperialis* have been described, such as *pini*, smaller and with more pink markings, and *nobilis*, from southern Texas.

Habits This moth, like many others, is attracted by ultraviolet lamps. The larvae live on various trees such as walnuts, limes, pines, elms, oaks, cedars, and maples. There is one generation a year in the north, with adults appearing in May–June, and two generations in the southern part of the range, with adults appearing from April to September.

165 ENODIA PORTLANDIA F.
pearly-eye butterfly

Family Nymphalidae, subfamily Satyrinae.

Geographical distribution Northern Illinois and Virginia to Florida and Texas in the south, especially in grassland.

Description and related species Wingspan 1¾–2 in. (45–50 mm). The subfamily Satyrinae is characterized by the presence on the wings of variously marked eyespots; in this species they are very prominently arranged along a submarginal band on all four wings; on the upper side the spots vary considerably in composition, but each displays a light pupil in the center, sometimes blue, surrounded by a yellow or brown ring. The species is subdivided into two subspecies according to the pattern of the underside of the wings and other features; in fact, these nowadays tend to be regarded as distinct species.

Habits This species is found in damp wooded areas near fields of *Arundinaria gigantea* and *A. tectia*, the food plants of its caterpillars. There are three generations each year, with adults appearing from May to September.

166 EPARGYREUS CLARUS Cramer
silver spotted skipper

Family Hesperiidae.

Geographical distribution Throughout North America, found by day in a variety of habitats.

Description and related species Wingspan approximately 1¾–2½ in. (45–60 mm). A large butterfly with strikingly long wings. The upper side of the wing is mainly brown, with a transverse yellow band and other small marks of the same color on the forewings. The coloration underneath is similar, but there is a large, irregularly shaped but prominent silvery-white area on the hind wings. This feature is not present in related species such as *Epargyreus zestos*, a southern group sometimes found in the south of Florida.

Habits This butterfly frequents varied habitats such as open woodland, grassy hills, and even parks and gardens. The caterpillars feed on numerous plants, including representatives of the genera *Gleditscia, Robinia, Wisteria, Desmodium, Phaseolus,* and *Glycyrrhiza*. There are as a rule one or two generations a year, more in the south.

167 ERYNNIS BRIZO Boisd. & LeCl.

Family Hesperiidae.

Geographical distribution The species is subdivided into four subspecies; one ranges from Manitoba to Massachusetts, southward to northern Florida and westward to eastern Texas; a second is found on the Florida peninsula, a third in the Rocky Mountains and the Great Basin, and a fourth in the Sierra Nevada mountains to the Bay of California.

Description and related species Wingspan approximately ¾–1½ in. (21–41 mm). An inconspicuous species, like many other members of the Hesperiidae, with mainly brown forewings marked with gray and black. The prevalent color of the hind wings is brown as well. The many other North American species of the genus *Erynnis* are distinguished by small details in their color patterns.

Habits This species is found in various dry areas close to its food plants, namely oaks and *Castanea dentata*. There are one or two generations each year according to latitude.

---

168 EUMORPHA LABRUSCAE L.

Family Sphingidae.

Geographical distribution A tropical species that reaches the southern United States. It may also be found as a straggler in more northerly regions such as Manitoba and Maine.

Description and related species Wingspan 4–5 in. (100–120 mm). The forewings, like the body, are largely grayish-brown. Small dark spots appear in a row on the submarginal area. A triangular stripe, darker than the rest of the wing, covers much of the median zone. The hind wings are very small, dark blue with a red stripe in the submarginal area, ocher-yellow on the inner margins and parts of the outer margins. The body, pointed at the tip, lacks the alternating spots that are so typical of many other species of sphingids.

Habits In the United States the caterpillar is found on *Vitis* and *Ampelopsis*. When at rest, the adult covers the brightly colored hind wings with its large forewings (which are cryptic in coloration), ready to open them suddenly if threatened.

169 EUPHYDRYAS PHAETON Drury

Family Nymphalidae.

Geographical distribution From Manitoba to Nova Scotia in Canada, southward to Nebraska, Arkansas, and Georgia.

Description and related species Wingspan approximately 1½–2½ in. (40–64 mm). The upper surface of the wing is mainly grayish-brown with indistinct black patterns and white dots and crescents. There is a neat, regular pattern of orange crescents on the outer margins of the forewings and hind wings; there are also traces of orange at the base of the wings. The underside colors are more contrasted, with a network of black and white in the postdiscal area and orange spots near the base and outer margins. The coloration of the margins clearly distinguishes this species from many others of related genera.

Habits The butterfly is found in damp grasslands and woodlands in the northeastern part of its range; elsewhere it also frequents swamps. It is a polyphagous species, which attacks both herbaceous plants and trees such as *Chelone glabra, Gerardia grandiflora* and *G. pedicularia, Plantago lanceolata,* and *Fraxinus americana.* There is a single annual generation, with adults emerging in May and June.

170 EUREMA NICIPPE Cramer

Family Pieridae.

Geographical distribution Much of the North American continent. In the United States from Florida to southern California and northward to Colorado, Nebraska, Michigan, Ohio, Pennsylvania, and New York.

Description and related species Wingspan approximately 1½–2 in. (35–50 mm). The upper side of the wing is dark orange with an irregular black outer marginal band, which on the forewing is extended along the costa. There is another small black spot on the forewing. The color of the underside is less regular, but yellow predominates and there is an orange area on the forewing of the males, variegated light brown on that of the females. It is fairly similar to *Eurema proterpia.*

Habits This species lives in various warm habitats where there are trees and in semi-desert areas. It also frequents river banks and mountain canyons. The larvae live on plants of the Leguminosae such as senna (*Cassia*) and trefoil (*Trifolium*). In southern regions there are two or three overlapping generations a year. In the north the flight period is shorter.

171 FENISECA TARQUINIUS F.
North American harvester

Family Lycaenidae.
Geographical distribution Eastern parts of North America, from Ontario to Florida and central Texas.
Description and related species Wingspan approximately 1¼ in. (28–32 mm). The upper side of the wings is orangish-yellow with broad irregular edges and brownish-black spots; the underside is lighter in color, the forewings mainly orange, the hind wings reddish-brown, with thin gray ring patterns. It cannot be confused with any other North American species.
Habits The habits of the harvester larvae present a rare exception within the order Lepidoptera, for the caterpillars are carnivorous, feeding exclusively on aphids of the genera *Schizoneura* and *Pemphigus*. The adults, too, feed on the honeydew of the aphids. There are one to three generations a year in central–northern parts of the range; more occur in the south.

172 GLAUCOPSYCHE LYGDAMUS Doubl.

Family Lycaenidae.
Geographical distribution A North American species with a wide range; in the north to Nova Scotia and Alaska, in the south to California, New Mexico, Oklahoma, Alabama, and Georgia.
Description and related species Wingspan approximately 1–1¼ in. (25–32 mm). In males the upper side of the wing is silvery-blue with dark margins and a short fringe of white hairs; females have a broad dark margin. Underneath, in both sexes, the dominant color is pale gray with white-rimmed black dots; some isolated dots are present in the discal area, others form a series of lines in the postdiscal zone of either wing. It resembles *Icaricia icarioides*, which generally displays a series of marginal spots on the underside of the wings. *Hemiargus isola* is distinguished by its smaller size and a more complex pattern on the underside.
Habits This species frequents various habitats from sea level to the mountains, including fields, open woodland, and cultivated areas. The caterpillars feed on many leguminous plants (*Lotus, Lupinus, Lathyrus, Vicia,* and *Astragalus*). There is one generation a year and it is one of the first species to make an appearance in spring.

173 HAEMATOPIS GRATARIA F.

Family Geometridae.
Geographical distribution The United States and southern Canada.
Description and related species Wingspan approximately 7–10 in. (180–260 mm). The species is easily recognizable by its yellow wings with almost parallel pink lines and two pink spots on the discal area of the forewings. The form *annettearia* has entirely pink wings and appears to have an extremely limited distribution (Ohio and the upper Mississippi river valleys).
Habits The caterpillars of the family Geometridae are known in Britain as loopers and in North America as measuring worms or inchworms because of their characteristic method of locomotion. They push the front part of the body forward, grip with their feet and then bring up the hind portion, so that the whole body forms a vertical arch. This gait results from the loss of several pairs of prolegs, which are normally found between the third and sixth abdominal segments. The caterpillars feed on trefoil, chickweed, and other herbaceous plants. The adults often fly in fields, even by day, from April to November.

---

174 HARKENCLENUS TITUS F.

Family Lycaenidae.
Geographical distribution North America, except in the extreme north and in the southern regions of the United States.
Description and related species Wingspan approximately 1–1¼ in. (25–32 mm). There is a striking difference between the wing shape of the males and the females; in the male the margins are straighter and the tips sharper. The color of the wing is brown above and predominantly light brown below, with scattered small dark spots encircled with white, and a band of orangish-red crescents near the hind margin. This feature distinguishes the butterfly from related species, together with the absence of tails on the hind wings.
Habits This butterfly frequents various open places where it can find suitable food plants, particularly those of the genera *Prunus* and *Amelanchier*, the young fruits of which are attacked. There is a single annual generation, with adults emerging from June to August.

175 HYDRIA UNDULATA L.

Family Geometridae.
Geographical distribution North America; north and central Europe to Siberia.
Description and related species Wingspan approximately 1¼–1½ in. (32–40 mm). The forewings display numerous thin wavy lines, white and pale ocher, with alternating stripes in varying shades of brown. There is an ocher-brown band on the median area and also two stripes partially joined to form a ring. In the submarginal zone the whitish line is less undulating. A black spot occurs on the cell. Alternating white and gray spots are present on the margins. The hind wings are similar but the basal zone is pale brown without stripes. *Hydria prunivorata* displays less brilliant colors with clearer separating bands between the various shades. These species are very much alike and can only be distinguished with certainty by characteristics of their genitalia or by the different biology of their larvae.
Habits The solitary caterpillars are reddish-brown with a pale line along the body, which joins together the spiracles at the sides. The ventral zone and the area below the lateral line are dark brown. They live on willows and birches. The adults are seen from May to August.

176 HYLES GALLII Rott.
bedstraw hawkmoth

Family Sphingidae.
Geographical distribution Canada, the United States, Europe; across temperate Asia to Japan.
Description and related species Wingspan 2½–3 in. (60–75 mm). The dark brown forewings are crossed at the apex of the base by a slightly undulating yellowish band. The marginal areas are nut brown. The hind wings are much smaller and more vividly colored. The basal area, the costa, and the submarginal zone are brown; the discal area near the inner margin is pale yellow while the remaining surface of the wing and the outer margin are various shades of pink. This hawkmoth has a stocky body and a tapering abdomen, with black and white bands at intervals between them. It is similar to the striped hawkmoth (*Hyles lineata*), but the latter has more slender white stripes on the forewing and thin white streaks on the veins. The subspecies *H. intermedia* is found in the United States.
Habits The bedstraw hawkmoth has become somewhat rare because of the discontinued cultivation of *Rubia tinctorum*, one of its food plants once used in the production of a red colorant. The caterpillar also lives on bedstraw (*Gallium*) and on various species of *Epilobium*. The adults fly from April to October. This is a migratory species.

177 HYLLOLYCAENA HYLLUS Cramer

Family Lycaenidae.

Geographical distribution Mainly northeastern regions of North America, from the Northwest Territories to Maine, westward to southern Alberta, Idaho, eastern Colorado, and back through Kansas, Ohio, Maryland, and New Jersey.

Description and related species Wingspan approximately 1¼–1½ in. (32–35 mm). As with many other related lycaenids, this species displays marked sexual dimorphism. The upper side of the male's wings is predominantly dark copper brown with blue reflections; only along the outer margin of the hind wings is there a broad orangish-red band. In the females the center of the forewings is light orange with a dozen or so black spots. On the underside the forewings are light orange with black dots, the hind wings grayish with black dots and an orange band along the margin. Related species such as *Epidemia dorcas* and *E. helloides* display different coloration on the underside of the wings.

Habits Found in and around wet, swampy zones. The larvae attack *Rumex crispus* and *Polygonum*. As a rule there are two generations a year, with adults appearing in June–July and August–October.

178 INCISALIA NIPHON Hüb.

Family Lycaenidae.

Geographical distribution Eastern parts of North America, from Nova Scotia westward to Alberta and southeastward to Texas and the states of the Gulf of Mexico.

Description and related species Wingspan approximately ¾–1¼ in. (19–32 mm). The upper side of the wing is completely brown in the males, with reddish tints in the females; the underside displays a complex series of irregular brown bands, in varying shades, alternating with broken brown and white lines. The closely related *Incisalia eryphon*, mainly found in the west, is distinguished by small details in the color pattern.

Habits This species frequents pinewoods, sometimes mixed with oaks, and the borders of woodlands. It is an undemanding species, which is also likely to be found in newly planted forests. The larvae feed on young pine needles, particularly of *Pinus virginiana*, *P. rigida*, and *P. banksiana*. There is only one generation a year, with adults emerging from March to June.

179 JUNONIA EVARETE Cramer

Family Nymphalidae.

Geographical distribution Mainly South America, ranging north to southern Florida and southern Texas.

Description and related species Wingspan approximately 2–2½ in. (50–65 mm). The upper side of the wings is predominantly brown, with elongated orange, black-bordered spots near the costa of the forewings and an irregular orange band crossing both forewings and hind wings. Close to this band are four black and blue eyespots. On the forewings is one small eyespot near the apex and another bigger one beneath it; the hind wings also display eyespots. The underside is mainly brown and orange, with far less contrasted coloration. *Junonia coenia* is very similar to this species but has a much larger anterior eyespot on the hind wings.

Habits This species lives along subtropical coasts and in open bushy grassland. The caterpillars are predominantly black with small yellow and blue dots and six groups of branching hairs. In the United States it lives on plants of the genus *Lippia*.

180 LEPTOTES CASSIUS Cramer
Cassius blue

Family Lycaenidae.

Geographical distribution Resident in southern regions of Florida and Texas, migrating northward. It also ranges southward to South America.

Description and related species Wingspan approximately ½–¾ in. (13–19 mm). A tiny species with translucent wings, so that the color pattern of the underside can be seen from above. The males are sky blue above, the females lighter, with a wide gray margin; underneath is a complex pattern of irregular brown bands on a white ground. The hind wings have two large black spots sometimes surrounded by yellow. Very similar to this species is *Leptotes marina*, which can be distinguished by its less vivid color contrasts.

Habits This species lives in parks and fields and also along roadsides. The caterpillars feed on the flowers of Leguminosae. There are many generations, seen all year round.

181 LYCOMORPHA PHOLUS Drury

Family Arctiidae.
Geographical distribution The United States and eastern Canada.
Description and related species Wingspan 1–1¼ in. (25–30 mm). Both the forewings and the hind wings are orangish-yellow at the base, black at the apex. The antennae are long and comblike. In the coloration of its forewings the species resembles the zygaenid moth *Pyromorpha dimidiata* and also the net-winged beetles (Lycidae), which are extremely distasteful to predators. In this way, the species *Lycomorpha pholus* acquires a certain measure of protection against enemies who cannot distinguish it from the former. This is a good example of phaneric mimicry.
Habits This species flies by day and frequently visits flowers together with net-winged beetles. The caterpillar feeds on lichens.

182 LYMANTRIA DISPAR L.
gypsy moth

Family Lymantriidae.
Geographical distribution Eastern United States and Canada, Europe, and Asia.
Description and related species Wingspan 1¼–1½ in. (30–40 mm) in the male, 2¼–2¾ in. (55–70 mm) in the female. There is marked sexual dimorphism both in the size and in other external characteristics of this species. The male has a tapered body and yellowish-brown wings, the hind wings being slightly paler, with several zigzag black lines on the forewings. The female has a stocky, cylindrical body and her wings are yellowish-white with zigzag black lines on the forewings and black spots along the apical margins of both pairs of wings.
Habits Groups of 200–500 eggs are covered with yellow hairs from the female's abdomen so as to form an oval cushion, which sticks to the bark of trees. There is a single annual generation, from June to August. The species was deliberately introduced into North America from Europe in 1868 or 1869 for silk production. Escaping from a laboratory in Massachusetts, it became a particularly serious pest of fruit and deciduous trees, probably because its natural enemies were not present on the American continent.

183 MALACOSOMA AMERICANUM F.
eastern tent caterpillar

Family Lasiocampidae.

Geographical distribution Southern Canada and the United States, and east of the Rocky Mountains.

Description and related species Wingspan approximately ¾–1¾ in. (22–44 mm). A moth with a stocky body and tawny wings. The forewings have two clear parallel lines on the boundary of the submedian and postmedian zones. Sometimes the median area is completely white. It much resembles the forest tent caterpillar (*Malacosoma disstria*), but has pale yellow or whitish bands on the forewings.

Habits This is a particularly harmful species, which, before the introduction of modern pest control systems, did serious damage to crops; the first reference to it as an insect pest dates from 1646. The caterpillar eats leaves voraciously and is recognizable by the characteristic silky white threads that appear during the spring in the forks of trees and shrubs. Once they are fully grown, the larvae abandon the food plants to spin their cocoons in sheltered places. Infestations tend to go in cycles, increasing for several years and then falling to low population levels. The adults appear in late May and June.

---

184 MEGISTO CYMELA Cramer

Family Nymphalidae, subfamily Satyrinae.

Geographical distribution East of longitude 100°W (the Dakotas, Nebraska, Kansas, Oklahoma, and Texas), from southern Canada to northeastern Mexico.

Description and related species Wingspan approximately 1¾ in. (44–48 mm). The upper side of the wing is uniformly brown, with two large eyespots of equal size on the submarginal band of the forewings, and two or three, only one of them large, on the hind wings. Each eyespot consists of two blue pupils surrounded by a narrow yellow ring. On the underside there are clearer eyespots and also two dark brown transverse lines. The pattern and shape of the spots distinguishes the species from the related *Megisto rubricata*, which also has a reddish area on the forewings.

Habits This species is found in broad-leaved woods with damp clearings as well as in various other habitats. The caterpillars live on various species of Gramineae and Cyperaceae. There are one or two generations a year, according to latitude, with adults appearing from March to October.

185 NYMPHALIS VAU-ALBUM Boisd. & LeCl.

Family Nymphalidae.

Geographical distribution Subarctic regions of North America, i.e. northern Canada and Alaska, southward to Minnesota, Colorado, and Oregon; also in the hills of Missouri and the mountains of North Carolina.

Description and related species Wingspan approximately 2⅓–3 in. (64–73 mm). The upper side of the wings is mainly ocher and brown, with a darker narrow band along the margins, and numerous black spots. In addition, there are two small white areas, one near the apex of the forewings, the other along the costa of the hind wings; these allow reliable identification of the species, particularly in comparison with various members of the genus *Polygonia*, a fairly similar genus but with more markedly angular wings. The underside of the wings of *Nymphalis vau-album* exhibits a dark cryptic coloration.

Habits This butterfly is normally found in the clearings of broad-leaved woodlands and sometimes along the banks of rivers and streams. The pale green caterpillars feed on the leaves of various trees, notably birch, willow, and poplar. There is only one annual generation, but the adults hibernate and can be found all year round.

186 PACHYSPHINX MODESTA Harris
big polar sphinx

Family Sphingidae.

Geographical distribution The United States and Canada.

Description and related species Wingspan approximately 4–5 in. (100–115 mm). This moth is easily recognized by the size of its body, its strongly indented outer margin, and its large hind wings, which exhibit a red band in the middle and a grayish-white band that turns black in the anal area; black also tinges the basal area. The brownish-black body is cylindrical in shape. The forewings are grayish from the basal to the submarginal zone, then turn darker in varying shades of brown. In southwestern states it is replaced by *Pachysphinx occidentalis*. Both these species resemble the European poplar hawkmoth (*Laothoe populi*), but differ from it by being larger and by having partially reddish-purple hind wings.

Habits The food plants of the caterpillar are poplar and willow. The adult appears in June–July in the more northerly zones, and from March to September in more than one brood farther south.

187 PAPILIO GLAUCUS L.
eastern tiger swallowtail

Family Papilionidae.

Geographical distribution Mainly the eastern parts of North America; also found from central Alaska and Canada to the Atlantic, southward to the southeastern regions of the Rocky Mountains and the Gulf of Mexico.

Description and related species Wingspan 3¼–5½ in. (80–140 mm). One of the most common large butterflies of the eastern part of the United States. As a rule it is yellow, with transverse black stripes and a marginal band in black streaked with yellow. There are completely dark-colored females that imitate *Battus philenor*, a species shunned by predators; these females resemble many other species that also mimic *B. philenor*. *Papilio glaucus* is similar to *P. rutulus*, which has a mainly western distribution.

Habits This butterfly lives in various habitats including woodland clearings, parks, and gardens; it is also found by roadsides and rivers. The caterpillars attack a wide variety of plants, especially trees of the families Salicaceae, Betulaceae, and Rosaceae. There are from one to three generations a year, with adults emerging from the spring to the fall.

188 PAPILIO POLYXENES F.
black swallowtail

Family Papilionidae.

Geographical distribution Eastern regions of North America, from southern Canada along the eastern face of the Rocky Mountains as far as Arizona and Mexico.

Description and related species Wingspan approximately 2¾–3½ in. (67–90 mm). The upper side of the wing is black and bluish-black with blue tints on the hind wings. There are yellowish marks on the postdiscal section and these may spread out to form a wide band. The hind wings, too, exhibit many submarginal blue spots and a red spot with a black pupil on the inner angle. The species resembles *Papilio bairdii*, in which the black pupil on this spot is longer, and *P. brevicauda*, which has shorter tails on the hind wings.

Habits This species lives in open spaces, including gardens and fields, and is only rarely found in wooded zones. The caterpillars are polyphagous; among their food plants are *Daucus carota*, *Ruta graveolens*, and *Thamnosoma texana*. There are two or three generations a year, depending on climate, with adults appearing from February to November.

189 PAPILIO TROILUS L.
spicebush swallowtail

Family Papilionidae.

Geographical distribution North America, from southern Canada to Florida and regions east of Texas and Kansas. It becomes rarer toward the west.

Description and related species Wingspan approximately 3¼–5 in. (80–115 mm). This showy butterfly is notable for the brownish-black coloration of both sexes. In the male, the apical half of the hind wing on the upper side is metallic blue, with two orange spots, while underneath there are two conspicuous groups of reddish crescents. It is similar to *Papilio polyxenes*, *P. glaucus*, and *Battus philenor*, but none of these has the orange spot near the costa of the forewings.

Habits This butterfly frequents both forests and open spaces, and may also be found in gardens. The caterpillars feed on various plants, including *Linderia benzoin*, *Sassafras albidum*, and certain species of *Persea*. The number of generations is variable, according to latitude, with adults appearing from the spring to early fall.

190 PARNASSIUS CLODIUS Mén.

Family Papilionidae.

Geographical distribution The only representative of the genus *Parnassius* endemic to North America. It ranges from southeast Alaska southward to the Santa Cruz mountains and the central Sierras of California; also found in Utah and north to Montana.

Description and related species Wingspan 2½–3 in. (60–76 mm). Individuals of both sexes are white or cream-colored with somewhat variable coloration according to subspecies. The patterns normally consist of black marks and dots on all four wings and of reddish spots encircled by black on the hind wings. It is generally distinguishable from *Parnassius phoebus* by the absence of red spots on the forewings.

Habits In the more northerly parts of its range the butterfly frequents forest margins at sea level; toward the south it is seen in wet, cool, and shady spots in the mountains. The caterpillars feed on the western bleeding heart (*Dicentra formosa*). There is one generation a year, with adults emerging at different times in various regions. Certain populations of this species have recently become extinct.

191 PHOEBIS SENNAE L.

Family   Pieridae.

Geographical distribution   Mexico, southern California, and states on the shores of the Gulf of Mexico to Florida. Migrates northward to Canada.

Description and related species   Wingspan 2¼–2¾ in. (55–70 mm). This is a large pierid, with elongated but not angular wings. The males are light yellow on the upper side of the wings, and yellow or spotted reddish-brown below. The females vary considerably, with colors ranging from lemon yellow to golden yellow or white on both sides, and with variable black spots and margins on the upper side. It is similar to *Anteos maerula*, which has angular wings; other related species are much smaller.

Habits   This species lives in a variety of open habitats such as gardens, river banks, and seashores. The larvae feed on various Leguminosae, such as *Chamaecrista cinera*, *Cassia*, and *Trifolium*. It migrates northward in enormous numbers – sometimes millions of individuals – covering relatively small areas.

---

192 PHYCIODES PHAON Edw.

Family   Nymphalidae.

Geographical distribution   From Florida northward along the coast to southern Virginia; westward to California and as far north as Kansas. It ranges southward to Guatemala and Honduras.

Description and related species   Wingspan approximately ¾–1¼ in. (21–33 mm). The species differs from its relatives by the contrasting coloration of both the upper and lower sides of the forewings; there is an area near the base that is mainly tawny with black markings, an irregular line of white spots bounded by the veining, and a blackish submarginal band with bright reddish-brown spots. The hind wings are similar in color pattern but less strikingly marked on the upper side, while the underside is light beige with a network of dark lines, some submarginal black dots, and a white crescent in the center near the outer margin.

Habits   This species lives on wasteland, in swamps, and in arid places. The larvae feed on *Lippia nodiflora* and *L. lanceolata*. There are one or two generations a year, with adults appearing from April to September. Toward the tropics they can be present throughout the year.

193 PHYCIODES THAROS Drury
pearl crescent

Family Nymphalidae.
Geographical distribution Much of North America, south to Mexico.
Description and related species Wingspan 1–1½ in. (25–40 mm). The upper side of the wing is predominantly tawny, with complicated black designs and a black stripe on the outer margins. The underside is mainly yellowish with less prominent markings. The overall appearance of the butterfly is similar to that of some other species of the genus *Phyciodes*, which differ in details that are often hard to observe.

Habits This species is commonly seen in meadows, fluttering just above the grass. Males have territorial instincts and often change their line of flight or leave resting places to approach virtually any living creature, humans included, that may be in the vicinity. The caterpillars live on plants of the genera *Aster* and *Machaeranthera* (Compositae). There are often several generations a year, with adults appearing from April to November.

194 PIERIS RAPAE L.
small white

Family Pieridae.
Geographical distribution Originally from the Palaearctic region, but accidentally introduced into Canada in the mid nineteenth century. Today its area comprises the whole of North America and Hawaii. It is also found in Australia.
Description and related species Wingspan approximately 1¼–2 in. (32–48 mm). The upper side of the wing is mainly white with a sprinkling of black at the base. The apex of the forewing is wholly black and there are submarginal black spots (one in the male, two in the female); another black spot is found along the costa of the hind wings. The main feature of the underside is the yellowish color of the hind wings. The small white differs from other related white pierids by the absence of black or greenish dots sprinkled along the veins.

Habits This species prefers fields and gardens, but may be found wandering almost anywhere. The caterpillars generally feed on Cruciferae but sometimes also attack cultivated Tropaeolaceae (nasturtiums). There are two or more generations a year, with adults emerging from the spring to the fall.

195 POANES HOBOMOK Harris

Family Hesperiidae.
Geographical distribution From Nova Scotia westward to Saskatchewan and southward to Georgia and Alabama, west to Kansas, and Arizona.
Description and related species Wingspan approximately 1–1½ in. (25–35 mm). The wings of the males are largely orangish-yellow above, with a brown margin; the color of the underside is similar, with a dark basal area to the hind wings. The females are rather more stocky, and on the upper side brown tends to predominate over the lighter tones; some specimens are almost completely dark in color. The other North American species of the genus *Poanes* are similar, with inconspicuous color differences.
Habits This species frequents broad-leaved woods and surrounding grasslands. The larvae live on plants of the family Gramineae and there is only one generation a year, with adults present over a long period from May to September.

196 POLYGONIA COMMA Harris
common anglewing

Family Nymphalidae.
Geographical distribution Eastern parts of North America, from Canada to central Georgia, and westward to Kansas, Nebraska, and Iowa.
Description and related species Wingspan 1½–2 in. (40–50 mm). The outer wing margin is characterized by pronounced "teeth," and on the hind wings these take on the appearance of two short tails. The upper side of the forewing and hind wing is reddish-brown with irregular black spots and a dark margin on both, more prominent on the forewings. The underside is brownish, covered with fine streaks, which camouflage the butterfly when its wings are closed. This background color may vary according to sex and seasonal generation, but all forms exhibit a violet comma-shaped mark. The other species of *Polygonia* are very similar, distinguishable by small details.
Habits This butterfly frequents open spaces on the fringes of woods close to water. The caterpillars are polyphagous; recorded food plants include *Humulus lupulus, Urtica dioica, Boehmeria cylindrica,* and even *Ulmus*. There are two generations each year in the north, three in the south, with adults appearing from the spring to the fall.

197 SATYRODES EURYDICE Johanns

Family Nymphalidae, subfamily Satyrinae.
Geographical distribution From Delaware west to Northern Illinois, north to central Quebec and the Northwest Territories. The subspecies *fumosa*, ranging from Iowa and South Dakota to Colorado, is now extinct in many regions.
Description and related species Wingspan 1½–2 in. (40–50 mm). The butterfly is mainly brown with a lighter postmedian area on the forewings; as in many other satyrines, there are series of eyespots on the submarginal zone of both the upper and lower sides, these ocelli being less distinct on the forewings. The related *Satyrodes appalachia* is darker above.
Habits This butterfly lives in damp meadows and marshy zones, where it feeds on plants of the genus *Carex*. The adults fly from June to September with one generation a year.

198 SMERINTHUS JAMAICENSIS Drury
twin-spot sphinx

Family Sphingidae.
Geographical distribution Alberta in Canada and the United States, except for the extreme south of Florida and Texas.
Description and related species Wingspan 2–3¼ in. (50–80 mm). The forewings are streaked in various shades of brown and the veins are emphasized by thin whitish lines that are particularly noticeable along the postdiscal area of the forewings. There is a black spot on the outer margin of the apical zone. On the hind wings are large blue eyespots, which in this species are often bisected by a black line. In certain specimens there is a small blue spot at the base of the hind wings, light brown along the margins and pink in the center. The eyespots vary considerably in size and this has led to many names being given to unusual individuals. Specimens from southern regions are lighter in color than those from the north. The twin-spot sphinx is similar to *Smerinthus cerisyi*, but is bigger, with more prominent veining on the forewing. In this, as in many other species of the subfamily Smerinthinae, the proboscis is small.
Habits The caterpillar lives on many different trees including apple, plum, ash, elm, and birch. It is a common species from April to October.

199 SPEYERIA APHRODITE F.
Aphrodite fritillary

Family Nymphalidae.

Geographical distribution British Columbia to Nova Scotia, southern Arizona, Nebraska, and northern regions of Georgia.

Description and related species Wingspan 2–2¾ in. (50–70 mm). The upper surface of the wing is a deep tawny color with many black dots, spots, lines, and semicircles. On the underside the tawny color is lighter; black patterns and silvery spots adorn the forewings, while on the hind wings silvery spots of varying size take on a regular pattern only toward the margin. It is very similar to other species of the genus *Speyeria*, and can be distinguished from them only by barely noticeable features.

Habits This species frequents scrubland or open woodland as well as broad-leaved and coniferous forests; it sometimes ventures into wet grassland. As is the case with other related fritillaries the food of the larvae consists exclusively of violet plants (*Viola lanceolata, V. fimbriatula, V. nuttallii, V. primulifolia*). There is a single generation each year with adults appearing from late June to September.

200 SPEYERIA ATLANTIS Edw.

Family Nymphalidae.

Geographical distribution From Alaska southeast to Nova Scotia and south to California, Arizona, and New Mexico; Michigan and the Appalachian Mountains south to Virginia. Found rarely in Iowa and Indiana.

Description and related species Wingspan approximately 1¾–2¾ in. (45–65 mm). This species is a member of a difficult group to identify. Coloration is typical of the genus, the upper wing surface being tawny with complex black designs. The underside of the wing is lighter in color; on the forewings there are black patterns and silvery spots near the apex, and on the hind wings silvery spots that tend to form parallel lines on a brownish ground, with a lighter band in the submarginal region. Most of the other species of the genus are distinguished by characteristics that need careful study.

Habits This species frequents flowery clearings in broad-leaved and coniferous woods, often alongside rivers or in wet meadows. The caterpillars feed on violets (*Viola adunca, V. purpurea, V. canadensis*). There is one generation a year with adults emerging mainly in July and August.

201 SPHECODINA ABBOTTII Swainson
Abbott's sphinx

Family Sphingidae.

Geographical distribution Southern Canada to the eastern United States.

Description and related species Wingspan approximately 2½–2¾ in. (58–72 mm). Easily recognized by its forewings, which are dark brown with a lighter band on the median area. This band is formed by a conglomeration of thin stripes, some of which extend to the outer margin and the discal zone. The outer margins are scalloped. There is a large yellow area on the hind wing running from the basal zone and widening along the costa and over much of the inner margin. The remainder of the wing is black with short gray stripes on the anal area. In body outline and in the markedly irregular indentation of the forewings it resembles *Amphion floridensis*, but may be distinguished from the latter by the partly yellow hind wing and the absence of yellow bands on the abdomen.

Habits The males of this species hover around the flowers of *Lonicera* and *Salix* at dusk, while the females appear to take the wing toward midnight. The caterpillar damages the leaves of *Parthenocissus* and *Vitis*. The adults are found from April to June.

---

202 STILPNOTIA SALICIS L.
satin moth

Family Lymantriidae.

Geographical distribution Europe, temperate Asia, Japan, western and eastern Canada, northern and eastern United States.

Description and related species Wingspan approximately 1¾–2¼ in. (44–55 mm). Shiny, silky white color with brownish antennae and black-ringed legs.

Habits This moth is originally from the Old World, accidentally introduced to both coasts of North America where it has become a serious seasonal pest in poplar and willow forests. The larvae are extremely voracious; initially gregarious, they live in a nest made of silk. Only after overwintering, around the end of June of the following year, do they separate in order to pupate in crevices of tree bark. The adults remain settled on leaves or trunks during the day and take wing after sunset. The fertilized females lay their eggs in white capsules (oothecae) attached to the bark or leaves. In North America there is only one generation, from June to August.

203 STRYMON MELINUS Hüb.
gray hairstreak

Family Lycaenidae.
Geographical distribution All parts of North America except in the north; southward to Venezuela and Colombia.
Description and related species Wingspan approximately 1–1¼ in. (25–32 mm). The upper side of the wing is gray with two distinct red crescents along the margin of the hind wings; the underside is predominantly gray with two transverse, broken black and white lines on both pairs of wings, and a large orange area near the apex of the hind wings, which are prolonged into two tails. These markings distinguish the species clearly from its relatives.
Habits This species is found in open places such as fields, woodlands, and parks. The caterpillars feed on a great variety of herbaceous plants and trees, sometimes attacking crops such as corn and cotton. There are two or more generations a year, with adults appearing from April to October.

204 TEGETICULA YUCCASELLA R.
yucca moth

Family Prodoxidae.
Geographical distribution North America and Mexico.
Description and related species Wingspan approximately ¾–1 in. (15–27 mm). A tiny moth, off-white in color, the females of which have strongly modified mouth parts, suitable for collecting pollen from the anthers of food plants.
Habits The female appears as soon as the flowers of the genus *Yucca* (Liliaceae) bloom. She first collects the pollen of a flower, rolls it into a ball, and then visits another flower, depositing the ball in the stigma and so pollinating it. At the same time she lays one or two eggs in the flower pistil. When, owing to the moth's intervention, the fruit develops, the eggs hatch and the young larvae proceed to eat some of the seeds, leaving enough to produce new yucca plants. This is one of the most famous examples of mutualism or symbiosis, for the moth, both in its larval and adult form, uses no other plant, while the plant in turn can only be fertilized by this particular insect.

205 UTETHEISA BELLA L.

Family Arctiidae.

Geographical distribution North America, Bermuda, and the Bahamas. Individuals of this species sometimes reach the British Isles.

Description and related species Wingspan approximately 1¼–2 in. (30–45 mm). The color of the wings is variable but very characteristic; it has yellow or pink forewings, with white-ringed black spots. The hind wings are pink, irregularly bordered in black along the outer marginal area. It is similar to *Utetheisa ornatrix*, but the forewings of the latter are lighter in color and the black spotting is more sparse.

Habits The caterpillar lives on *Crotalaria* and other Leguminosae. The European species of *Utetheisa* feed on *Heliotropum* and *Tournefortia* (Boraginaceae), which contain substances that are toxic to vertebrates. These substances are absorbed by the larvae, are present in the hemolymph, and are secreted as a yellowish, foul-smelling foam, evidently as a defensive mechanism. In northern regions the adults emerge from the chrysalis from June to September; in the south broods are continuous.

206 VANESSA VIRGINIENSIS Drury
American painted lady

Family Nymphalidae.

Geographical distribution From the Atlantic to the Pacific coasts of the United States, from Canada in the north to Colombia in the south. In southern regions it is only found at high altitudes. A resident in the Canary Islands, it is also found as a stray in Hawaii, in the islands of the Azores and Madeira, and occasionally reaches Europe.

Description and related species Wingspan approximately 1¾–2¼ in. (44–54 mm). The upper side of the wing is largely tawny with black patterns; the apex of the forewing is black with white streaks. There are two black, blue-centered eyespots on the hind wings. On the underside the butterfly displays a complex pattern, with two big eyespots, the pupil blue with a black outline, prominent on the hind wings. Another four similar species are to be found in South America. *Vanessa cardui*, closely related, has smaller but more numerous eyespots on the underside of the hind wings.

Habits This butterfly frequents open countryside. Populations vary in numbers of individuals from one year to another. The caterpillars live mainly on plants of the family Compositae. There are two or three generations a year.

207 XYLOPHANES PLUTO F.

Family Sphingidae.
Geographical distribution Southern United States through Central America to Brazil.
Description and related species Wingspan approximately 2¼–2¾ in. (55–65 mm). The forewings are olive green with brown streaks on the marginal and basal areas. Pale violet lines occur on the median zone. The hind wings are much smaller, the outer margin being sinuate near the anal angle; they are black at the base, orangish-yellow on the discal area and inner margin, and dark green to brown on the outer margin. The body is particularly pointed at the lower tip and is completely brownish. In body shape it resembles *Eumorpha labruscae*, but the latter has very differently colored wings.
Habits A rare species in southern Texas and Louisiana, but sometimes common in Florida where it is often observed on *Verbena* flowers. The caterpillar feeds on leaves of *Eythroxylon* and *Chiococca*.

208 ZERENE CESONIA Stoll.

Family Pieridae.
Geographical distribution South America and southern parts of North America; in the south it reaches Argentina; in the United States its range extends from southern California to Florida, and sporadically northward.
Description and related species Wingspan approximately 2–2¾ in. (48–65 mm). The predominant color of the upper side of the wing is yellow, with a wide black band on the outer margin of the forewing, bordered inside by an irregular line. The hind wings likewise have a more or less distinct black stripe on the outer margin. Two black spots occur on the forewings and two orange ones on the hind wings. The underside is mainly yellow, sometimes with a sprinkling of pink dots. The pointed apex of the forewing characterizes this species and the related *Zerene eurydice*.
Habits This species lives in open woodlands and sometimes frequents desert areas. The caterpillars feed on various Leguminosae, including *Amorpha californica*, *A. fruticosa*, and species of *Trifolium*. In northern regions it flies in mid to late summer; in the south it occurs all year round.

209 ADELPHA COCALA Cramer

Family Nymphalidae.
Geographical distribution Central America, Guyana, Brazil.
Description and related species Wingspan 2½–2¾ in. (60–70 mm). The brown forewings have an orange band running across from the costa, tapering gradually to the inner margin. At the front this band broadens like a claw to surround a circular zone in the costal area. There is also a smaller, pale pink band on the hind wings that tapers to the inner margin. To either side of this band, on the submarginal and marginal zones, there are thin, wavy stripes of a light brown color. The related *Adelpha beotia* has isolated spots on the hind wings like those in the apical area; *A. cytherea* has rounded hind wings, a much bigger orange band, and a far narrower pink band.
Habits Another species, *A. fessonia*, from Central America (but which strays into Texas), feeds on Rubiacae of the genus *Rondia*, while *A. bredowii*, from some parts of the United States, feeds on oak trees.

210 ANARTIA FATIMA F.

Family Nymphalidae.
Geographical distribution South and Central America, across Mexico to Texas and, more rarely, Kansas.
Description and related species Wingspan 2–2¼ in. (50–55 mm). The upper side of the wing is dark brown. The forewings display a series of small whitish spots on the discal area and a cream-colored band across the median area. This band, fairly wide with ragged edges, gradually turns lighter in the submarginal part of the hind wing; the discal area of this wing also bears a quadrangular reddish band formed of tiny juxtaposed dots. A thin white discontinuous stripe runs along the margins. The underside is paler brown with whitish bands mirroring the pattern described on the upper side.
Habits Erratic in flight, this species is found in temperate regions from March to May and from October to December and in the tropics throughout the year. It likes open sunny places, flowery grasslands, and areas close to rivers and streams.

211 ARAWACUS AETOLUS L.

Family Lycaenidae.

Geographical distribution Colombia, Bolivia, and Venezuela to Trinidad.

Description and related species Wingspan 1½–2 in. (40–50 mm). This lycaenid is whitish on the upper side of its wings. The forewings, along the costal zone, apex, and marginal strip, are brown; and there is a large brownish spot on the median area. On the underside the alternating black and white bands of the costal zone merge to almost all black, with some white spots toward the tails. Seen from above, with closed wings, the body of this species looks particularly thin, except for the anal angle of the wings which widens to form a false head. This illusion is perfectly enhanced by white spots, which look like eyes, at the base of the tails, and by the tails themselves, which resemble antennae. A very similar species is *Arawacus togarna*, found in Mexico and Bolivia, but the patterns on the upper and lower sides of the wings are smaller. *A. jada* occasionally strays into Arizona from the south.

Habits As soon as it alights, this butterfly turns round rapidly so that its false head faces the opposite direction from which it came, or upward if the support is vertical. Predators will thus attack its tail rather than its head, giving the butterfly a better chance of escaping. The food plants of the caterpillar are species of the genus *Solanum*.

212 ASCALAPHA ODORATA L.
black witch

Family Noctuidae.

Geographical distribution Throughout South and Central America, and the southern United States; rarely reaches Canada.

Description and related species Wingspan 4–6 in. (100–150 mm). A moth with brownish or blackish patterns and marks typical of the owlet moths. Females of the species have a violet pink band with undulating margins, which cuts through the middle of the forewings and hind wings. Males lack this band. In the median zone of the forewings near the costa are two eyespots, deeply notched on the outer circumferences. On the hind wings, close to the outer margin and toward the anal angle, there is a large violet red crescent with a black border; its outer margin, in the shape of a double arc, outlines one black spot and one brownish spot the same basic color as the wing.

Habits The caterpillar lives on Leguminosae of the genera *Cassia* and *Pithecellobium*. The black witch has recently been introduced to the islands of Hawaii where it has done much harm. It is a migratory species.

213 ASTRAPTES NAXOS Hew.

Family Hesperiidae.
Geographical distribution Brazil and Colombia.
Description and related species Wingspan approximately 1¼–1½ in. (30–35 mm). In this species, as in many others of the genus, the wings are black with a brilliant blue basal area. The down on the back of the thorax is likewise a splendid bluish-green. The forewings have a few whitish dots extending from the costa to the apical area. A short band, repeatedly broken, runs from the costa through the discal area but not to the apex. The hind wings are completely brown except for the metallic blue basal zone. The species much resembles *Astraptes pheres* and *A. hopferi* but these have no white speckles on the wings. In *A. fulgerator*, a tropical species that reaches southern Texas, the wing bands are lighter in color and larger, and the one across the forewings reaches the apical area.
Habits This species is an excellent flyer with a streamlined body. The flight pattern is extremely rapid and unpredictable. The caterpillar has a constriction in the zone behind the head.

---

214 AUTOMERIS CORESUS Boisd.

Family Saturniidae.
Geographical distribution All tropical countries of South America.
Description and related species Wingspan 2½–3¼ in. (60–80 mm). The upper side of the forewing is grayish-brown with streaks and patches in various shades of the same color. A poorly defined dark brown band also appears. On the postdiscal area of each orange hind wing is a large eyespot. These markings are signals designed to confuse likely predators, causing them to become intimidated or drawing their attention away from the vulnerable parts of the moth's head. This type of coloration is suddenly exposed only when the moth is disturbed.
Habits The caterpillars are armed with many elegantly branched irritant spines, which may cause serious wounds because they contain toxic substances accumulated in tiny vesicles beneath the skin. The larvae of *Automeris armida* and *A. erischtoni* can damage cacao plants.

215   CALIGO EURILOCHUS Cramer

Family   Brassolidae.
Geographical distribution   This species, subdivided into many subspecies, inhabits Central America, Colombia, and Bolivia.
Description and related species   Wingspan 4–5 in. (100–120 mm). The male is slightly smaller than the female in this species, which is brown, with an iridescent blue patch in the center of the wing. As in other examples of the same genus, the underside of the wing displays prominent eyespots. The sexes differ not only in size but also in the different forms of the ocher brown stripes arranged irregularly along the outer margins of the forewings. In the female these stripes are double, in the male single.
Habits   This species is sometimes seen flying by day although it appears to prefer the hours surrounding dusk. It often frequents river banks, alighting on the leaves of water plants or on wet rocks. The species will feed, in the larval stage, on monocotyledons and as a consequence do damage to banana plantations.

216   CALIGO IDOMENEUS L.

Family   Brassolidae.
Geographical distribution   Brazil and Surinam.
Description and related species   Wingspan 5 in. (120 mm). This species belongs to the family of butterflies known as "owls" because of the two enormous eyespots situated on the underside of the hind wings. The colors of the upper surface of the wings are brown except for a lighter strip, which runs lengthwise across almost the entire front wing, fading toward the inner margin. On the basal and discal areas of the hind wings are large, very dark blue patches; this color is also found along the outer margins of the hind wings. In between these areas is a brown zone, much darker than that which appears on the forewings.
Habits   These butterflies feed on monocotyledons. The gregarious larvae eat banana leaves and can thus do considerable damage to plantations. The adults, which live in forests, fly at dusk and are attracted by fermenting fruit.

221 DIAETHRIA AURELIA Guen.
"89" butterfly

Family Nymphalidae.

Geographical distribution The species is known only from the island of Trinidad. The related *Diaethria asteria* is a rare stray in south Texas.

Description and related species Wingspan approximately 1½–2 in. (35–45 mm). The upper side of the forewing is dark with a short green band in the center. This band continues, together with a thinner one of the same color, on the marginal area of the hind wing. There is another short greenish stripe on the discal part of the forewing. The underside of the forewing is red, patterned with alternating black and white bands in the discal area. On the hind wings the alternate black and white bands form a graceful figure "89" giving the species its common name. There are no appreciable differences in coloration between the sexes.

Habits The flight pattern of this species is graceful and determined. It prefers high altitudes. The caterpillar feeds on *Trema micrantha* (Ulmaceae).

222 DISMORPHIA SP.

Family Pieridae.

Geographical distribution The various species of this genus are distributed throughout the entire tropical area of South and Central America, and in the southern United States.

Description and related species The many species constituting this genus are of modest size (wingspan 1½–2½ in. or 40–60 mm) and varied coloration. They range from forms that are almost entirely white to those that are streaked with yellow, black, and orange. There are numerous mimetic associations with butterflies of other families, such as Acraeinae (Nymphalidae). The abdomen is slender and threadlike, the wings large. In many species, marked sexual dimorphism is evident, affecting both the coloration and the shape of the wings; in particular, the hind wings of the males are much bigger, and the margins pointed rather than rounded in the usual way. The males also exhibit secondary sexual features such as patches of androconial scales on the hind wings.

Habits The caterpillars of these butterflies live on forest trees.

223 DOXOCOPA PAVON Latr.

Family Nymphalidae.
Geographical distribution From Bolivia across northern regions of South America to Mexico; occasionally found in southern Texas.
Description and related species Wingspan 2–2½ in. (50–60 mm). This species is notable for its spectacular blue tints. Its sexual dimorphism centers on color. The upper surface of the male's wings is brown with a deep red strip along the costal area widening into an orange patch on the apical zone. There are bluish reflections over large parts of the wings, crossed by two ocher yellow bands, one on the discal area and the other near the margins. The female is dark brown with an orangish yellow patch on the discal area and a band of paler brown across the wings. In both sexes the underside of the wings is maroon with white stripes. In color the species resembles *A. fessonia*, but the latter has brighter orange zones and, in the female, orange patches on the hind wings.
Habits This species frequents forest glades. The caterpillar feeds on leaves of the genus *Celtis* (Ulmaceae).

---

224 EMESIS ZELA Butler

Family Riodinidae.
Geographical distribution Venezuela, Colombia, Central America, and Arizona.
Description and related species Wingspan approximately 1¼–1½ in. (28–38 mm). The forewings are triangular, the male's pointed at the apex, the female's broadly curved. The outer margins are brown. The male's forewings are brownish with darker spots arranged in stripes along the postbasal, median, and submarginal areas. The hind wings are ocher, with black spots. The coloration of the female is similar except that the spots tend to be more prominent. The hind wings of a related species, *Emesis ares* (also found in Arizona), are deep orange, and the black spots are separated, not arranged to form stripes as in *E. zela*.
Habits The male vigorously defends his territory, which may be in small valleys between mountains and dry canyons. The caterpillars live on *Caesalpina mexicana*, which was introduced into the United States as an ornamental plant.

225 CYLLOPSIS SP.
(formerly EUPTYCHIA SP)

Family Nymphalidae, subfamily Satyrinae.

Geographical distribution The species of this genus are especially widespread in South America. Some may venture across the United States into Canada.

Description and related species Generally of small or medium size, these species may constitute over 70% of the satyrine population in some places, such as the island of Tobago. Many of these butterflies are fairly plain, generally shades of brown on the upper wing surface, but much more decorative below, with stripes and patches of often brilliant color. However, the principal regular features of these species are the eyespots, particularly in the submarginal area. *Cyllopsis innocentia*, from Venezuela, is one of the most conspicuous species both in size and color, violet blue with shaded bands and brown reflections on the underside of the wings. There is little sexual dimorphism.

Habits These species fly in the open late in the afternoon and may often be seen by the roadside, attracted by car headlights, or indoors, drawn there by the lights. The caterpillars, so far as is known, live on Gramineae.

226 EUREMA SP.

Family Pieridae.

Geographical distribution The numerous species of this genus are found in the West Indies, Central and South America, and in southern North America. Also known from the Old World.

Description and related species The species that make up this vast genus are notable for their fairly small size, with a wingspan of 1–2 in. (25–50 mm). Their dominant color is orangish-yellow, although some species are completely white, except for a dark apical area; in this respect members of this genus resemble the typical Pieridae of temperate regions. To the human eye these colors appear somewhat monochromatic but they in fact give off a diverse range of ultraviolet radiation, perceptible to other butterflies. As is the case with the related species *Colias*, mechanisms of interspecific isolation exist in this genus among individuals that are apparently very alike and live in the same surroundings; this separation at least partly depends on the range of ultraviolet emissions from the wings.

Habits The butterflies of these species pursue a zigzag flight pattern. Some of the species to be found on Tobago are particularly attracted to mimosa.

227 EURYBIA LYCISCA Ww.

Family Riodinidae.
Geographical distribution Central America, Colombia, Ecuador, and Peru.
Description and related species Wingspan 1¾–2¼ in. (45–55 mm). There are two eyespots on the dark brown forewings, consisting of a reddish circle bounding a black area, situated on the median zone near the costa. The hind wings, with blackish margins, have an iridescent blue surface caused by tiny metallic scales. The underside is brownish with darker marks along the margins of the forewings and hind wings. In this large family many groups of species are specialized in imitating inedible butterflies of various genera.
Habits This butterfly flies rapidly. It has the habit of settling on the undersurface of leaves, wings outspread. Although represented by numerous species, these butterflies are rarely found in collections because of the difficulty in capturing specimens.

228 EURYTIDES PROTESILAUS L.
swordtail

Family Papilionidae.
Geographical distribution From eastern Venezuela to Brazil, and from eastern Ecuador to eastern Peru and Bolivia.
Description and related species These medium-sized butterflies have a wingspan of up to 3¼ in. (80 mm). The sexes are much alike. Their color is transparent with black streaks and two bright red spots on the anal region and hind wings, tapering slightly in the middle to form two short blackish bands. On the forewings the black bands vary in length, extending from the basal zone and marking the borders of the submarginal and marginal zones. A characteristic black stripe runs from the edges of the apical area to the angle of the inner and outer margins. The species of this group closely resemble one another, but *Eurytides protesilaus* can be distinguished from *E. glaucolans* and *E. molops* by the much larger red anal spot and the more strongly indented outer margins of the hind wings.

229 HELICONIUS ERATO L.
small postman

Family Nymphalidae, subfamily Heliconiinae.
Geographical distribution Various parts of Central and South America, and as a stray in southern United States.
Description and related species Wingspan approximately 2¼–3¼ in. (55–82 mm). Like *Heliconius melpomene*, this species is also found in numerous forms, with variable coloration. There are variations, too, in the shape of the wings, as with *H. erato cyrbia*, the female of which has fringes on the outer and inner margins of the hind wings. Recent genetic studies of these species have led to the formulation of new hypotheses concerning the evolution of Müllerian mimicry. These are, in fact, polytypical species exhibiting marked color diversity in certain areas, this coloration controlled by a few genes and selectively maintained in different mimetic conditions.
Habits Although they may have migratory habits, most individuals of this species tend to return to the same place to spend the night. In Trinidad they are known to live on average for about fifty days. The solitary caterpillars feed on poisonous species of the genera *Passiflora* and *Tetrastylis*.

230 HELICONIUS MELPOMENE L.
postman

Family Nymphalidae, subfamily Heliconiinae.
Geographical distribution From Bolivia through Brazil and Colombia to Central America.
Description and related species Wingspan approximately 2½–3½ in. (60–85 mm). Some of the numerous forms of the postman (*Heliconius melpomene*) are subdivided, probably with justification, into subspecies, and are hard to distinguish from the corresponding variations of the rather more common *H. erato*, known as the small postman. The hind wings are generally dark brown, crossed by a yellow band, but they may be bluish or exhibit radiating orange stripes.
Habits This species flies lazily in the shade of secondary growth forest trees, usually low to the ground, but it is alo found on flowers in full sunlight. Numerous individuals of the same species often assemble at dusk to spend the night on tree branches. Prior to mating, the male alights on his partner and brushes her hind wings with his forewings. She emits pheromones (sex-scents) from special glands to excite her mate, stimulating him to fly closer and in his turn to release, from glands located in a special area of his hind wings, a pheromone that stimulates the female.

231 HYALYRIS COENO Doubl. & Hew.

Family Nymphalidae, subfamily Ithomiinae.
Geographical distribution From Bolivia to Venezuela through Peru, Ecuador, and Colombia.
Description and related species Wingspan approximately 2½ in. (60–65 mm). This species is variable in color and is subdivided into many subspecies. Some of these include individuals whose brown or black wings are interspersed with orange areas, reminiscent in this respect of species of the ithomiine genera *Mechanitis* and *Melinaea*. Others have transparent wings surrounded by a blackish band, on which there are tiny white dots regularly set along the outer margins. The female is more uniformly brown, especially in the basal zone. The discal area of the hind wings is yellowish, but in some individuals orange predominates; alternatively the wings may be almost completely black.
Habits The species flies in the low undergrowth of the rain forest. These unpalatable butterflies are imitated by others of different families whose members are not always inedible. Thus the entire mimetic chain is made up of some species that exhibit Müllerian mimicry and others that display Batesian mimicry.

232 HYPOLERIA OCALEA Doubl. & Hew.

Family Nymphalidae, subfamily Ithomiinae.
Geographical distribution Northern regions of South America and perhaps in Brazil.
Description and related species Wingspan 2¼ in. (55 mm). The wings are faintly tinged light brown in the almost transparent basal areas. Both sets of wings have dark brown borders; on the forewings this color covers almost the whole apical area, broken by thin, short stripes of paler brown. From the costa the brown color extends in a broad band to the outer margin, and this band divides into thin stripes that cover the veins. On the hind wings the dark edging is absent on the inner margin, especially near the base. The sexes are much alike both in size and coloration. *Hypoleria gephyra* is very similar but its wings are more heavily streaked with dark brown.
Habits This species is sometimes found in large numbers at the start of the rainy season. It flies lazily in shady areas and often rests with closed wings on the tips of leaves close to the ground.

233 ITHOMIA PELLUCIDA Weymer

Family Nymphalidae, subfamily Ithomiinae.
Geographical distribution From Brazil to Colombia, Venezuela, Trinidad, and Tobago.
Description and related species Wingspan approximately 1¾ in. (43–46 mm). This is a delicate butterfly of a soft transparent green color. In the male the margins of the forewings are surrounded by a brown band, which broadens near the apex, continues into the median zone, and tapers off, as the color turns paler, at the inner margin. The hind wings have a brown band along the outer margin. The coloration of the female is similar. *Ithomia pellucida* and the related *I. jucunda* from Costa Rica, *I. drymo* from Brazil, and *I. ardea* from Bolivia form a group whose individual identification is not easy. The subfamily to which these species belong is characteristic of South America but one genus may also be found in Asia and Australia.
Habits This species flies slowly and does not migrate. Many species belonging to this genus are found in very restricted areas, possibly indicating their evolution along with plants of the families Apocynaceae and Solanaceae on which the caterpillars feed.

---

234 LYCOREA CLEOBAEA Godart

Family Nymphalidae, subfamily Danainae.
Geographical distribution From regions of Peru and Brazil to Trinidad, Cuba, Haiti, Mexico, and the southern part of Texas where it seems to have reestablished itself after the climatic catastrophe of 1960.
Description and related species Wingspan 3–3½ in. (75–90 mm). The forewings are brownish-black with yellow streaks and two long, transverse orange stripes from the base to the median area. On the hind wings the brown margins are punctuated by yellow spots, and an orange band, angled in the center, bounds the postdiscal zone. The pattern is completed by a yellow stripe running from the base to the discal area. The few species of this genus are associated with a complex pattern of mimicry with Heliconiinae, other Ithomiinae, and moths of the families Arctiidae and Castniidae.
Habits A solitary flyer, this butterfly lives in forests and in scrubland. The caterpillar feeds on *Asclepias curassavica*, *Cacica papaya*, and species of the genus *Ficus*.

235 MARPESIA MARCELLA Fldr.

Family Nymphalidae.
Geographical distribution Central America and northern regions of South America.
Description and related species Wingspan 2–2½ in. (50–60 mm). The forewings are brown with thin black stripes in the basal area. The median and postmedian areas are red, becoming brownish on the outer margin. The discal zone of the hind wing is violet blue and the apical zone red. This species also has two brown tails, the longer one on the outer margin, the other, less prominent, close to the anal angle. The female is brown with a white strip along the forewings, without the blue tints on the hind wings. A species of this typically American genus is also found in Africa.
Habits This species flies vigorously at low levels, in forest clearings and other open spaces. Some caterpillars of its genus have been found on *Mora excelsa* and on various species of fig. It is common in much of its area of distribution and does not migrate.

236 MELINAEA MNASIAS Hew.

Family Nymphalidae, subfamily Ithomiinae.
Geographical distribution The western Amazon, primarily in Brazil.
Description and related species Wingspan approximately 2¾–3 in. (65–75 mm). The coloration of the wing consists of various alternating yellow, brown, and orangish-red stripes. The sexes are similar and numerous subspecies of the species have been described from various parts of its range.
Habits The conspicuous colors of the individuals of *Melinaea mnasias* cause them to stand out clearly against the greens and browns of their natural environment. As with all other Ithomiinae, this is an inedible species, and together with other species, even from other families, it forms part of a complex mosaic of Müllerian mimicry – that type of mimicry in which many inedible species tend to imitate one another. This is doubly advantageous, for not only does it reduce the number of distinguishing characteristics that each predator has to learn but it also decreases the ratio of losses that the protected species must inevitably suffer. This butterfly usually flies slowly, in the open, and at fairly low levels. The gregarious larvae live on Solanaceae of the genus *Heliotropium*.

237 MORPHO CATENARIUS Perry

Family Nymphalidae, subfamily Morphinae.
Geographical distribution Southern Brazil, Paraguay, and Uruguay.
Description and related species With its wingspan of 5¼ in. (130 mm), this is one of the smaller species of the genus. The coloration of the male is pale blue; there are some dark brown spots on the apex and along the outer margins of the fore-wings. A dark stripe, narrowing in the middle, covers the costa and extends to form the outer margin of the discal cell. The hind wings display isolated spots at the point where the veins make contact with the outer margin, and a series of small spots alternating with the others, along the sub-marginal zone. It is a species very similar to *Morpho laertes*, but in the latter the brown spots on the wings are smaller or wholly absent. There are two subspecies of *M. catenarius*, the nominal form coming from the zone lying between São Paolo and Santa Caterina. Seasonal variations are to be found, including a summer form with broad, rounded wings, in which all the marginal and apical patterns are much less distinct.
Habits This species lives in the canopy of tropical rain forests.

---

238 MORPHO PELEIDES Kollar

Family Nymphalidae, subfamily Morphinae.
Geographical distribution From Mexico to Venezuela and Trinidad. Some varieties, not yet formally described, come from Peru and Colombia. Nevertheless, a very large number of varieties have already been described, some having been raised to the rank of subspecies.
Description and related species Wingspan 4½ in. (110 mm). Compared with related species, *Morpho peleides* is the smallest. Color varies according to subspecies and season (dry or rainy). Normally there is a large blue area on the outer margins of the forewings and hind wings, this being sur-rounded by a darker band speckled with small whitish spots. In the subspecies *zonares* the blue changes to a soft cyclamen color, while the lateral band becomes ocher. Seen from below, the dark color is fairly uniform, except at the margins where there are alternating narrow bands in varying shades of brown. Both wings display large eyespots. Another sub-species, *marinita*, is chestnut brown; the blue color is limited to a narrow strip on the forewings. *M. peleides* is very similar to *M. granadensis* and *M. achillaena*, and is often confused with them.
Habits This species lives in the canopy of tropical rain forests.

239 OLERIA ESTELLA Hew.

Family Nymphalidae, subfamily Ithomiinae.
Geographical distribution Ecuador and Peru.
Description and related species Wingspan approximately
1½ in. (43–46 mm). This species is a transparent green color.
On the outer margins of the forewings is a black zone with a
few white spots in the area of the apex. Continuing along the
lines of the outer margin is a narrow curving band, chestnut in
color, which extends from the costa to the base; toward the
inside of this band is a thin blackish stripe. From the middle of
the costa a triangular black patch runs to the center of the
median area. The costal and outer margins of the hind wings
are surrounded by a chestnut-colored strip, which extends to
the inner margin. This strip is bounded by two black stripes,
the outer one with a few white spots and the inner one
merging near the anal zone. It is similar to *Oleria faunula* but
the latter lacks the brownish band on the forewings; in *O. zea*
there are no white spots on the outer margins.
Habits The adults fly in the forests and are protected from
predators by their unpleasant scent and taste, as well as by
being exceptionally coriaceous. The caterpillars live on various species of Solanaceae.

240 OPSIPHANES CASSIAE L.

Family Nymphalidae, subfamily Brassolinae.
Geographical distribution Central America to southern
Brazil.
Description and related species Wingspan (males) approximately 2¾ in. (65 mm). There are numerous subspecies. The
male of this species is brownish on the upper side of the
wings, broken by a yellowish-orange band in the center of
the forewings. The female is similar in color but there are
two small light spots at the apex of her forewings. The apical
zone of the outer margin of the hind wings is orange. The
hind wings of the male, as in other species of the genus, bear
scent scales. It is very similar to *Opsiphanes cassina
merianae*, but differs in that the band on the wings is thinner.
Habits This species is found on banana plantations, particularly on mud near river beds that have not yet dried out. The
green caterpillar is highly cryptic and extremely difficult to
detect on leaves. Males of the related *O. cassina*, when
captured, give out a pleasant sweetish scent, possibly to mark
territory and possibly of importance in mating.

241 PARIDES PERRHEBUS Boisd.

Family Papilionidae.
Geographical distribution Widely distributed in the Neotropical region. It is found in Argentina, Uruguay, Paraguay, and southeastern Brazil.
Description and related species Wingspan approximately 2¾ in. (65–70 mm). The dark brown coloration is heightened by a series of hourglass-shaped spots along the marginal area of the hind wings. The inner margin of the hind wings is whitish. The sexes are much alike, but the female is slightly bigger and has a distinct bronze sheen on the lower surface of the hind wings. The species *Parides photinus, P. alopius, P. dares*, and *P. montezuma* are all very similar, but only the last is likely to be mistaken for *P. perrhebus*, which is distinguishable by the much longer tails on the hind wings.
Habits The food plants belong to various families including Lauraceae, Hernandiaceae, Rutaceae, and Aristolochiaceae.

242 PEDALIODES SP.

Family Nymphalidae, subfamily Satyrinae.
Geographical distribution The high mountain regions of the Andes from western Venezuela to Bolivia; also found in Costa Rica.
Description and related species The members of this family, mainly represented in South America, seldom have striking colors. They are of average size and have a swelling at the base of the wing veins. This special structure appears to be an apparatus for sound reception. The species of the genus Pedaliodes are dark in color but there are often blurred reddish-brown or whitish bands or spots on the forewings and hind wings. The underside of the wing frequently displays dark rounded spots encircled by a pale ring and with a white dot in the middle. These eyespots may be isolated or arranged in a line on the submarginal part of the hind wings.
Habits These butterflies fly at low levels, well concealed and making full use of any form of shelter. They are attracted to rotting fruit and are occasionally found indoors, attracted to the lights, during the early evening. They have the same habits and frequent the same sorts of localities as species of the genera *Erebia* (alpine meadows) and *Oeneis* (tundra) of the northern hemisphere.

243 PERISAMA BONPLANDII G. Mén.

Family Nymphalidae.
Geographical distribution Colombia, Brazil, and Peru.
Description and related species Wingspan approximately 2–2¼ in. (48–55 mm). This species belongs to a vast genus of South American butterflies, the members of which generally display contrasting, iridescent colors on the underside of the wings, and varying shades of brown with green stripes and bands on the upper side. The forewings of *Perisama bonplandii* are brown above, with a narrow, elongated bluish-green patch at the apex and a curving green band in the median zone. The hind wings are chestnut with broad yellow or greenish patches on the submarginal area. The underside of the hind wings is ocher with a wide, paler band on the discal zone. The colorful underside of the forewings is red at the base, brown with green spots and ocher on the discal area. *P. cabirnia* is very similar but the green band on the forewings bends sharply before reaching the costa. In *P. vaninka* the green bands are much broader.

---

244 PHILAETHRIA DIDO L.
scarce bamboo page

Family Nymphalidae, subfamily Heliconiinae.
Geographical distribution From Peru, Brazil, and Trinidad to the southernmost part of Mexico.
Description and related species Wingspan approximately 3½ in. (85–92 mm). The basic colors of this species are the brownish-black bordering the wings (except for the innermost zone of the hind wings) and the green which forms spots of varying size, lengthened on the cells bordering the wing veins. On the underside the color becomes translucent and the brownish-black takes on a light chestnut tone. It is similar to *Philaethria wernickei*, but in this species the color of the wings is less intense. Some scientists claim that this genus could be the American representative of the Oriental genus *Cethosia*. There are, in fact, many affinities both in the larval stages and in the choice of food plants.
Habits This species circles for hours in full sunlight, at a great height above particular groups of trees, especially those situated on high ground. The caterpillars live on *Passiflora laurifolia*.

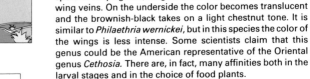

245 PHOEBIS PHILEA L.
yellow apricot

Family Pieridae.

Geographical distribution This species and its various subspecies are found from Mexico to Brazil, Paraguay, northern Argentina, and Peru.

Description and related species Wingspan 3–3¼ in. (75–80 mm). This butterfly exhibits some sexual dimorphism. The male is apricot yellow, with orange tints on the median area of the forewings close to the costa and along the outer margin of the hind wings. The female is a deeper yellow with numerous dark spots along the outer margin of forewings and hind wings; both sexes are broadly suffused with red in the postdiscal and marginal areas. The underside is much paler yellow, the black spots are more blurred, and there is no red at all. The most closely related species, the apricot (*Phoebis argante*), is deep yellow without any orange tints in the male and has a thin dark brown stripe on the outer margin and along the costa of the forewings. The female has no red on the hind wings.

Habits This species flies in full sunlight at some distance above the ground; specimens are most numerous in the early part of the rainy season.

---

246 PHYCIODES SP.

Family Nymphalidae.

Geographical distribution Much of North, Central, and South America.

Description and related species Study of the species of this genus is often complicated by the extraordinary variability displayed and the fact that their subdivision into numerous subspecies is not always clearly defined. *Phyciodes ianthe*, with a wingspan of approximately 1¼–1½ in. (32–36 mm), is a white and black butterfly, the underside of the wings duplicating, in weaker tones, those of the upper side. It flies in places sheltered from direct sunlight, in the forests of Venezuela, Colombia, and the West Indies. *P. ianthe leucodesma* (a subspecies of *P. ianthe*) from Venezuela, has a precise flight pattern, often gliding just above the forest floor around leaves that have been torn away by violent tropical rains. The pearl crescent (*P. tharos*), with a wingspan of 1–1½ in. (25–38 mm), has streaked dark red wings above, which are wholly reddish below.

Habits Like the related genera *Chlosyne* and *Eresia*, these butterflies often imitate protected forms in tropical regions. The ten or so species inhabiting the temperate regions of North America are, however, somber in coloration.

247 **PIERELLA HYALINUS** Gmelin

Family Nymphalidae, subfamily Satyrinae.
Geographical distribution Only found in Guyana.
Description and related species Wingspan approximately
2–2¾ in. (50–65 mm). The colors of this butterfly are fairly
modest. Brown predominates on the narrow elongated forewings and on part of the hind wings. The latter are quite

different from the former, large, with the outer margins
curved to form a short, broad-based tail at the meeting point
with the inner margins. The coloration of the hind wings, too,
is different; although brown near the body, there are also
long blue spots on a dark ground, which extend to form short
bands in the discal and marginal areas. Other species are

ocher with black spots or iridescent patches, particularly on
the forewings, which change hue according to the angle at
which they are viewed.
Habits This butterfly, like other species of its genus, favors
shady parts of the tropical forest. The caterpillars live chiefly
on Gramineae and may attack cultivated plants such as
bamboo, sugar cane, and palms.

248 **PYRGUS COMMUNIS** Grote
checkered skipper

Family Hesperiidae.
Geographical distribution From southern Canada to
Argentina.
Description and related species Wingspan approximately
¾–1¼ in. (19–32 mm). An extremely variable species. The

head and basal zones of the wings are often bluish; the wings
are dark with broad white streaks on the discal area, becoming gradually thinner and more irregular toward the outer
margins, which are almost completely brownish on the hind
wings. The underside of the forewings is similar but paler
than the upper side. The hind wings are light in color with

alternating bands of dark olive green and grayish-green. The
spots usually merge into stripes delicately outlined in black
and dark chestnut. The dark gray and white colors decorating
the fringes are arranged in a checkered fashion, from which
the common name is derived.
Habits Males of this species are rather aggressive; indeed,
they patrol their territory, ready to attack any moving creature. The adults are present all year round in the south, and
from April to October in the cooler zones. Among the food
plants are many genera of Malvaceae, including *Hibiscus,
Malva,* and *Sidalcea.*

249 URANIA LEILUS L.

Family Uraniidae.
Geographical distribution The tropical belt of South America, and the West Indies.
Description and related species Wingspan approximately 2½–3½ in. (58–85 mm). This elegant species belongs, with a few others, to the only genus representing the family Uraniidae in South America. In its color pattern it resembles species of the genus *Chrysiridia* from Africa and Madagascar. The blackish forewings are crossed by narrow, brilliant green stripes, which get broader and divide in the submedian area. The hind wings, furnished with long, slender tails, have a wide band in varying shades of greenish-yellow, broken by black transverse stripes. Thin blurred lines, likewise green, run from the base to the zone of the anal angle. The very similar *Urania sloanus* has brighter green spots with a golden iridescence.

Habits The species flies by day and the caterpillar, with long, clublike hairs on its body, feeds on species of the genus *Omphala*, poisonous plants of the family Euphorbiaceae.

---

250 URBANUS PROTEUS L.
long-tailed skipper

Family Hesperiidae.
Geographical distribution Central and South America as far south as Argentina; north to the United States.
Description and related species Wingspan approximately 1½–2 in. (38–52 mm). The long-tailed skipper has a large, robust body. Its slender hind wings extend at the apex into two long tails. The upper side of the forewing is dark with brownish spots. The base of the wings, the head, and the thorax are iridescent green; the underside is lighter. The forewings are speckled and the hind wings have two dark bands near the tip. *Urbanus metophis* has a shorter, broader tail; *U. harpagus* is bigger and has white spots on the upper side of the wings.

Habits A species to be found in gardens and on river banks. In the United States there are three or more generations a year. The caterpillars live on plants of various families, particularly Leguminosae and Cruciferae. Sometimes, though rarely, they also attack species of the monocotyledonous genus *Canna* and has been known to be a pest of beans (*Phaseolus*).

251　ACRAEA SP.

Family Nymphalidae, subfamily Acraeinae.
Geographical distribution This genus is essentially African, represented by over 150 species.
Description and related species The various species in this group are subject to seasonal polymorphism. The most characteristic colors are reddish-brown, orange, and yellow with black spots, particularly on the hind legs.
Habits The genus is found in all habitats, from desert to rain forest, and at every altitude, from sea level to over 10,000 ft. (3,000 m). It is probable that all of the included species are distasteful to potential vertebrate predators, and for this reason many are imitated by other, edible butterflies. As a result many of the African species closely resemble one another and this similarity is an advantage to them because the absence of conspicuous distinctive features causes predators to identify all butterflies bearing these particular colors as distasteful and to reject them as a source of food. This mutual imitation among species that effectively become protected is a classic example of Müllerian mimicry. The butterflies of *Acraea* generally fly slowly. Their caterpillars live on toxic plants of the families Passifloraceae and Compositae.

252　ANTHENE LARYDAS Cramer

Family Lycaenidae.
Geographical distribution Central and West Africa.
Description and related species Wingspan approximately 1 in. (22–25 mm). The upper surface of the male's wing is entirely blackish; in the female it is various shades of brown with a line of small white spots along the submarginal area of the hind wings and black crescents on the outer margin close to the anal angle. In both sexes the underside is light brown with black spots and white lines. These white lines outline bands of darker color on the forewings or surround the black spots near the basal area of the hind wings. *Athene larydas* belongs to the group of species in which the underside of the forewings is crossed by two bands situated in front of the postdiscal area. It is very similar to *A. crawshayi* but the latter is decidedly lighter in color. The basal area of the female's wings is also slightly bluish.
Habits This species is particularly abundant in forest regions.

253 ARGEMA MITRAEI G. Mén.
Malagasy silk moth

Family Saturniidae.
Geographical distribution Madagascar.
Description and related species Wingspan 6½–7 in. (160–180 mm). This species is the largest of its genus. The color of the male is predominantly pale green, and that of the female yellow. On the forewings the costal margin to and including the apex is brown; a pair of similarly colored small lines branch out from the median area to touch two large eyespots. These are black in outline and in the center, with an inner ring of chestnut brown and a yellow crescent beneath. An undulating brown band runs from the middle of the inner margin almost to the apex. On the anal angle there is a triangular, brown-speckled spot. Two more eyespots appear in the discal zone of the hind wings; stemming from the anal zone are two extremely long (up to 8 in. or 200 mm) and elegant appendages, twisted and enlarged at the tip. The species is similar to *Argema mimosae* but differs from the latter by its much longer tails.
Habits The larvae, green with several yellow tubercles and black and yellow hairs, live on *Eugenia* and *Weinmannia*. Their lacelike cocoons have a silvery sheen.

254 BELENOIS AUROTA F.

Family Pieridae.
Geographical distribution Africa, Madagascar, Saudi Arabia, Turkey, Australia, and India.
Description and related species Wingspan 1½–2½ in. (40–60 mm). The species is usually whitish and displays relatively few variations. The outer margins of both wings and the apical area of the forewing are edged with black. Each of the black patterns encloses a white spot, rounded on the hind wings, elongated on the forewings. The veins on the underside of the hind wings are marked with black. Specimens from Madagascar display prominent yellow spots on the hind wings.
Habits A migratory species, very common in parts of Africa. The caterpillar lives on Capparidaceae.

255 BUNAEA ALCINOE Stoll.
common emperor

Family Saturniidae.
Geographical distribution Tropical Africa and Madagascar.
Description and related species Wingspan 4–6½ in. (100–160 mm). A very common species, its color ranging from red to purple and various shades of brown. The typical form has a reddish basal area clearly outlined by a narrow white band. There is a characteristic transparent mark, shaped like a quadrilateral, in the median area. On the discal zone of the hind wings are two huge eyespots; these are orange with a double black and white border. The marginal area of both pairs of wings is white, merging gradually with the chestnut tone of the outer margins. Many subspecies have been described, apparently differentiated one from another by chromatic variations. The *plumicornis* form from Madagascar has angular forewings.
Habits The larva is black with long black and white spines that are orange in tropical forms. It feeds on the leaves of various plants, including *Celtis, Croton,* and *Terminalia.*

---

256 CATOPSILIA FLORELLA F.
African migrant

Family Pieridae.
Geographical distribution Saudi Arabia, Iran, India, China, Syria, Egypt, Mauritania, the Canary Islands, and central Africa.
Description and related species Wingspan approximately 2–2¾ in. (50–65 mm). There is slight sexual dimorphism. The female is generally yellow, the male white with a barely perceptible green tinge. Both sexes have a black mark on the median area of the forewing, the costal and outer margins of which are brown. The underside of the female's wings is yellow; two white dots surrounded by brown occur on the discal area of each hind wing. Numerous forms have been described; in *pyrene* the females are identical to the males described above; females of the form *hyblaea,* however, are intermediate in color, in other words, white with yellow zones. A related species is *Catopsilia thauruma* of Madagascar, in which the coloration of the two sexes is reversed: in the male the basal and discal areas are yellow, in the female they are white, while the remaining parts are white and yellow respectively.
Habits The caterpillar lives on Leguminosae of the genus *Cassia.* It is a migratory species and the adults fly rapidly.

257 CHARAXES BRUTUS Cramer

Family Nymphalidae.
Geographical distribution From Guinea to western Nigeria.
Description and related species Wingspan 3–3½ in. (75–90 mm). The upper side of the wing is dark brown with a white transverse band; on the forewings this band breaks up into increasingly small spots with irregular outlines. The outer margin of the hind wing displays small, sharp dots, two of which are markedly longer. The underside, similarly crossed by a light band, is various shades of brown with a complex white pattern. There are eyespots along the marginal areas of the hind wings; other triangular spots appear on the marginal zone of the forewings.
Habits This species flies strongly at high levels, sometimes gliding with outspread wings into clearings. It often settles on patches of wet mud and on animal excrement in quest of mineral salts, and feeds on rotting fruit and on sap from tree wounds. The caterpillars of certain species feed on Leguminosae of the genera *Afzelia*, *Tamarindus*, and others.

258 COLOTIS DANAE F.
scarlet tip

Family Pieridae.
Geographical distribution Africa, Iran, Pakistan, India, and Sri Lanka.
Description and related species Wingspan 1¾ in. (45 mm). A large genus of butterflies notable for the appearance of a scarlet spot on the apex. The sexes are very similar, although the female may either be white, like the male, or yellow. There are also small black spots along the outer margins of the hind wings and on the underside of both pairs of wings. This pattern, however, is variable; in the dry season both the markings and the size of the individuals tend to be smaller.
Habits These butterflies fly in woodlands, savannahs, and over grasslands in full sun. Adults spend the night grouped in large communities on food plants. The caterpillars feed on *Cadaba*, *Capparis*, and *Maerua*, genera of Capparidaceae.

259 DANAUS CHRYSIPPUS L.
African monarch

Family Nymphalidae, subfamily Danainae.

Geographical distribution Tropical Africa and Asia, Australia; also some areas of the Palaearctic region (Egypt and Greece).

Description and related species Wingspan 2¾–3¼ in. (70–80 mm). This is a highly variable species and some forms tend to be more prevalent in particular parts of the range than in others. The forelegs of the males are almost completely atrophied; there are areas of androconial scales on the hind wings and groups of hairs at the tip of the abdomen. Various subspecies of this species have been described (e.g. *aegyptius*) as well as numerous color varieties. The basic color is a variable chestnut with black on the margins and on the apical zone of the forewings. This color is sprinkled with white dots, some bigger, some elongated or variously merged.

Habits This species prefers flying in the open but can also be found in towns. Apart from the North American monarch (*Danaus plexippus*), this is the only species of the genus that extends into Europe, in this instance from Africa, where it is one of the most common butterflies. In tropical zones there may be as many as twelve generations a year, while in temperate zones there are only one or two. The yellowish eggs, a little over 1 mm in length with some twenty longitudinal ridges, are laid on the stems of food plants. The larva feeds on species of *Calotropis* and other poisonous Asclepiadaceae, and has also been observed on Rosaceae and Scrophulariaceae. After rapid incubation, the egg hatches and the caterpillar immediately begins feeding. It grows quickly, becoming white with black bands, the broader bands bearing pairs of yellowish-green spots. On the upper part of the second and seventh abdominal segments are pairs of thick black filaments, which contract when the caterpillar is even slightly disturbed. Once mature, the larva is transformed into a jade green chrysalis in the form of a conical cylinder, which is attached to the food plant or a nearby twig. The butterfly is protected from predators by its unpleasant taste and its associated warning coloration. For this reason it is imitated by nymphalines such as *Elymnias hypermnestra* and *Hypolimnas misippus*. The latter is the best-known mimic and exhibits two distinct forms, each of which imitates the corresponding color variety of *Danaus chrysippus*. It has been established that only the females, which from the biological standpoint constitute the more important sex, assume the protective coloration of the danaines, whereas the males, with more ordinary colors, are not totally protected. The African monarch is imitated by other diurnal butterflies of various families as well as by moths, including species of the genus *Phaegorista* (Agaristinae).

260 EUCHLORON MEGAERA L.
verdant hawkmoth

Family Sphingidae.

Geographical distribution Africa south of the Sahara.

Description and related species Wingspan 2½–4½ in. (72–120 mm). A beautiful moth with an unmistakably brilliant green body and forewings, the latter speckled with black and gray spots. One prominent blackish mark adorns the curve of the inner margin. The hind wings are a contrasting orangish-yellow. The marginal area from the anal angle to about the middle of the outer margin displays a gray spot of irregular outline that gradually turns reddish-brown. A larger and darker patch, also with very irregular edges, stems from the inner margin and extends to the discal area. Other pairs of dark spots are to be seen on the lower and upper halves of the basal area of both the forewings and hind wings. The subspecies *serrai* from São Thomé lacks the black spots on the inner margin of the forewings; the subspecies *lacordairei* from Madagascar differs in a few barely perceptible characteristics.

Habits The caterpillar, which has been observed feeding on leaves of *Parthenocissus* and *Vitis* (both Vitaceae), has a pair of menacing eyespots close to the forehead, which discourage small birds from attacking it.

261 EUCHROMIA LETHE F.

Family Arctiidae, subfamily Ctenuchinae.

Geographical distribution West Africa and the river basin of the Congo.

Description and related species Wingspan 1¾–2¼ in. (45–55 mm). The forewings are dark brown with lighter elongated patches on the postmedian and postbasal areas; between the two zones is a bluish crescent. The basal and postbasal areas of the hind wings are yellowish-white. The abdomen is elongated with orange, red, and white rings alternating with black. It is very similar to *Euchromia guineensis*, which lacks the yellow band on the terminal part of the abdomen and has larger yellow areas on the wings. The family to which this species belongs is cosmopolitan but is best represented in the tropics where some extraordinary examples of mimicry with Hymenoptera have evolved. For example, the eighth abdominal segment of certain Ctenuchinae is extended to resemble the ovipositor of ichneumon flies (Ichneumonidae). Ctenuchines also mimic lycid beetles and poisonous moths of other families such as Zygaenidae.

Habits This species feeds mainly on herbaceous plants, flying slowly by day and tending to group in large numbers.

262 EUPHAEDRA NEOPHRON Hopffer

Family Nymphalidae.
Geographical distribution From the coastal forests of eastern Kenya through Tanzania into Mozambique, Malawi, Zimbabwe, and Natal.
Description and related species Wingspan 2½–3 in. (60–75 mm). Sexual dimorphism is evident in the size and sometimes in the colors of this species. The wings of the smaller male are navy blue except for several wide bands on the forewings, the first of which is black and runs from the middle of the costa to the basal angle; this is followed by an orange, a black, and another orange band, the last reduced to a spot on the apical area. In addition, two black spots occur near the costa. The female has the same coloration. In the subfamily *littoralis*, however, the ground color of the male's wings is cobalt blue, whereas the female's is purple. The undersides of the wings in both sexes are various shades of hazel.
Habits This species flies rapidly but not for long distances, settling with wings open. It prefers to live in forests. The caterpillar has feathery side processes and lives on species of *Deinbollia* (Sapindaceae).

263 EUPHAEDRA PERSEIS Drury

Family Nymphalidae.
Geographical distribution From Sierra Leone to the Ivory Coast.
Description and related species Wingspan approximately 2¾–3½ in. (70–85 mm). The forewings of both the males and the females are blackish except for the base, which is dark red, and a large irregular band of the same dark red color covering much of the inner margin. Two yellowish spots occur on the median zone, a yellowish band outlines the apical area with an elongated yellow dappling on the apex. The hind wings are largely dark red apart from the inner and outer margins, which are black. On the latter is a row of white speckles. The pattern of the underside of the wings is similar to that of the upper side, except that the inner margin and the basal zone of the forewing are generously tinged with red. The abdomen is blackish with symmetrical lines of white dots. It greatly resembles *Euphaedra zaddachi*, and more precisely *E. z. elephantina*, except that the upper surface of the wing displays more red.
Habits It is probable that this species has close mimetic associations with *E. zaddachi* and with certain species of moths belonging to the noctuid subfamily Agaristinae.

264 EUPHAEDRA THEMIS Hübner

Family Nymphalidae.

Geographical distribution From Sierra Leone to Nigeria.

Description and related species Wingspan approximately 2¾–3½ in. (70–85 mm). A variable species with gaudy colors; many variations and aberrations have been described. The ground color is brownish-black, adorned with a large zone of brilliant bluish-green with yellow tints on the discal and postdiscal areas of the hind wings. The same coloration continues in a semicircular area, the base of which is positioned in the middle of the inner margin of the forewing. The basal zone of the latter is dark reddish-brown; a broad yellow band marks the inner boundaries of the apical area. Noteworthy features of the underside are the dark red basal areas and the overall yellow color spotted with black along the submarginal areas and on the margins of both wings. There are other black and bluish markings on the discal zones, while the inner margin of the forewings is tinted blue. The female is larger, and yellow prevails over the bluish-green tones. It is similar to *Euphaedra justicia*, and the two are not easy to distinguish.

---

265 GRAPHIUM PYLADES Fabricius

Family Papilionidae.

Geographical distribution Kenya, south to Tanzania, Mozambique, Zimbabwe, Transvaal and Natal; inland across Zambia and southern Zaïre to Botswana and Angola.

Description and related species Wingspan approximately 2¾ in. (65–70 mm). The forewings are brownish-black. A large grayish-white area extends from the base to the discal zone and inner margin. Spots of the same color, mostly isolated and of varying size, are set along the outer margin, deeply recessed in the center, and in the discal, costal, and postdiscal zones. The hind wings are similarly blackish, except for a more extensive light area running from the base that covers over half the wing. In the dark zone there are two series of whitish spots; the outer ones are more angular and correspond to the recesses of the outer margin. The pattern on the underside is similar, but the ground color is light chestnut. The female is very like the male, except that the margins of the forewings are less recessed. Various subspecies have been described (*baronis* from Ethiopia and *pylades* from western Kenya, Uganda, Sudan, Nigeria, and Senegal). A related species is *Graphium taboranus*, with far fewer white spots.

266   GRAPHIUM POLICENES Cramer

Family Papilionidae.

Geographical distribution Throughout west, central, and east Africa and southward to Natal.

Description and related species Wingspan 2¾–3 in. (70–75 mm). The ground color is brownish-black, with predominantly whitish stripes and spots. The sexes are similar in coloration. The upper side of the forewing has two light stripes in the basal and postbasal zones, which continue along the costal area, gradually getting smaller until they become small spots at the apex. A further series of small spots marks the inner boundary of the marginal area. The hind wings display a light stripe along the inner margin, terminating in a pink spot. Parallel to this stripe, stemming from the costa, runs another band. The outer margin is deeply indented, with narrow, pale half-moons and a long tail. The underside of the wing more or less repeats the patterns of the upper side, but the ground color is light brown. The species is similar to the common *Graphium antheus* and to *G. porthaon*, but in these the stripes of the costal area are sinuous in form.

Habits This species flies among forest vegetation. Its food plants include species of Anonaceae.

267   JUNONIA TEREA Drury

Family Nymphalidae.

Geographical distribution From Senegal to Nigeria.

Description and related species Wingspan approximately 1½–2 in. (43–47 mm). The lateral areas are brown, there is a large ocher yellow band on the discal zones, and the marginal areas are brownish-black. White spots stand out against the dark background of the apical zones of the forewings. A row of contiguous eyespots is situated in the submarginal area of the hind wings. The underside of both pairs of wings is predominantly yellow with light brown spots, stripes, and streaks. The wing margins are indented and the hint of a tail extends from the anal angle of the hind wings. The outer margin of the forewings, near the apical area, is recessed. One of the various forms of this species, *tereoides*, lacks the yellow band as in the related *Junonia natalica*.

Habits A very common forest species. The caterpillar lives on Acanthaceae.

268 BELENOIS SUBEIDA Feld.
(formerly PIERIS SUBEIDA)

Family Pieridae.
Geographical distribution Tropical Africa from Guinea to Ethiopia and Tanzania.
Description and related species Wingspan 2–2¼ in. (50–55 mm). The species is subdivided into numerous subspecies. As a rule it is white with varying degrees of brown on the outer margins of both the forewings and hind wings. There are a few black dots on the discal area and near the costa of the hind wings. On the forewings a dark band runs from the costa to the median area. Sometimes this band is completely broken, culminating in an isolated spot; alternatively it appears as a series of interlinked spots. In the typical form, in both sexes, the veins on the underside of the hind wings are not black. Among the various subspecies, *instabilis*, as the name suggests, displays considerable variability, especially in the females, which exhibit numerous examples of intermediate colors. *Belenois subeida* is very similar to the related and common species *Belenois aurota*, although the former is much darker in color.
Habits This species lives mainly in the rain forests.

---

269 SALAMIS PARHASSUS Drury
mother of pearl

Family Nymphalidae.
Geographical distribution Tropical Africa with the exception of the western part of Cape Province in South Africa.
Description and related species Wingspan 3–4 in. (75–100 mm). The wings are a translucent shade of green, tinged pearly gray, with pale violet spots and dark margins. Eyespots are particularly conspicuous on the undersides, both on the forewings and hind wings. A thin brown line crosses the median area of both pairs of wings. A short reddish tail protrudes from the outer margin of the forewings, close to the apex. Another short tail juts out from the middle of the outer margin of the hind wings. A smaller form of this species has been described from the Upemba Park. Other species of the genus *Salamis* exhibit more vivid colors, and the underside of their wing resembles a dry leaf.
Habits This species is common in forests and dense shrub up to 6,500 ft. (2,000 m). The caterpillar feeds on species of *Asystasia* and *Isoglossa* (Acanthaceae).

270 ATTACUS ATLAS L.
Atlas moth

Family Saturniidae.

Geographical distribution India, Sri Lanka, China, southeast Asia, Malaysia, and Indonesia.

Description and related species Wingspan 6½–12 in. (160–300 mm). Females of this species are among the biggest of all Lepidoptera. The forewings, with their broad, rounded apex, are various shades of brown and yellow. On both forewings and hind wings the marginal area is yellow sprinkled with chestnut brown; it is bounded on the outside by an irregular black line and inside by a narrow, curved pink band. The median area of the forewing is reddish, shaped somewhat like an hourglass, and is bounded by a narrow white band on either side. Further forward is a large translucent, triangular white mark, bordered with black. There is a comparable mark in the discal area of the hind wing, which is similar in coloration to the forewing.

Habits The large caterpillars are mainly green with black streaks; they feed on leaves of diverse shrubs and trees.

---

271 CETHOSIA CHRYSIPPE F.

Family Nymphalidae.

Geographical distribution The typical form is found at Cape York in Queensland, Australia. The species is subdivided into numerous subspecies inhabiting islands of the Molucca archipelago, New Guinea, and neighboring islands. It is very likely, however, that some of these so-called subspecies will prove to be seasonal variations of the same species.

Description and related species Wingspan approximately 3½ in. (85 mm). The female of this butterfly is mainly brown, except for a large central area that is sometimes tinted violet on the basal and discal zones of both forewings and hind wings. On the subapical zone of the forewings, stemming from the costa, are two short, light-colored bands. Thin crescent-shaped stripes, also pale in color, surround the fringes of the outer margin on the hind wing. The male is very similar to the female, except for the presence on the basal half and upper part of the forewing of purplish-red shadings and the less evident bluish sheen on the distal half of both wings.

Habits The caterpillars of one subspecies of this butterfly are known to have gregarious habits and to feed on *Adenia populifolia*.

272 COSCINOCERA HERCULES Miskin
Australian Atlas moth

Family Saturniidae.
Geographical distribution Northern Australia, New Guinea, and the Bismarck Archipelago.
Description and related species Wingspan approximately 6½–8 in. (165–210 mm). This species is one of the giants of the order Lepidoptera. The forewings are characteristically sickle-shaped, like those of other members of this family, while the hind wings are provided with long tails, much bigger in the males. The ground color is reddish-brown, against which pearly white spots, one on each wing, stand out conspicuously. A wide band parallel to the line of the body – white outside and black-bordered inside – runs across the wings for their entire length. This stripe outlines the basal area with its somewhat irregular and much darker reddish-brown spots. By reason of its large size and, in part, its coloration, it resembles *Attacus atlas*, but is immediately distinguishable by the presence of tails on the hind wings.
Habits This species is a powerful flyer in tropical rain forests. The caterpillar lives on various trees.

273 DELIAS MYSIS F.

Family Pieridae.
Geographical distribution An Australian species from Queensland; also found in other parts of the Papuan region such as the islets of the Torres Strait, New Guinea, the islands of Misool, Aru, etc.
Description and related species Wingspan 2½–2¾ in. (60–70 mm). This species belongs to a very large genus. Like related species, the upper side of the wings is white with blackish margins. The underside of the hind wing, however, displays vivid colors; there is a bright red band with a deep black border along the submarginal zone, the area of the scales is off-white, and the basal area and part of the discal area, facing the inner margin, are orange. The forewings are whitish, except for a black band along the costa that broadens at the apex and extends beyond the middle of the outer margin. A few long, yellowish-white dots appear inside the black band on the apex. The species is fairly similar to *Delias doylei* but in the latter the orange area is more extensive.
Habits This species flies slowly in tight circles above the treetops of the forest and wherever flowers bloom. The larvae are particularly associated with *Loranthus* species, the adults with species of *Lantana*.

274 EUPLOEA SP. F.

Family Nymphalidae, subfamily Danainae.

Geographical distribution Species of this genus inhabit the westernmost islands of the Indian Ocean across to India, Australia, the Solomon Islands, China, and the Philippines.

Description and related species All species and races of this genus are dark brown or black, with whitish spots and stripes; many display an iridescent blue sheen. Males may be distinguished by the widely curving inner margin of the forewings, which in the females is straight. Other distinctive features of the male are the presence, in some cases, of patches of androconial scales on the forewings, and similar areas on the costal margin of the hind wings. This genus has presented quite a few problems of classification because the constituent species, many of them subdivided into numerous subspecies, are difficult to identify.

Habits These butterflies are generally distasteful to birds and other predators because their larvae feed on poisonous plants such as oleander, *Ficus eugenoides,* and *Hoya australis*, and pass on these plant poisons to the adult.

275 EUTHALIA DIRTEA F.
archduke

Family Nymphalidae.

Geographical distribution A variable species of which numerous subspecies have been described. It ranges from India and Pakistan to Hainan and from Malaysia to the Philippines.

Description and related species Wingspan approximately 3¼–4 in. (80–105 mm). The genus to which this butterfly belongs shows a marked resemblance to the species of the genus *Apatura*. The female is brownish and has many small irregular yellowish-white spots on both the forewings and hind wings. On the forewings this speckling appears to spread out from a point near the base of the wings, but on the hind wings the dots are arranged in two transverse lines. On the submarginal area of the hind wings there are dark brown areoles outlined by a thin yellowish border. A few triangular reddish marks also occur, the tips of which face toward the slightly jagged outer margin. The abdomen displays isolated reddish spots. The male's wings, by contrast, are bright blue or green.

276 GRAPHIUM ANDROCLES Boisd.

Family Papilionidae.
Geographical distribution The island of Sulawesi (Celebes).
Description and related species Wingspan 3¼–3½ in. (80–90 mm). A large butterfly, magnificently adorned with long tails on the hind wings. The coloration is mainly grayish-white. The forewings have large black stripes on the basal area, the outermost one cut in half. A broad black zone, crossed by two narrow grayish-green bands, covers the apical area and part of the discal area. There are, too, somewhat irregular black crescents along the outer margins of the hind wings. The tails, like much of the wings, are grayish-white. On the underside there are yellowish bands, especially near the body, and the black spots, which on the upper side assume no clear pattern, are here very distinct. Melanistic forms of this species are known, as well as a variety with broad greenish-yellow areas on the hind wings. It resembles *Graphium dorcus*, but is easily distinguished from it by its bigger size and by the presence of the two grayish-green bands on the dark surface of the forewing.
Habits This species flies with considerable agility, usually along the banks of streams in mountain zones. The female is seen more rarely than the male.

---

277 GRAPHIUM SARPEDON L.
blue triangle

Family Papilionidae.
Geographical distribution Widely distributed from northern India to China, Japan, and the Solomon Islands. The subspecies *choredon* ranges from the islands of Misool, Salawati, Aru, and Kai, across West Irian and the islands of the Torres Strait to New South Wales in Australia.
Description and related species Wingspan approximately 2¾ in. (70 mm). There is little difference between the two sexes of this beautiful butterfly. Its dark color is broken by a continuous wide band from the forewings to the hind wings, greenish above, bluish below. Stemming from this band, which is pointed at the tip, are roundish spots of the same color, extending to the apex of the forewings. There are also narrow, elongated dots on the underside, reddish in the postdiscal area, lighter and sickle-shaped near the outer margin. The related *Graphium gelon* is smaller, with a much reduced greenish band.
Habits This species is a rapid flyer, which may be found on *Lantana* flowers. The caterpillar feeds on *Geijera salicifolia, Tristania laurina, Cryptocarya, Macaranga, Persea gratissima* (avocado), *etc.*

278 HYPOLIMNAS BOLINA L.
common eggfly

Family Nymphalidae.
Geographical distribution Widely distributed in the Oriental and Australian regions. This species can be divided into two groups: the first ranges from India to Taiwan; the second inhabits the Malayan peninsula and the Australian region.
Description and related species Wingspan 2¾–4½ in. (70–110 mm). The males of the two above-mentioned groups differ in color. Those from Asia exhibit a small white mark in the submarginal area of the underside; in those from Australia this distinctive mark is absent. Males and females display widely different wing coloration. Males are dark with violet blue patches on the scaly zones of both forewings and hind wings. Females are generally brownish, fading towards the margins where there are streaks of lighter browns. On the hind wings another pattern of small pale stripes adorns the outer margin.
Habits Species of this genus are frequently seen in gardens, the males often fiercely defending their territory. They can appear in large numbers after a heavy downpour of rain, but are not particularly active, confining themselves to short, rapid flights when disturbed.

279 IDEA DURVILLEI Boisd.

Family Nymphalidae, subfamily Danainae.
Geographical distribution Subdivided into various subspecies, this species ranges from the Moluccas to the western part of New Guinea.
Description and related species Wingspan 5–5¼ in. (120–130 mm). The male is slightly smaller than the female of this species. The basic color is white, against which are etched dark veins and blackish stripes. Along the outer margins of the wings is a prominent black band surrounded by rounded white spots. The dark streaking of the wing is not as conspicuous in the males as in the females, especially along the outer margins and on an irregular band crossing the discal area of the forewings. In other species of this genus the black band of the discal area is broken into large spots with irregular outlines; in some instances these may be missing altogether, as in *Idea aza*.
Habits The caterpillar, like that of other species in this subfamily, probably lives on the foliage of Asclepiadaceae, Apocynaceae, and Moraceae.

280 KALLIMA INACHUS Boisd.
Indian leaf butterfly

Family Nymphalidae.

Geographical distribution From the Himalayas to southern China.

Description and related species Wingspan approximately 3½–5 in. (92–120 mm). The species of this genus constitute one of the most classic examples of cryptic mimicry. There is a striking difference in the appearance of the upper side and underside of the wings. The upper side of the forewings is vividly colored: a white spot stands out against the black apical zone, there is an orangish-yellow band and, finally, a grayish-blue basal area with contrasting white spots. The upper side of the hind wings is largely violet gray with reddish tints, particularly evident along the costa. The undersides of both pairs of wings, on the other hand, display chestnut brown streaks, exactly reproducing the coloration of a dead leaf. A thin dark stripe extends from the tail to the apex; and from here run other even thinner dark stripes, which combine to give the appearance of the veining of a leaf.

Habits This species, together with others of the genus, lives in forests. It appears to fly in a straight line; as soon as it alights, it closes its wings, and appears to be a dead leaf. The caterpillar lives on *Acanthus*.

---

281 ORNITHOPTERA PRIAMUS L.

Family Papilionidae.

Geographical distribution The Moluccas, New Guinea, and the Solomon Islands; northern Australia.

Description and related species Wingspan approximately 6½–8 in. (170–200 mm). The species is subdivided into various subspecies spread over its large area of distribution. There is considerable sexual dimorphism both in size and coloration. The male is emerald green with a large black area crossing the whole surface of the forewing. The wing margins are black and there are round spots on the discal area of the hind wings. These spots are bigger on the underside, and are present on each of the cells of the hind wings. Two yellow dots occur near the costa. The abdomen is bright yellow. The female is dark in color with irregular lighter colored bands, often divided and situated mainly on the outer margins of the discal area of the forewings. It is very similar to the female of *Ornithoptera victoriae*.

Habits This butterfly is found near the coasts. The caterpillar feeds on species of *Aristolochia*.

282 ORNITHOPTERA VICTORIAE Rotsch.
Queen Victoria's birdwing

Family Papilionidae.
Geographical distribution This stupendous butterfly, dedicated by its discoverer to Queen Victoria, is found with its numerous subspecies on the New Georgia archipelago of the Solomon Islands.
Description and related species Wingspan 5½–6½ in. (140–170 mm). The female of this species is very different to the male both in size and coloration. It is dark brown with short bands of whitish spots in the subdiscal and submarginal areas. On the underside there are also yellow zones in the basal area and on the costa of the discal area. In the male almost the entire underside of the hind wing is yellow; on the upper side the discal and postdiscal areas are green and the yellow is limited to large spots in the submarginal area. On the upper side of the forewing only the apical area is yellow, while the basal area is green; the underside is yellow, except along the margins, which are dark brown.
Habits This species flies among the treetops of tropical forests. The caterpillar lives on various species of *Aristolochia*.

---

283 PACHLIOPTA POLYDORUS L.
red-bodied swallowtail

Family Papilionidae.
Geographical distribution This species, subdivided into different subspecies, inhabits the Australian region, except for New Zealand, New Caledonia, and other islands lying south of the Solomon Islands.
Description and related species Wingspan 3 in. (75 mm). The size of this species varies slightly according to the subspecies and the sex (the females are slightly bigger). The most brilliant colors are found on the underside of the hind wings. The shape of the wing also differs slightly in the two sexes; the female's wings are broader and more rounded. Their coloration is brown with whitish streaks which become fainter along the discal and postdiscal zones of the forewings. The underside of the female's hind wing exhibits a group of short whitish bands in the discal area, and rounded red spots along the submarginal zone. The abdomen is dark, with the exception of the apex, which is bright red. It resembles *Pachliopta polyphontes sejanus*, but in the latter short lobate tails are found on the hind wings.
Habits The larva of this species is brownish-black with red tubercles. It lives on plants of the genus *Aristolochia*, on which it completes its cycle in about two weeks.

284 PAPILIO ANACTUS Mcleay
dingy swallowtail

Family Papilionidae.
Geographical distribution Australia, from Queensland to Victoria, and the western part of South Australia.
Description and related species Wingspan 2¼–2½ in. (55–60 mm). The dominant coloration of both sexes is dark with spots in various shades of gray; these spots are elongated crosswise in the discal and postdiscal areas, small and roundish along the outer margin of the forewings. The hind wings, however, display lighter colored markings in the discal cell and arranged like a fan in the interstices of the veins stemming from it. The postdiscal area has small blue spots, set in a curving line; and close to the outer margin are five circular spots, one of which, though not set flush with the others, is reddish.
Habits The butterfly is very common in gardens. It has a leisurely flight pattern but, if disturbed, will dart away swiftly. The caterpillar feeds on various species of the genus *Citrus* (Rutaceae).

---

285 POLYGRAMMODES SP.

Family Pyralidae.
Geographical distribution This species is found all over the world but is most prevalent in the tropics. It is found in the Nearctic and Palaearctic regions (excluding Europe), in Africa, and in the Indo-Malayan region.
Description and related species This genus belongs to the subfamily Pyraustinae, with about 3,500 known species. The wing patterns are fairly uniform, consisting of zigzagging transverse bands, often mingled with lighter or translucent round spots.
Habits Typical of this genus and also of the majority of the subfamily Pyraustinae is the resting position with extended wings, as shown in the specimen illustrated here. Most species fly at night or at sunset; few can be called diurnal. Like all the Pyralidae, they have an abdominal tympanum or ear that can pick up ultrasounds emitted by predatory bats.

286 TELLERVO ZOILUS F.

Family Nymphalidae, subfamily Danainae.
Geographical distribution Sulawesi, New Guinea, and Queensland, Australia to the Solomon Islands. Various subspecies have been described from parts of New Guinea and associated islands.
Description and related species Wingspan 1½–1¾ in. (40–45 mm). Both sexes of this small danaine are similar in size and coloration. This coloration is dark with sky blue patterns consisting of a large spot in the center of the hind wings and small dots on the forewings near the subapical area. Underneath, the blue is more extensive, broken into small spots along the inner and costal margins of the hind wings. There are numerous spots on the forewings, in addition to the three primary ones, especially along the outer margin. The species is distinguished from all other danaines by the absence of tufts of hair on the tip of the abdomen. It is a model for the nymphaline mimic *Naptis praslini*, although the latter is bigger.
Habits This species flies in forests and is particularly difficult to catch because it hides in dense thickets when pursued. The caterpillar lives on Asclepiadaceae, Apocynaceae, and Moraceae.

287 TENARIS ARTEMIS Voll.

Family Nymphalidae, subfamily Amathusiinae.
Geographical distribution Known only from New Guinea.
Description and related species Wingspan 2¾–3½ in. (70–90 mm). The forewings are whitish with a black border along the costal zone. The entire apical area is black. The hind wings are pale yellow with a black band along the whole of the costal and outer margin, gradually narrowing toward the anal angle. In the postdiscal and submarginal areas are two large blue, black-centered eyespots, surrounded by a black border that becomes wider toward the base of the wing and blurred near the inner margin.
Habits The larva is cylindrical, thick in the middle, and its whole body is covered with soft hairs. The adult flies at dusk together with butterflies related to *Brassolis*, with which it shares a taste for ripe bananas, sometimes doing damage to plantations.

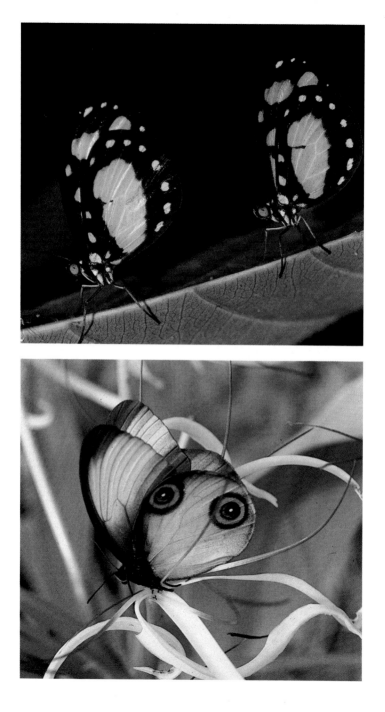

288 TROGONOPTERA BROOKIANA Wall.

Family Papilionidae.

Geographical distribution This extremely beautiful butterfly has been subdivided into various subspecies, which inhabit Borneo (the typical form), the Malayan peninsula, Sumatra, Thailand, and southern Burma.

Description and related species Wingspan approximately 5–5¼ in. (125–130 mm). The adult has large black and green wings (the female's slightly bigger than the male's). The green band on the forewing is "toothed," the points of the "teeth" directed toward the outer margin. The female exhibits varying shades of brown and white. The front of the thorax in both sexes is an intense deep red. The related species *Trogonoptera trojana* is slightly larger, differing in the coloration of the scent areas of the male's wings and of the lower half of the female's forewings.

Habits This species lives in primary rain forests, appearing in greatest numbers during the monsoon season and flying even during rain. The males of some subspecies tend to assemble in clearings and on river banks, attracted by water, urine, and decaying substances. The males fly from early morning until afternoon while the females appear only in late afternoon. Both sexes visit flowers of trees and shrubs such as *Lantana*, *Bauhinia*, and *Ixora*. The food plants of the caterpillar are species of the genus *Aristolochia*.

---

289 UTHETHEISA PULCHELLA L.
crimson speckled moth

Family Arctiidae.

Geographical distribution Australia, Asia, southern Europe; also found rarely in central Europe, where it is probably not a resident species.

Description and related species Wingspan approximately 1½ in. (35–42 mm). The forewings are straw yellow, generously and irregularly sprinkled with deep pink and black spots. Near the apex is a thin, incomplete gray margin; a gray band occurs in the postmedian area. A regular line of black dots marks the marginal zone. The hind wings are white and much bigger than the forewings; a brownish-black mark with uneven outlines appears on the apex and on the outer margin.

Habits The caterpillar feeds on Borraginaceae, plants which contain substances toxic to vertebrates. It appears to require exposure to the sun before it begins to feed. The wide distribution range of this moth may be explained by its migratory habits.

GLOSSARY

Adectic Chrysalis whose jaws, when present, are unjointed and immobile.

Afrotropical region Zoogeographical region comprising the African continent south of the Sahara and the southern part of the Arabian peninsula.

Androconial Scales of a particular type which emit odors secreted by attached glands.

Antennae Pair of sensory organs, usually filamentous, on the head of an insect.

Apex Related to the wings, the meeting point of the outer margin and the costa.

Basal Pertaining to the base (of the wing).

Batesian A type of mimicry in which organisms unappetizing to predators are imitated by other unprotected organisms so as to enjoy the same advantage.

Chaetotaxy Distribution of hairs on the body of a larva.

Costa Anterior margin of the wing.

Cryptic Mimetic coloration used by animals to confuse predators.

Dectic Chrysalis whose jaws are free and functional, thus being used to break out of the cocoon.

Diapause State of almost total immobility, very similar to hibernation in vertebrates.

Discal Situated in the area of the wing cell.

Distal Opposite the base (of the wing).

Endemic Restricted to a particular area and not found in other zones.

Exarate Chrysalis with abdominal segments 1–7 free.

Family Systematic category which includes genera with common features.

Frenate System of wing attachment in butterflies and moths in which bristles situated on the hind wings lock into groups of hooked hairs on the forewings.

Galeae External lobes of the jaws, elongated and hollow inside, which constitute the proboscis.

Genus Systematic category which includes one or more related species.

Hemolymph Liquid circulating in the body of many invertebrates, corresponding to the blood of vertebrates.

Holometabolism Process of insect development represented by complete metamorphosis (larva, chrysalis, adult).

Indo-Australian region Zoogeographical region comprising India and Indonesia linked with Australia, Tasmania, New Guinea, New Zealand and lesser islands.

Jugate Pertaining to the jugum, a wing attachment in butterflies and moths consisting of a lobe at the base of the forewings which hooks on to the hind wings.

Melanism Phenomenon whereby an individual displays a special blackish coloration, unusual in the population to which it belongs.

Metamorphosis The combined transformations which appear in butterflies and moths from the larval to adult stage.

Molt Special process in which the caterpillar renews its skin covering and some of its internal organs.

Müllerian Particular type of mimicry in which, theoretically, the more poisonous species possess the same warning colors, the less the number of individuals in each species lost while predators are learning from experience.

Nearctic region Zoogeographical region comprising North America and part of Mexico north of the 20th parallel.

Neotropical Zoogeographical region comprising Central and South America, the West Indies and the Galapagos.

Obtect Chrysalis whose various appendages and abdominal segments are welded to the walls of the body.

Ocellum Detail of wing pattern represented by a round spot with a small central dot (eyespot); the same term is applied to the two simple eyes on the head of certain groups.

Osmeterium Retractile organ of the caterpillars of certain butterflies and moths which, when erected, often give out an unpleasant odor.

Palaearctic region Zoogeographical region comprising Europe, Africa north of the Sahara, and central and northern Asia.

Pheromone Chemical substance secreted by special glands, acting as a sexual attractant.

Phytophage Organism which feeds exclusively on plants.

Polymorphism Presence in a population or a species of some genetic variability which results in different individual forms.

Proboscis Organ formed by the union of the galeae, with which butterflies and moths suck liquids; when at rest it is rolled spirally beneath the head.

Sexual dimorphism Presence of more or less striking differences between the two sexes of the same species.

Species Group of organisms with the capacity to interbreed and procreate indeterminately fertile young.

Systematics Sector of natural sciences concerned with the classification of organisms.

Taxon Systematic biological category at any level.

Veins Tubelike structures which support the wings of butterflies and moths and permit the flow of hemolymph.

Wing cell Central area of each wing, generally enclosed by veins.

BIBLIOGRAPHY

Ancillotto, A., Grollo, A., and Zangheri, S. *I bruchi*, Milan, 1970.

Arnett, R. H., and Jacques, R.L. *Guide to Insects*, New York, 1981.

Barcant, M. *Butterflies of Trinidad and Tobago*, London, 1970.

Berger, L.A. *Les papillons de Zaire*, Brussels, 1981.

Berio, E. *Fauna d'Italia: Lepidoptera Noctuidae I*, Bologna, 1985.

Carter, D., and Hargreaves, B. *A Field Guide to the Moths of Eastern North America*, Boston, 1984.

D'Abrera, B. *Butterflies of the World: Australian Region, Afrotropical Region, Neotropical Region*, Melbourne, 1971.

Haugum, J., and Wilson, D. *A Monograph of the Birdwing Butterflies*, Klampenborg, 1978-79.

Higgins, L.G., and Riley, N.D. *Field Guide to the Butterflies of Britain and Europe*, London, 1980.

Howe, W.H. *The Butterflies of North America*, New York, 1975.

Klots, A. *The World of Butterflies and Moths*, London, 1958.

Klots, A. *Butterflies of the World: a handy guidebook to more than 50 butterfly, skipper and moth families*, London and New York, 1976.

Le Moult, E., and Real, P. *Les Morpho d'Amerique du Sud et centrale*, Paris, 1963.

Lewis, H.L. *Butterflies of the World*, London, 1973.

Novak, I. *Butterflies and Moths* (trans. from Czech by O. Kuthanova), London, 1986.

Novak, I. *Field Guide in colour to Butterflies and Moths*, London, 1981.

Pinhey, E.C.G. *Moths of Southern Africa*, Cape Town, 1875.

Pyle, R.M. *The Audubon Society Field Guide to North American Butterflies*, New York, 1981.

Rougeout, P., and Viette, P. *Guide des papillons nocturnes d'Europe et d'Afrique du Nord*, Lausanne, 1978.

Sbordoni, V., and Forestiero, S. *The World of Butterflies*, London and New York, 1985.

Seitz, A. *Macrolepidoptera of the World*, Stuttgart, 1907-1954.

Watson, A., and Whalley, P.E.S. *Dictionary of Butterflies and Moths in color*, New York, 1975.

Wickler, W. *Mimicry in plants and animals* (trans. from German by R.D. Martin), London, 1968 and New York, 1986.

Williams, J.G. *A Field Guide to the Butterflies of Africa*, London, 1969.

INDEX OF ENTRIES

Picture Sources

Introduction illustrations: Mondadori Archives: pp. 8–9, 66–67 — Giambattista Bertelli, Brescia: pp. 20, 22, 27, 30, 33, 34–35, 37, 42–43, 56 — Gabriele Pozzi, Milan: pp. 19, 24–25, 38, 40–41, 49, 50 — Aldo Ripamonti, Milan: pp. 11, 12, 13 — Romano Rizzato, Milan: pp. 46–47 — Vittorio Salarolo, Verona: pp. 15, 17, 52, 53, 59, 60, 61, 62–63.

Entry photographs: Agence Nature, H. Chaumeton: 29, 76, 99, 131, 134, 140, 176, 188, 241, 284; P. Da Costa: 47; Y. Lanceau: photograph opposite title page, 11, 35, 38, 65, 78, 102, 103, 118, 132, 253, 257, 259b, 268; F. Sauer: 13, 17 — A. Ancilotto: 5, 8, 10, 27 — Ardea Photographics, I. R. Beames: 49, 54, 58, 90; H. & J. Beste: 272, 277; J. B. & S. Bottomley: 161; E. S. Burgess: 168, 189; B. Gibbons: 196; D. W. Greenslade: 93, 239; A. Lindau: 81; E. Lindgren: 69, 278, 286, 289; J. L. Mason: 14, 15, 24, 25, 30, 72, 88, 106, 115b, 120, 126, 145, 211, 249, 285; S. Roberts: 143; A. Warren: 209, 232, 242, 244; A. Weaving: 262 — Peter Arnold: J. Macgregor: 173, 175, 183, 198, 201; C. A. Morgan: 153, 204 — Bruce Coleman, J. Burton: Caterpillars section: opening illustration, 9, 34, 51, 66, 108, 128, 259a; B. & C. Calhoun: 151, 206; R. Carr: 171; A. Compost: 276; A. P. Davies: 119; M. Dohrn: 56, 85; G. Doré: 114, 115a, Afro-tropical region: opening illustration; I. Everson: 63; M. Fogden: 229, 275; N. Fox-Davies: Palaearctic region: opening illustration, 84; D. Green: 43, 45, 59, 83; P. Helo: 23, 107; F. Lanting: Nearctic region: opening illustration, 162b; J. Markham: 7; A. J. Mobbs: 104; A. Purcell: 55; H. Reinhard: 135; H. Rivarola: 220, 228; F. Sauer: 36, 67, 87, 109; W. Schmidt: 235; J. Shaw: 141, 149, 150, 152, 154, 156, 158, 159, 160, 167, 169, 174, 177, 178, 180, 184, 185, 187, 192, 193, 194, 195, 197, 199, 200, 203, 224; J. Taylor: 12; K. Taylor: 40, 50; P. Ward: 213; L. West: 172 — Deltaprint, Verona: 96, 98, 110, 111 — Tom Fox: Neotropical region: opening illustration, 170, 191, 210, 215, 217, 218, 221, 225, 230, 233, 237, 240, 247, 248, 250 — Eiji Hamano: 52 — Jacana, R. C. I. Banco: 264; J. M. Bassot: 281; J. P. Champroux: 263; A. Ducrot: 100, 112; Ermie: 89; Y. Gillon: 252, 260; B. Hawkes: 234; J. P. Hervy: 265; R. Konig: 74; J. M. Labat: 71; N. Le Roy: 82; D. Lecourt: 138; C. & M. Moiton: 42, 48, 60, 80, 86, 116; P. Pilloud: 91, 117; A. Roux: 137; VarinVisage: 122, 280; G. Ziesler: 270 — N.H.P.A. (Natural History Photographic Agency), ANT: Indo-australian region: opening illustration; A. Bannister: 1, 251, 254, 256, 258, 269; G. I. Bernard: 16, 222, 226; D. Boyd: 44, 274; N. A. Callow: 77; G. J. Cambridge: 125; J. Carmichael: 148, 219, 227, page 376; S. Dalton: 2, 62, 79, 105, 113, 124, 127, 133, 162a, 163, 212, 223, 231, 246; E. Elms: 271; R. J. Erwin: 155, 190; R. Fotheringham: 6, 92; E. A. Janes: 73, 129; L. H. Newman: 70, 288; H. Palo junior: 245; J. Shaw: 165; M. F. Tweedie: 273; D. Woodfall: 95; W. Zepf: 53, 75, 130 — The National Audubon Society Collection/Photo Researchers, Inc., D. Brass: 166, 186; K. Brate: 142; R. Coleman: 157; S. Dalton: 207; J. Lepore: 144, 164; K. B. Sandved: 208 — Panda Photo: E. Stella: 4, 33, 61, 214, 255 — T. Racheli: 216, 236, 243, 279, 282, 283, 287 — Ricciarini: 20, 21, 26, 28, 31, 39, 57; Ricciarini/ Cappelli: 22, 37, 64, 68, 101, 182, 202 — Edward R. Ross: 32, 146, 147, 181, 205 — W. Rossi: 18, 19, 94, 136, 139, 261, 266, 267 — V. Sbordoni: 238 — Kazuo Unno: 46, 97, 121, 123.